— THE —
DINGHY CRUISING
COMPANION

Tales and advice from sailing a small open boat

THE DINGHY CRUISING COMPANION

Tales and advice from sailing a small open boat

ROGER BARNES

ADLARD
COLES

LONDON · OXFORD · NEW YORK · NEW DELHI · SYDNEY

ADLARD COLES
Bloomsbury Publishing Plc
50 Bedford Square, London, WC1B 3DP, UK
29 Earlsfort Terrace, Dublin 2, Ireland

BLOOMSBURY, ADLARD COLES and the Adlard Coles logo are trademarks of
Bloomsbury Publishing Plc

First published in 2014
This edition published 2022

A catalogue record for this book is available from the British Library

Library of Congress Cataloging-in-Publication data has been applied for

ISBN: 978-1-4729-9429-5
ePub: 978-1-4729-9428-8
ePDF: 978-1-4729-9427-1

10 9 8 7 6 5 4 3 2 1

Page design by Louise Turpin
Typesetting and page layouts by Susan McIntyre
Typeset in 9 on 12pt Grotesque MT Light
Printed and bound in China by C&C Offset Printing Co., Ltd.

To find out more about our authors and books visit www.bloomsbury.com
and sign up for our newsletters

CONTENTS

PREFACE TO THE SECOND EDITION

I welcome the opportunity to revise this book. Although the essential skills of cruising in a small open boat are probably eternal, the technology of the modern world inevitably intrudes upon our lives, even in a cruising dinghy. So the sections about electronic equipment have been updated, and I have revised the information on suitable dinghies you might wish to buy to reflect changes in the boats now manufactured. At the same time, a few annoying errors in the first edition have been corrected – such as the place where Cook careened HM *Bark Endeavour* in Australia. More major alterations are the inclusion of completely new sections about capsizing and sailing in heavy weather, contributed by Jacques van Geen and Jeremy Warren.

Roger Barnes, Douarnenez 2021

In a peaceful tidal creek, a cruising Wayfarer makes ready to go sailing.

INTRODUCTION: ON THE EDGE OF THE WILD

My aim in this book is to encourage you to use a small open boat to explore local and more distant waters. We will discover the amazing flexibility of a dinghy, small enough to be trailed behind a car and launched almost anywhere there is navigable water. A little boat, honed to her purpose, can carry you sure-footedly over the waves into the most beautiful and remote places.

Over the horizon

Loctudy has a melancholic end-of-season air. The café-bar at the marina is closed, and its canvas canopies slat mournfully in the chill north-east wind. It is very late in the year for a sailing holiday, but I had a sudden whim to go cruising. Unlike most cabin yachts, my dinghy is not laid up ashore half the year, waiting to be craned back into the water in the spring. I am free to go sailing at any time I like. This means I can take advantage of the magical spells of settled weather that sometimes occur in late autumn, just before the onset of winter.

I scull my dinghy away from the slipway, hoist the lugsail and sheet in. The brown sail fills, her hull heels and she comes alive. Skirting the rows of white yachts sulking on their pontoons, I head towards the harbour mouth. The ebb tide sucks my boat swiftly into the narrows, and soon her bows rise to breast the rounded green swells of the Bay of Biscay beyond.

The local fishing fleet is returning to port. A flotilla of gaily painted vessels plunges pugnaciously past me, a thicket of black flags flapping on the danbuoys racked in their sterns. A yellow arm waves from the last boat, and then vanishes back inside the wheelhouse. The fishing boat rounds a red beacon and enters the harbour. Very suddenly, I am alone. Avel Dro sails on towards the empty horizon.

The coastline astern becomes grey and less distinct, and eventually it begins to slide below the waves. The sail curves out over the seas to leeward, the sheet tugs at my hand and the tiller frets under my fingers. My boat lifts lightly to the swells and then swoops down into the troughs beyond. Occasionally a flurry of spray breaks over the weather bow. The only sounds are the scrunch of her bow wave and the murmur of the wake spreading out astern.

I have grown used to the loneliness of the open sea, and usually I find peace in its wide horizons. But the sea is not peaceful today. The long swells are dismal grey and ominously choppy. Avel Dro begins to sail hard-mouthed and slews into the wind in the gusts.

I stop to pull in a reef close to the rust-streaked east cardinal buoy protecting the isolated Men Dehou rock, 4 miles offshore. With sail lowered and the centreplate raised, Avel Dro lies stern to the wind, her buoyant transom lifting to the waves. I work in her heaving hull, rolling up the foot of the sail and tying the row of reef knots. The surly seas hiss past, cold and hostile.

A line of rocks leers above the horizon, like a row of stained and broken teeth – my first sight of the islands. I wonder what desperate foolishness has brought me out onto this horrible waste so late in the day. Suddenly a sunbeam slips beneath the cloud wrack and lights up the distant archipelago. It glows golden like a promised land. My sail shines red and comforting in the low sun, and the seas no longer seem quite so threatening. I sail on with new hope.

Skirting the eastern side of the archipelago, I close with a wave-dashed west cardinal beacon rising from an offlying rock, which marks my chosen passage into the heart of the Glénan group. Hardening up the sail, I round the beacon and enter a long channel that cleaves into the heart of the archipelago. Waves break ominously on the rocks on both sides. Guided by the very dangers she must avoid, Avel Dro close-reaches into the jaw of the shoals.

The channel leads to a shallow passage between two long, low islands. Soon I can see the sandy bottom slipping past, close beneath my keel. Then the water deepens

again and Avel Dro emerges into the main anchorage of the archipelago. An ancient castle towers sheer-faced from a tiny islet at its centre, reminding me that vessels flying the Red Ensign were not always so welcome in these waters.

I bring my dinghy alongside the stone quay on the Île St Nicholas and clamber up the iron ladder. There is no one about. The island appears to be all shut up for the winter. Eventually I find a small bar that is still open. There are only five people on the island it seems, and all of them are standing at the bar counter:

'Were you on the "vieux gréement" we saw sailing into the islands?' they ask – so respectfully you would have thought I had arrived in a windjammer, not a 15ft dinghy.

AVEL DRO alongside the quay at the Île St Nicholas.

THE GREAT WILDERNESS

Ancient and elemental, awesome in its power and vast beyond comprehension – the sea is the last great wilderness of the world. The lives of most sea creatures still remain a mystery to us and we know less about the ocean depths than the surface of the Moon. Venture onto even the fringes of the wild ocean and it is impossible to remain unmoved or unchanged.

On land we inhabit an increasingly artificial environment. We enjoy the comforts of modern civilisation, but perhaps we feel that something has been lost. For why is it that so many of us take long aeroplane flights to distant lands, where life seems simpler and less artificial? It is as if we want to chase down the last remaining scraps of primitive authenticity before they too are lost, and in doing so we contribute to their inevitable destruction.

But real nature is more accessible than most people think. There is no need to cross the world to live simply in its wild embrace. Venture just two miles offshore and the land will start slipping into the sea, for that is how close the horizon appears when viewed from a small boat. Out on the wide ocean you can actually see the curvature of the Earth, bending away on all sides. No maritime culture has ever believed that the Earth was flat. Keep on sailing towards the far horizon, and soon you will be alone in a vast seascape, which has not changed over the whole span of human history. The waves still run, the gulls still swoop and glide, the breakers still wash the shores – just as they did when our ancestors first built boats capable of navigating on open waters.

Beyond the shallows, punctuated by wind farms and navigation buoys, away from the production platforms rising from oil and gas fields, outside of the shipping lanes where

A fleet of Wayfarers rounds Old Harry rock near Swanage.

the lines of cargo ships follow their well-trodden paths, the deep ocean remains profoundly empty. The sea still offers the promise of freedom and escape to anyone with the confidence to venture out upon it.

The wild ocean divides countries one from another, isolates offshore islands and consigns remote archipelagos to marginality – or so it seems from the land. But the world looks quite different from a boat at sea. Out there, the sea is revealed as a unifying medium, linking coastlines and continents. The sea can be a savage place, but humanity has long since learnt how to navigate it with confidence. Ancient sea paths cross the waters of the world, the arteries of culture and trade since prehistory, rooted deep into the hinterland by rivers and canals. Water is the medium

of civilisation. The great cities of the ancient world were always established on the coast or beside a navigable river. Sail a simple boat close along the shoreline, and you travel back to the very origins of human society.

On the shifting boundary between land and sea, you also find many natural wonders – wetlands and marshland, shallows and deep estuaries, cliffs and rocky inlets, sand and surf, reed beds and sea marsh. You can only properly appreciate the beauty of the coast when you see it from the sea, and if you want to explore its deepest mysteries, you need to be in a small boat. Dinghies are for the interesting bits of the sea – the delightful fringes where sea and land blend into a landscape of cliffs and beaches, intricate channels and forgotten pools: the final frontier of dry land.

A dinghy explores a creek at Traeth Bach in Wales. (DCA)

THE BOATS OF THE WATERLANDS

Only the very old can remember the last days of working sail. Few inshore sailing craft survived the difficult aftermath of the Second World War, and the last ocean-going windjammers gave up the struggle at about the same time. For at least seventy years, major developments in sailing technology have focused on pleasure boats. Sailing craft no longer need to work for a living, and this has profoundly influenced their design.

Once small working sailing boats were everywhere on the coastline, populating the waterlands. They bobbed at the foot of quayside steps; they lay on the mud at low water; they were pulled up on shingle beaches. In the days of sail, small craft filled many workaday roles – fishing, ferrying people about, moving small cargoes and communicating with larger vessels at anchor. These modest boats were sea-kindly, stable and simple. Created for an era before motors, they performed effectively under both sail and oar, and were weatherly in rough conditions.

The modern racing dinghy has become something rather different. Mass-produced for a fiercely competitive leisure market demanding fun beach boats or fast dinghies for class racing, they accelerate rapidly in a gust, plane thrillingly off the wind and give instant feedback to their crew. Modern dinghies are astonishingly close-winded and respond to the slightest zephyr. They are extraordinarily effective at the purpose for which they were designed, but so was the traditional dinghy. There are other ways to judge a dinghy than pure windward efficiency. The owners of small working boats were not uninterested in sailing performance, but their chief priority was

A traditional Clovelly Picarooner, still being used for fishing under sail in the twenty-first century.

that their small craft would be a safe place to spend many hours each day, working at sea.

In recent years there has been an upsurge of interest in these historical designs. All over the world, naval architects have started looking again at traditional small workboat types and gently updating them to suit contemporary requirements. In doing this, they are creating boats that feel timeless, but also very modern. In these dinghies a new generation of boatmen and women are relearning the old ways, and rediscovering the simple delight of being in a capable boat.

Rather than go to sea in a cabin yacht, a growing number of people are choosing to sail in small craft instead. They are not interested in buying a lavish boat to display their wealth: their desire is to own a simple, beautiful and well-designed craft in which to experience an intimate and sympathetic relationship with the natural world.

Island anchorage

I do not know what woke me. Perhaps it was the rocking of my boat, or the noise of wavelets lapping against the clinker strakes of her hull, or the squeak of the hurricane lamp swinging above my head. But there is no need to get up just yet. I snuggle deeper into my sleeping bag. It is the first morning of my cruise and I want to savour the sensation of waking up aboard my dinghy at anchor. Normally I would be at work now, but today I can lie here as long as I like, surrounded by the happy gurgles of a small boat afloat. Soon the watery reflections shimmering on the tent canvas become too alluring to stay in bed any longer. I sit up in my sleeping bag, fold open the boat tent and look out on the world outside.

I can vividly remember sailing to the archipelago, but it is still a surprise to wake up anchored at the heart of Les Glénan, eight sea miles off the southern coast of Brittany. My dinghy is encircled by low islands thatched with pine trees, their shorelines fringed by bleached rocks and gilded white sand. She sits lightly on the brilliantly clear water, suspended above the sandy bottom just below her keel. Leaning over the transom, I can see fish nibbling at seaweed fronds, waving softly beneath me. The sky is clear blue but the air is chilly, still awaiting the warmth of the morning sun. There is just the barest breath of wind, and only the most delicate ripples disturb the smooth surface of the sea.

I am alone in the anchorage. The local yachts that crowd these islands in the height of the season have long since departed for their winter lay-up. My little dinghy has brought me away from the bustle of life onshore and out into another world, into the great wilderness of the sea.

Cruising dinghies are amazingly flexible: masterpieces of minimalist design. The same boat can be rowed, sailed or powered with a small outboard motor, according to taste and the weather conditions. They can be used singlehanded, for family outings or with a group of friends. In them you can venture across the lake to a sheltered beach, or take the flood tide up a winding watercourse, feeling your way to a remote upriver quay or an ancient waterside community long abandoned by modern patterns of trade. Dinghies can also be used for effective coastal sailing and even be used for extended cruises; their crew sleeping aboard each night, just like in a cabin yacht.

DINGHY SAILING IS ABOUT DETAIL, NOT DISTANCE

It is rarely necessary to make long open-water passages in a dinghy. Large expanses of seawater are more conveniently crossed by putting your dinghy in the hold of a car ferry, cradled on her road trailer. Nonetheless, substantial open-sea passages have been made in cruising dinghies. Small boats, intelligently handled and properly equipped, are extraordinarily effective sea boats. Not every dinghy sailor wants to cross the wide sea in their small craft, but it is comforting to know that your boat is capable of such things.

Cabin yachts are undoubtedly very fine things to own. I sailed a classic six-ton cutter

Cruising dinghies just setting off from the quay after mooring for lunch on the River Tamar. (John Perry)

for many years, and her ability to keep the sea in conditions that would send a dinghy scurrying to shelter was awe-inspiring. But when I sold her and returned to my first love of dinghy cruising, I found that I covered more sea miles each year in my little dinghy than I ever did in the seagoing yacht. A dinghy may not be quite as fast as a yacht, but you use her much more often.

Yachts have their advantages of course. Their greater size imparts a great sense of security to her crew, and a larger boat is undoubtedly more capable of riding out dirty weather at sea. On the other hand a small dinghy can wriggle into little havens inaccessible to a deep-keel vessel, so she has more opportunities to seek shelter. Yachts

have to hold the sea on a dirty night, afraid to enter shoal waters, while a dinghy can slip into the shallows to find peace and security.

A yacht moored in a sheltered haven is undoubtedly a very comfortable place to be, but when she's pitching into a steep head sea, she becomes one of the most unpleasant environments you could possibly experience. She may have comfy couches to lounge on, a convenient kitchen to serve you food, a drinks cabinet for your refreshment and a bathroom for your ablutions, but so does a dinghy beached close to a convivial pub.

So dinghies have many advantages. Not only are they substantially cheaper than a yacht to purchase and maintain, but their unpretentious charm wins them friends.

From the islands to the city

The sun rises over the Glénan archipelago as I eat my breakfast afloat. Then I strike the boat tent, pack away my camping gear and weigh the anchor. The wind has died away completely now, so I do not bother hoisting sail. I weigh the anchor and start rowing. The water parts smoothly before the prow of my boat and slides silkily astern, stained by little whirlpools from my oar strokes. I wander among the little islands, resting occasionally and staring down through the clear water into shallow rock pools populated by waving anemones and tiny darting fish. Towards evening I find another anchorage in a small bay at the eastern extremity of the archipelago and spend the night under the revolving red beam of an ancient lighthouse.

My holiday plan is to sail on eastwards, island-hopping along the southern coast of Brittany: first to the Île de Groix, then Belle Île, and finally the rocky islands of Houat and Hoëdic in Quiberon Bay. But this requires a period of settled weather, and the next morning's weather forecast, received on the crackly VHF, soon scotches that idea. A high-pressure system is building to the north, rotating clockwise like a Catherine wheel hundreds of miles across, creating strong easterly winds to thwart the plans of small boats, here in the Bay of Biscay.

Cruising dinghies are like trading vessels in the age of sail. They do not battle mindlessly against the wind, but endeavour to sail with it. So I hastily revise my plans. Rather than continue into the eye of the wind, I decide to bear away to the north-west and explore one of the rivers that wind deep into the hinterland of southern Brittany.

A pair of adorably pretty lighthouses marks the transit past the elegant seafront of Bénodet, and into the mouth of the Odet river beyond. The waterway leads me onwards, deep into the verdant Breton countryside. The wind is stronger now and sudden williwaws tumble down from high wooded escarpments on each side. My boat lurches from their blows and then wallows languidly in the sudden calms that follow. Suddenly I hear a throaty throb astern. A coaster is coming up fast behind me, a massive presence in the narrow river. Her bluff bows heap up the water before her and send it frothing past her rusty sides.

I drop the sail and slide close to the bank, out of the way. The coaster throbs past, rounds a green navigation perch just ahead of me, and then disappears behind a sharp bend in the river. As the noise of her engine dies away, it reveals a peculiar rippling noise, like a mountain stream tumbling over boulders. I look around me, trying to locate the source. Then I see that the tide is racing past the perch, throwing up a considerable bow wave and creating the puzzling sound. At that moment Avel Dro swings abruptly out of the back eddy. The tide grabs her and flings her bodily forward. I clutch at an oar and promptly drop it over the side. My dinghy spins round the corner of the river, the floating oar swirling after her. I find myself being swept broadside up a wooded gorge, like a spider in a spout. Lunging at the oar with one arm, I retrieve it from the water and drop it into a rowlock. Unstowing the other oar, I start to row, and slowly begin to re-establish some control over my wayward dinghy.

The river snakes inland, walled by rocky banks and dark overhanging woodland.

Eventually it widens into a lake, surrounded by fields and low wooded hills, a soft breeze blowing across its placid waters. It is now early evening, and the low sun ripples the wavelets with golden light. I hoist sail and begin to tack slowly across this empty inland sea, like a lonely explorer venturing into the interior of a mighty continent.

At the head of the lake the first outskirts of the city of Quimper come into view. The same coaster is lying alongside a wharf, discharging shingle dredgings onto heaped piles. Just beyond her a concrete road bridge spans the river, barely high enough to clear my mast and sail.

I have lost the fair tide. The ebb is running out swiftly against me now. I row hard to make progress, close against the stone banks of the river. Various inhabitants of the locality stroll past, enjoying the evening sun. Some call out to me in encouragement. Soon the tide becomes too strong to row against, and I start towing Avel Dro from the bank instead, walking along the edge of the quayside, hauling her along with a pair of warps. I am getting close to the centre of the city now. The twin spires of the cathedral rise above the huddled slate roofs of the surrounding houses. A series of low bridges span the river ahead, decked with flowers on their iron parapets. I drop back down into Avel Dro, lower the mast and begin to scull her beneath them, standing in the stern.

I have to duck as the dinghy slides under the low bridges. Then there is a fork in the river, but I carry straight on, and finally bring my little vessel alongside a flight of stone steps close beside the prefecture in the heart of the city, where I make her fast to the iron railings. The bustle and noise are striking after the peace of the Glénan archipelago. Here I am, a scruffy vagrant just in from the sea, preparing to spend the night alongside the quays of an elegant tree-lined boulevard, full of prestigious shops and the best cafés in Quimper.

My Avel Dro moored in the centre of Quimper.

A cruising dinghy is always welcome in a small working harbour, whereas a visiting yacht feels like an alien intrusion, and may be refused entry. A dinghy fits in comfortably among the working craft in a small fishing port. Yachts are more at home in deep water anchorages or marinas, but a dinghy is free to use small drying harbours, unknown to yachtsmen. In these little havens a small dinghy is soon made to feel at home by the local mariners.

Even in popular sailing areas, a dinghy can always find uncrowded places to sail, or she can follow minor channels into the depths of the countryside, and discover quiet anchorages among the wildlife of the littoral.

'Gunkholing' has become a popular activity in the USA. Groups of small-boat sailors sail out to a secluded haven, pull their light boats up out of the water, erect a tent and spend the night beside the water, lighting a fire to cook the fish they caught during the day.

In France, a movement called 'voile-aviron' (sail and oar) is sweeping the coastline. Ordinary people are rediscovering the delights of sailing in simple, traditionally inspired boats, mostly without engines, and are relearning the skills of the old working boatman. Voile-aviron rallies have become immensely popular and attract anything from a score of dinghies to many hundreds. Crowds of dinghies sail together up a river, or congregate convivially in an anchorage for a shared meal.

A more competitive type of dinghy cruising is provided on 'raids'. Typically these take the form of a cruise in company along a river or through an archipelago, which can last a week or more. Some legs of the route will be races under sail or oar, and sometimes these become very competitive. The raid scene has spawned new and innovative dinghy designs, as progressive designers use these events to experiment with new designs or to hone existing ones.

There are more relaxing boat festivals too, where little boats meet to cruise in company and spend friendly evenings

AVEL DRO dried out among the working craft at Clovelly.

together. Maritime festivals have become extraordinarily popular in recent years. Hordes of boats flock on the water, while on the shore there is live music and dancing, clouds of bunting, fireworks, and a powerful sense of festive occasion. You can now spend all summer trailing your boat from one festival to another – just assuming you can cope with long days out sailing, followed by many late nights of partying.

Camping in a dinghy is a pleasure well worth discovering. The ability to sleep aboard the boat frees the dinghy sailor from being tied to the land, and immeasurably improves the cruising experience, especially on a long passage. It is generally far easier to find a sheltered anchorage in which to spend each night afloat in your dinghy than to find a secure mooring close to shore accommodation every evening. And nothing matches being lulled to sleep by the gentle rocking of your boat and the noise of waves lapping against her hull.

A 'voile-aviron' rally on the River Aulne in France. (Ronan Coquil)

Avel Dro approaching harbour in rough conditions, with three reefs in the sail. (Ronan Coquil)

A choice of boats to the mainland

The roar of a car ferry rumbling into her berth awakens me. Clambering out of my dinghy tent, I join a huddle of yacht skippers outside the harbour office. Someone wipes the wet glass so we can see the forecast more clearly. The weather has definitely broken. This is my third morning on the island, and each morning the forecast gets worse.

I have enjoyed my stay on the Île de Groix, but now I want to be off sailing again. When I arrived in Port Tudy after a two-day passage from Quimper, I was instantly attracted by its faded grandeur. Its warehouses and fine villas still bear witness to the past prosperity of the local tuna fishery, but the powerful 'thoniers' whose masts thicketed the harbour only two generations ago have long gone. Their carcasses now rot in the mud of Breton rivers. And I want to depart too. I want to shape a course south-east across the rolling seas of the Bay of Biscay. But Biscay is a bully and does not give a damn about smashing up little boats. When the sun glistens on the waves the weather seems less dangerous – but I know this is an illusion.

It is blowing well over Force 7 in the rain squalls. My intended passage to Belle Île is over 20 nautical miles, with a perilous coast to leeward. The question is no longer whether Avel Dro *can get to Belle Île, but whether she can leave the Île de Groix at all. The shortest passage is to head directly for the mainland, straight into the port of Lorient, but even this is dodgy in this weather. I look at the boxy car ferry. Has it really come to that?*

I walk along the breakwater to assess the conditions. A big sea is running in the five-mile-wide strait between the island and the mainland shore, but there is no way to assess the conditions in the shallows at the entrance to Lorient. I picture my little dinghy swept by a breaking sea, pitching me helplessly into the water. Is it reckless to attempt the passage?

It is certainly reckless to make decisions before breakfast. No one thinks straight on an empty stomach. I appropriate a table in my favourite harbour café. There are the tidal streams to consider, the wisdom of the north Biscay pilot to consult, the chart to study and markup. Finally, when I am full of coffee and croissants and the chart is covered with crumbs, I have decided what to do.

Preparations for a rough passage inevitably become a solemn ritual. I reef the big lugsail methodically, ensuring that the bunt is rolled neatly and securely tied down. Then I input a waypoint into the GPS at the entrance to Lorient, tune the VHF to the harbour working channel, put the chart in its waterproof case and slide it under the shock cords on the stern seat. Just before casting off, I make a final check that all the rest of the gear is securely lashed in place in the dinghy and the chinstrap is pulled tight on my sea hat.

It is time to go. I scull Avel Dro *past the working craft at the fish quay, and out between the little lighthouses at the harbour mouth. There, under the lee of the high stone breakwaters, I hoist my heavily reefed sail.* Avel Dro *wallows heavily in the wind shadow, before emerging abruptly into the full force of the weather.*

Her sail fills with a sudden bang, she heels sharply, and suddenly she is off, thundering towards Lorient on a beam reach.

Long seas sweep in from abeam, scooping her up and rushing away as she settles down into the troughs behind. They are vast and mostly unthreatening, but if a crest were to break as it hit my boat, she would easily be overwhelmed. I concentrate on my steering, avoiding any crests that look on the point of breaking. Avel Dro is sailing at the limit of what she can safely handle, but the danger adds to the stark beauty of the scene. I am sweeping over a landscape of blue rolling hills, shimmering in the sunlight – ever moving, ever changing, and awesome in their power. It is breathtakingly spectacular.

The seas grow steep and ever taller as I close the entrance to Lorient, and their direction changes. They lift Avel Dro's stern and send her hurtling forward. There is breaking water on a raft of black rocks close to leeward of us and a confused mass of lateral marks fills the channel ahead. I am thankful for my careful preparation before departing from the island.

The wind eases as my boat slips into the lee of the huge fortifications guarding the entrance to Lorient. The Île de Groix ferry passes close alongside. I look up at her brick-like bulk as she heads out to sea. I could easily have been on board her now with my car and trailer, returning to the island to recover my dinghy. Instead here I am, sailing triumphantly into harbour. It feels good. I did not get to Belle Île, but beyond the narrows a wide river opens up ahead of me. Here is a whole new sailing ground to explore.

'A whole new sailing ground to explore.' (François Vivier)

1 FINDING A GOOD BOAT

THE ORIGIN OF THE DINGHY

The word 'dinghy' normally describes a small craft without a fixed keel or cabin, and under some 20ft long (6m). Originally of Indian origin, the Royal Navy adopted the word 'dinghy' during the British Raj to describe the smallest boat carried by a warship. It replaced the former naval term 'jolly boat', which features in a number of important scenes in Stevenson's classic novel TREASURE ISLAND, for instance.

Naval dinghies were generally between 12ft and 16ft in length (3.6–4.8m), with a lifting centre plate and a modest sailing rig. Designed to cope with the harsh naval life and repeatedly being hoisted aboard a ship, they were very robust in construction and much heavier than most modern dinghies. Effective sailing vessels nonetheless, they were often used for informal races in harbour. When pensioned off into civilian use, they laid the foundations of the modern sport of dinghy sailing.

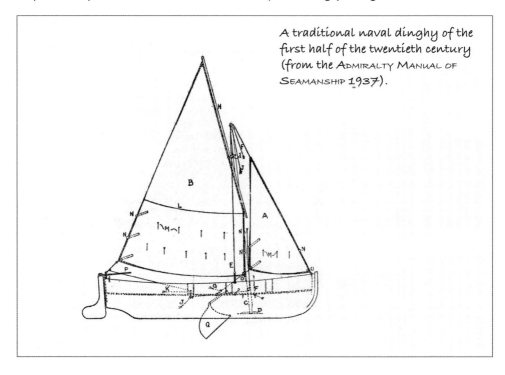

A traditional naval dinghy of the first half of the twentieth century (from the ADMIRALTY MANUAL OF SEAMANSHIP 1937).

The demands of leisure sailing are very different from those of the Navy, and the design of pleasure dinghies soon departed radically from these naval origins. Designers vied to produce ever faster and more responsive craft for the racing circuit. Dinghy rigs became more close-winded. Their hulls developed flat underwater sections so they would plane off the wind. Nowadays some racing dinghies can even rise up on hydrofoils, and skim above the water at improbable speeds. The dinghy has come a long way from its naval origins.

Small workboats

There was another tradition of small boat design that owed nothing to the naval dinghy. In the days of working sail, coastal watermen used small vessels for fishing and other workaday activities. These little craft were never called 'dinghies'. They were often just called 'boats' (although where I used to live in the south-west of England, they are usually referred to as 'punts'). These small vessels evolved over many centuries to suit their local sailing conditions. Typically they had deep hull sections to grip the water when going to windward and carried ballast for stability. A centreplate was rare. Working seamen considered them a needless expense and a source of leaks. Windward performance was not of prime importance in a workboat. Their owners were more interested in durability and practicality; their boats needed to be a stable place to coil ropes or haul nets. When confronted with a head wind, the crew did not waste time tacking against it – they just lowered the mast and bent to the oars.

The post-war dinghy boom

In the 1950s, dinghy sailing became immensely popular as a leisure activity. New designs of dinghy were developed for the affluent post-war generation that could be towed behind a small car, and this opened up sailing to the masses. Suddenly, everyone could own a boat; they were no longer restricted to the wealthy or people lucky enough to live on the coast.

The boom in leisure boating was accompanied by the development of new forms of hull construction. First plywood and then glass-reinforced plastic (GRP) supplanted the old skills of wooden boatbuilding. Traditional boatbuilders went out of business all along the coastline, to be replaced by large factories that mass-produced dinghies using the new materials. This process has accelerated in recent years as GRP is being replaced by rotomoulded polypropylene, massively undercutting the old production methods.

Many people continue to use the older types of class dinghy, however, and the most popular designs of the 1950s and 1960s are still in production. Common examples in my local waters are the Wayfarer and Mirror dinghies, but similar designs were produced all over the world in the dinghy boom of those years. Sailing dinghies of this period were much less extreme than modern racing boats. Often they were designed as general-purpose family boats, and were intended to be raced, cruised, rowed or used with an outboard. Many classes of dinghy originally intended for plywood construction have long been built in GRP, and the older wooden examples now can be picked up second-hand for modest sums. These boats make an ideal choice for a first venture into dinghy cruising. A wooden dinghy is more easily modified for cruising than a more modern GRP or polypropylene boat.

THE WAYFARER

The Wayfarer is a typical example of the plywood dinghy designs of the late 1950s, and remains very popular in its modern GRP incarnation. The dinghy is an effective performer under sail, and owners benefit from the expertise of the Wayfarer Class Association, which has a wealth of experience of adapting the dinghy for effective offshore cruising. Wayfarers have crossed oceans.

This is a big dinghy, with a large sail area, but the beamy hull has good form stability and they are a popular sailing school boat for this reason. When used for training, the dinghy is often sailed with five adults on board, but is a good two-person boat when used for cruising. Rather a handful when sailed singlehanded, the slightly smaller but very similar Wanderer, by the same manufacturer, is a better choice for those who prefer to sail alone. The boat is rather too beamy for efficient rowing, so an outboard motor is often carried.

Over the long life of the design, many varieties of Wayfarer have been created, but the ones that keep closest to the original design are generally more suitable for cruising, as they provide more stowage space for cruising gear and are less likely to turn turtle in a capsize.

Two people can sleep comfortably on the bottom boards, either side of the centreboard case. There is a big aft locker for the crew's gear or an outboard motor, and the forward buoyancy tank can also be used to carry a large amount of camping gear. The mast is set in a tabernacle and the rig is simple and practical, so that the mast can be raised and lowered while the dinghy is afloat; an invaluable feature.

The Wayfarer is the quintessential fast cruising dinghy, and provides its owners with almost unlimited possibilities, from class racing to ambitious cruising. They are also good family dinghies.

Dinghy T
LSC Poole

OCEAN CROSSING WAYFARER

In 1959 an English garage owner called Frank Dye purchased a brand-new plywood Wayfarer, as exhibited that year at the Earls Court Boat Show. Soon he had adapted his little dinghy for ambitious cruising, and embarked on a number of epic voyages from Scotland to the Faroes, Iceland and Norway. His account of these trips in *Ocean Crossing Wayfarer*, published in 1977, popularised the Wayfarer class as a cruising dinghy.

More than forty years after it was designed, the Wayfarer is still popular among the cruising fraternity, and it remains common in sailing club racing fleets. Wayfarers are capable of fast sea passages in fair weather, but despite their fine performance under sail, they are also stable and forgiving, and remain a popular training dinghy for this reason.

More modern designs of class dinghy have not become popular with cruising sailors in the same way as the Wayfarer, and this reflects the decline of the 'general-purpose' dinghy in the face of the new generation of modern vessels competing for a slice of the contemporary leisure market. The design of most dinghies now is determined by price, fashion and the demands of the racing fleet, not their suitability for cruising.

A Wayfarer dinghy set up for cruising. Notice the reefing arrangement on her mainsail. (Chris Yerbury)

The return of the tanned sail

As the design of class dinghies moved ever more distant from traditional forms, this presented a growing problem for the cruising dinghy sailor. It was the lack of a modern dinghy designed to workboat standards, and up to the rough and tumble of the sea, that led the former Royal Navy officer John Watkinson to design a new type of sailing dinghy. Since then, his Drascombe Lugger has become as common as fish and chip shops in British harbours, and popular well outside their home waters. They have become so ubiquitous, we forget how outrageous they seemed when they first appeared half a century ago.

Inspired by the traditional cobles of north-east England, Watkinson created a sturdy and stable dinghy, safe for his young family to go out sailing in. He drew a long lean hull with a well-flared bow, designed to ride easily over the seas. More radical still, he chose an old-fashioned rig, designed for practicality rather than ultimate sailing

A Drascombe Lugger in the open sea off Solva in Wales.

efficiency. The Drascombe Lugger was revolutionary. It made tan-coloured sails trendy overnight.

But it would be a mistake to see the Lugger as simply a romantic 'retro' design – as if John Watkinson was to dinghies what Laura Ashley was to women's clothing. Watkinson did not simply copy the looks of a traditional workboat – he completely rethought the design of the contemporary dinghy to produce an immensely practical vessel. Put into GRP production by Honnor Marine, the Lugger soon built up an enthusiastic following. Watkinson then went on to develop a series of similar dinghies that shared the Lugger's philosophy: pragmatic, workaday boats for the cruising sailor.

Luggers never race, so they are rarely seen in the dinghy parks of sailing clubs.

Their natural habitat is the tidal estuary, where they lie on drying moorings like sleeping seabirds. They appeal to people who want a sturdy dinghy that they can take their children out sailing in, that will not frighten anyone or flip over unexpectedly, and that can be motored home when everyone has had enough of sailing for the day.

The small boat revolution

Until recently, boats like the Lugger were often dismissed as a reactionary backwater of dinghy design – an irrelevance, compared to the exciting challenge of producing ever-faster dinghies for club racing. But times change. Specialist magazines, like *Le Chasse-Marée* in France, *Water Craft* magazine in the UK and *Small Craft Advisor* in the USA, are promoting dinghy cruising as an ideal form of recreation for the contemporary world, perfect for people who want to get close to nature using the minimum of resources.

There has been an explosion in the production of dinghies designed unashamedly for cruising. Designers such as François Vivier in France, Iain Oughtred in the UK, John Welsford in Australia, Paul Gartside and Chuck Paine in the USA are combining the best features of the working and racing traditions to develop new forms of dinghy eminently suitable for modern leisure sailing.

Choosing a dinghy

Many of the less extreme dinghy designs, dating from the 1950s and 60s, can be adapted for modest cruises without major modification. If you own one of these dinghies, the best boat to begin your cruising

in could well be the one you already have. As you gain experience, you will discover what features you would look for in a more specialised cruising boat. Do you want a light, responsive craft that is exciting to sail, or something heavier and more forgiving, which will not spring any unpleasant surprises? It is better to experiment with the dinghy you already own than to splash out lots of cash on a new boat that may prove unsuitable.

If you are definitely looking to buy a new boat, the best way to assess the performance and abilities of your chosen design is to take one of them out sailing in real conditions. Contact some experienced dinghy cruisers and ask them about their boats. Most people are glad of a chance to show off their dinghy. Popular cruising dinghies usually have Internet forums through which you can contact other owners, and some class associations

Larger sister of the Lugger, a Drascombe Longboat motorsails up the River Severn. (John Christie)

A group of dinghies hauled up on the beach on a misty morning in the Bay of Morlaix, France.

organise cruising rallies. Dinghy cruising groups, like the Fédération Voile-Aviron in France and the Dinghy Cruising Association in the UK, are another way to get in touch with other enthusiasts.

Weight and size

Every dinghy is a compromise between performance, weight and weatherliness. When dinghy skippers meet in longshore taverns, the arguments about the best cruising boat are long and passionate, so I approach this subject with great circumspection. As a rough rule of thumb, singlehanded sailors should choose a dinghy less than 15ft long (4.5m), whereas couples will be happier in a boat up to around 18ft in length (5.5m).

Weight is a more important consideration than length, however. The heavier the dinghy, the more stable and forgiving she will be at sea. Weight in the hull creates a dampening effect and makes the boat less flighty under sail. Heavier sailing dinghies heel over less rapidly when hit by a squall and give their crews more time to react. As a guide to what I mean by 'light' and 'heavy', a light 12ft (3.6m) dinghy would weigh under 200lbs (90kg), whereas a heavy 12-footer will displace over 300lbs (140kg). The corresponding figures for a 16ft (4.9m) dinghy are 350lbs (150kg) for a light boat and over 650lbs (300kg) for a heavy one. These are 'all up' weights of the hull and rig, but exclude any cruising gear you might put aboard.

The weight of dinghy you choose will be strongly influenced by where you intend to keep her. If your dinghy is to be kept in a sailing club dinghy park, you will want to be able to wheel her down the slipway on a launching trolley, and so she must be light enough to be manhandled by her usual crew. Sailing clubs generally ban road trailers in the dinghy park, and any boat that needs vehicle assistance for launching is ruled out.

If you intend to keep your boat at home and tow her to a slipway each time you go sailing, the dinghy will spend most of the time sitting on her road trailer. A boat used for 'trailer-sailing' can be rather heavier than a sailing club dinghy, as you will be able to use the car to pull the boat up the slipway and to manoeuvre her around on land. (Extensive advice on towing and launching a dinghy is given in Chapter 11.)

People who live near the coast can often keep their boat on a mooring in a local creek, and only need to take her out of the water in winter. If this is the sort of dinghy you are looking for, you will be tempted to purchase a heavy and robust boat that can put up with lying afloat for much of the year and that will be more forgiving in rough weather. But be cautious about buying a boat that is too large and heavy. A big dinghy can be difficult to beach, and you may need to use a tender every time you want to get ashore. One of the beauties of

dinghy sailing is casually running your boat up onto the shoreline in order to make a landing. If you have to inflate a rubber dinghy every time the crew want to stretch their legs, you may as well buy a yacht.

Hull form

In dirty weather it is not usually the boat that gives up first, but the people on board. The crew call out the lifeboat because they are too cold, wet, tired or seasick to carry on. A good cruising dinghy must look after her crew. Ideally she will have a buoyant hull with generous freeboard. It may be exciting to see spray crashing over the weather bow into the crew's face on a brief sail about the lake, but this becomes tedious on a long beat to windward in the open sea. A capable cruising dinghy will have good flare in the bow, so that it rises smoothly over the waves and deflects spray from the interior of the boat. A buoyant stern, which lifts easily to following seas, is

A Drascombe Longboat (left) and a BayRaider on moorings at Holy Island, Northumberland, waiting for the tide. (John Hughes)

My old 12ft Tideway dinghy pulled up on the beach, with cruising gear aboard. Note the reefing lines on the boom.

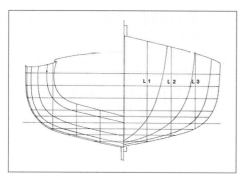

A good cruising dinghy hull is full bodied with ample form stability. These are the lines of the Ilur dinghy designed by François Vivier.

also desirable. It is fashionable for modern racing dinghies to have vertical transoms, or even no transom at all, but a transom that slopes outwards will deflect a following sea downwards, and keep the boat dry when running before the wind.

Many dinghies have large areas of decking up forward. This helps to keep spray out of the well, which is desirable. On the other hand, many proven cruising dinghies have no decking at all. These include the popular Mirror class dinghy and the Drascombe Lugger. A lack of decking allows more

space to work within the boat. Indeed, an excessively long foredeck can be dangerous on a dinghy. Clambering onto an unprotected deck to lash down a jib should not be contemplated at sea. Such boats should be rigged with a downhaul line so that the jib can be dowsed safely from the interior of the boat, or preferably fitted with roller furling.

Hull materials

Despite the advantages of more modern materials, many dinghies are still made out of wood. Timber remains an excellent choice for boat construction. It is lighter for its strength than most modern materials, and is ideally suitable for individually built boats or for amateur construction. Modern techniques of computer-aided design and the laser cutting of plywood have revolutionised the production of kit boats for home builders. There is a wide variety of beautiful designs available which are very well suited to dinghy cruising.

Many people are afraid of buying a wooden boat because they fear it will demand innumerable hours of scraping, sanding, painting and varnishing, whereas boats built of modern materials like GRP or polyethylene are popularly believed to need no maintenance at all. A wooden boat certainly requires some attention every year, but the work is not all that onerous on a vessel as small as a dinghy, and many people get a great deal of pleasure from maintaining their wooden boats. Above all, a wooden dinghy is a work of delightful craftsmanship, inspiring to own and a joy to use. Beside them, plastic boats feel sterile and impersonal, no matter how much wood trim they may incorporate. A wooden boat is like a musical instrument – beautiful in its functional efficiency, a lovely and poetic human creation. Wooden boatbuilders often work long hours for little money, purely out of love for what they do. If you have the chance to commission and then sail in a work of bespoke craftsmanship from one of these talented and committed people, do not hesitate.

Stability

Hull stability is a vital consideration in the choice of a cruising dinghy. The Dinghy Cruising Association has an old rule of thumb that a dinghy should not capsize when all the crew are standing on the gunwale at the same time. A decent cruising boat will heel over during this test, but you should not be afraid that she might suddenly lurch and tip you into the water.

Unlike a yacht or a dayboat, a dinghy relies largely on 'form stability' to keep her upright, rather than the weight of a ballast keel. Stability is a function of beam, weight and hull shape. As a general rule, a beamy and heavy dinghy will be more stable than a light and narrow one. To quantify this, a beamy 12-footer (3.6m) should be nearly 5ft in the beam (1.5m), whereas a 16-footer (4.9m) will have a beam of over 6ft (1.8m). But, as always with boat design, things are not as simple as that. Greater beam undoubtedly helps a dinghy to stand up to her sail, but a beamy dinghy can become very difficult to row. There is a conflict between the demands of a rowing hull and one built for sailing. All 'sail and oar' boats are inevitably a compromise. If you are looking for a dinghy that can be rowed, her beam should be no more than about 5'6" (1.7m). More beamy dinghies generally have to rely on an outboard motor for auxiliary propulsion.

Traditional sailing dinghies often had heavy centreplates fabricated from galvanised steel, with a tackle to hoist them up. It might be thought that a heavy lifting keel provides a useful righting force, but this is a misconception. A weighted keel only produces an effective 'righting moment' at large angles of heel, and a dinghy is best sailed level. Ballast carried low down in the hull is just as effective as a heavy centreplate. Traditionally, dinghies often carried pigs of lead or even stones from the beach as internal ballast. A contemporary update to this technology is the water ballast often fitted to purpose-designed cruising dinghies, such as Swallow Boats' 'BayRaider'. The tank is flooded when the boat is put into the water and drained out again when she is hauled back out onto her trailer. This makes the boat light for trailing and manoeuvring on land, but heavy in the water – an ideal combination. Another advantage is that the water ballast has neutral buoyancy should the hull become flooded, so extra buoyancy tanks do not have to be provided to counteract the weight of the ballast.

Going on the plane

Racing-dinghy hulls typically have long, flat after-sections under the waterline and a big wide transom. Their smooth underbody reduces 'wetted area', making the dinghy faster. Traditional dinghies generally have a shallow full-length external keel, running into a deep skeg aft. A racing dinghy will plane in strong winds, skimming over the surface of the water in a cloud of spray, and will surf down the faces of the waves in a following wind. A heavy traditional dinghy, by contrast, only planes very reluctantly. Her crew has to reduce sail in a strong following wind to prevent the dinghy from broaching. A traditional hull form has other virtues, however. It will track straight under sail, so that the dinghy demands less attention from the helmsman, be easier to row, and will heave-to comfortably in heavy weather.

Swamping

It is not the wind strength that is the chief concern of the crew of a cruising dinghy, but the state of the sea. If a big sea breaks aboard, it can flood a dinghy to the gunwales, and she needs to have the ability to stay afloat while you bale her out again. There must be sufficient buoyancy spread out around the edges of the boat to keep her afloat and stable enough to resist the 'free surface effect' of the water sloshing around in her.

Traditional dinghies often still carry buoyancy bags, and these remain a good solution. Unlike a defective buoyancy tank, it is obvious when a bag is leaking, as it will slowly deflate. But the tendency in modern dinghies is to have built-in buoyancy, which is usually contained beneath an internal moulding on GRP boats. A dinghy adapted for cruising will often have waterproof hatches fitted to the buoyancy tanks so that they can also be used for gear storage. If the integrity of the buoyancy tank is not to be compromised, these hatches must be quality products and properly waterproof.

It is becoming common for modern cruising dinghies to be designed so that the interior of the boat is self-draining. This is an extremely desirable feature. Not only does it contribute greatly to safety at sea, but the crew will not need to keep pumping water out of the dinghy during a wet beat to windward.

Capsizing

Racing dinghies are often sailed very 'close to the edge' in strong winds, and frequently capsize. The propensity of racing boats to turn turtle has given all sailing dinghies a bad

Avel Dro hit by a sudden squall on the River Aulne. She dips her lee gunwale but does not capsize. (Ronan Coquil)

reputation for instability. In fact, a decent cruising dinghy is very resistant to turning over. The crews of Drascombe Luggers, sailing in coastal waters, never imagine that their boat is likely to capsize. In very severe conditions any dinghy can suffer a knock down, however, and even though this may only be a remote possibility for a well-designed cruising boat, it should always be taken into consideration.

It is important to discover how your dinghy will behave after a capsize. Some dinghies sit so low in the water, they are impossible to bail out once flooded. Others become completely inverted and are very resistant to being righted. A capsize in the open sea is a much more serious situation than being flipped over during a race, with plenty of rescue boats buzzing around. If the dinghy is difficult to bring upright, the crew will become tired and possibly hypothermic, and soon be unable to assist themselves.

Dinghies that are less resistant to capsizing must have a strategy to deal with it. It is well known that some versions of the Wayfarer have a tendency to become stable when inverted, for example. Experienced cruising sailors take this into account. They practise righting their dinghies so that they are confident they can achieve this in all conditions, or they add masthead buoyancy to their dinghies, to stop them dipping their masts under the water. Most of all, they reef down early and sail their boats well within their limits.

Multihulls

Although single-hulled craft remain the most popular form of cruising dinghy, some experienced cruising sailors swear by multihulls. The cruising catamaran was popularised by the British designer James Wharram, and the smaller craft built to

Catamarans can make good cruising dinghies. This is John Hughes's 'Hitia' catamaran sailing in the Irish Sea. (John Hughes)

his designs are very well suited for dinghy cruising. Catamarans are very stable and extremely fast off the wind, but tend to be wet to windward. Waves break right over the bridge deck straight into the crew's faces. Unless the weather and the water are very warm, the crews of 'cats' need to wear full waterproofs or perhaps even drysuits when sailing in open water. On the other hand, they get to their destination far faster than people sailing conventional dinghies.

A big disadvantage is that catamarans are impossible to row. Should the wind drop, a catamaran must be propelled by a small outboard or by paddles, but their performance under sail is breathtaking.

Rigs for cruising dinghies

Bermudan rig

The most common rig for a modern dinghy is still the Bermudan sloop. Although traditional rigs are much more popular than they were, they are still considered rather eccentric. The Bermudan rig deserves its popularity, as it has many benefits. A Bermudan dinghy will leave most traditionally rigged boats standing when beating to windward. The rig is also intrinsically simple. It relies on a minimum number of spars and only needs one halyard for the mainsail. It is thoroughly understood by anyone who has been through a sailing school dinghy course, and does not require new techniques to be learnt.

The windward performance of the Bermudan sail is chiefly the result of its long luff. This needs a tall mast – and that is also the rig's greatest liability. When rigging the boat, the mast can be difficult to raise to the vertical and hold in place while the standing rigging is set up. Elderly dinghy sailors sometimes cite the increasing difficulty they have in stepping the mast as a reason they will soon have to give up sailing. If a Bermudan mast is mounted in a tabernacle, it can be raised and lowered more easily, but it inevitably projects far beyond the transom when lowered and this is an encumbrance when using canal locks or if the mast needs to be lowered at sea.

Standard Bermudan dinghies will generally need some adaptation for cruising use. The mainsail must be altered so that it can be hoisted and lowered more easily, and you will need to give some thought to reefing it. There is much that can be learnt from a well-set-up cruising Wayfarer. Many features have been developed to adapt the dinghy for cruising use, and have been progressively refined over the years. Cruising Wayfarers can be reefed down in a matter of seconds without lowering the sail, and this is only one of the many clever refinements that have been developed from years of experience cruising these dinghies.

Gaff rig

Gaff rig was largely ignored for years, but it has recently enjoyed a great resurgence. Like many traditional rigs it sets a four-sided sail, with a spar at head and foot. Modern gaff sails are generally 'peaked up' higher than was traditional, in the interests of improved windward performance, and a well-tuned modern gaffer, exploiting the benefits of modern synthetic ropes and sailcloth, can approach the Bermudan rig in windward efficiency.

A gaff sail has one great advantage over other rigs: the peak halyard can be eased to depower the sail on any point of sailing, even if the sail is full of wind. A gaff sail with peak lowered spills most of its wind, while retaining a small triangle of sail that still sets properly. The ability to adjust the 'throttle' of a gaff sail by playing the peak halyard is extraordinarily useful when manoeuvring in confined waters under sail, and it is worth choosing the gaff rig for this feature alone. It is no accident that modern Bermudan-rigged yachts usually lower their sails and turn on their engines for close-quarters manoeuvring in confined waters.

Lugsails

Another old rig now regaining its place in the sun is the lugsail. This rig is astonishingly simple, and spreads a huge sail area very efficiently on short spars. This simplicity is deceptive, however, as the rig is extremely powerful and effective. In the days of commercial sail, the lugsail

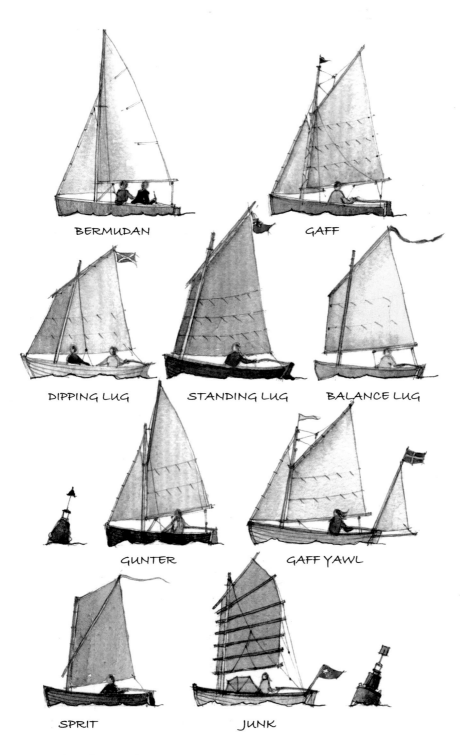

BERMUDAN

GAFF

DIPPING LUG

STANDING LUG

BALANCE LUG

GUNTER

GAFF YAWL

SPRIT

JUNK

Comparative dinghy rigs.

was considered to be the fastest and most efficient working rig. The only disadvantage of a lugger was that it demanded a large and strong crew, so alternative rigs were adopted in more prosperous areas where seamen's wages were higher. Big well-crewed luggers could give contemporary racing yachts a run for their money. After the celebrated schooner *America* had secured the America's Cup by competing against contemporary British yachts in the Solent in 1851, she was afraid to accept a challenge from the fastest Yarmouth lugger *Reindeer*, because the *America*'s owners were unable to face the possible embarrassment of losing to a crew of longshore seamen, or so the story goes.

No lugsail is quite as efficient to windward as a Bermudan sail, but the rig has many advantages, chief among them being its ability to be deployed and struck very rapidly. The sail can be lowered completely into the boat, and does not remain swinging about in the air above your head, like a Bermudan or gaff sail. Once lowered, it can be quickly bundled up and lifted out of the way, so that the boat is ready for other activities.

Lug-rigged dinghies have a reputation for not being very close-winded. This is because there are far too many nowadays with poorly set-up rigs, where the boatbuilder wanted a romantic look but did not consider the demands of efficient performance. The lugsail is perhaps the most misunderstood of the traditional rigs. Far too many modern luggers can only sail effectively to windward with the help of an engine – a painful sight for any seaman. In order to form an efficient aerofoil, a lugsail requires a huge amount of luff tension. There has to be a powerful tackle on the tack, led aft to the helm so it can be adjusted while sailing. The

tackle should be relaxed when sailing off the wind and hardened up for close-hauled work. Lugsail dinghies from the boards of designers who thoroughly understand the rig – such as Nigel Irens and François Vivier – are swift and efficient designs, and show the true potential of the modern lugger.

A recent example of a fast lugger is the Goat Island Skiff (GIS), designed by Michael Storer. It sets a single large balanced lug sail which is highly efficient and quick to rig. This is a versatile boat that rows well and sails like a rocket.

Lugsails come in a confusing variety of guises: dipping lug, standing lug and balance lug. The **dipping lug** was the traditional working boat rig. It is probably the most efficient lug rig, but it is a complex business to tack the sail. There are various methods of bringing a dipping lugger about, but none of them are particularly easy or fast, even with a well-trained crew. Some dipping lugsails must be lowered completely every time the boat goes about, lifted round the mast by the crew and then re-hoisted on the other side. This is acceptable in the open sea, but a frightful nuisance in confined waters. The dipping lug is breathtakingly beautiful and extraordinarily fast in experienced hands, however – a real seaman's rig. If you always sail with a crew of two or three people, who can be well trained in its quirks, it would be worth considering for a cruising dinghy that will mainly be sailed on open water.

The **standing lug** is a more practical set-up for a small dinghy. Before the Second World War it was very popular for pleasure dinghies. Unlike the dipping lug, a standing lugsail remains on the same side of the mast on both tacks. The dinghies in Arthur Ransome's celebrated book *Swallows and Amazons* were both standing luggers.

A gaff-rigged yawl sails across a lake in winter (a Kittywake 14).

This yole sets a dipping lugsail on her main and foremasts.

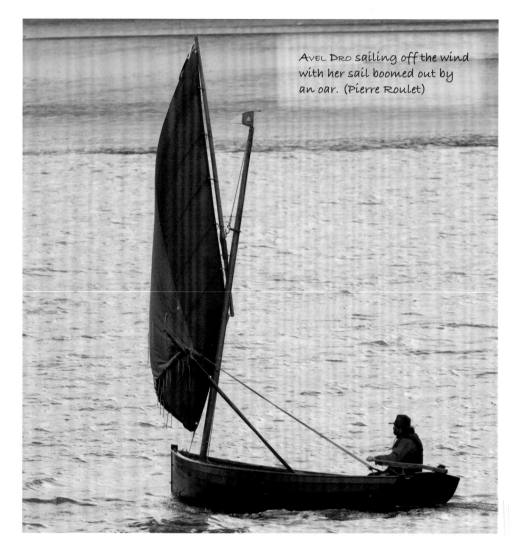

AVEL DRO *sailing off the wind with her sail boomed out by an oar.* (Pierre Roulet)

Working boats would usually set a boomless standing lugsail, whereas pleasure dinghies spread the foot of their sails along a boom, creating a more efficient sail shape when sailing off the wind. A boomless sail is much easier to hoist and lower, however, and is less cumbersome when lowered. It is also more easily cleared to one side of the boat to leave space for nets or coiling down warps. For this reason, working fishermen never had booms on their lugsails. A cruising dinghy sailor may agree with their choice, and enjoy never being banged on the head

by the boom ever again. On long reaches off the wind, a boomless sail can be poled out with an oar, which takes the twist out of the sail.

The **balanced lugsail** was once very popular on dinghies sailed on inland waters, but traditionally it was considered too rigid to be used at sea. The boom of a balance lugsail extends forward of the mast, and a downhaul is bent onto the boom a little way back from the luff of the sail. This operates in a similar way to a modern kicking strap, preventing the boom from lifting when sailing off the wind. If properly set up, a balance lug will not twist on any point of sailing. As with all lug rigs, it is frequently misunderstood, and you often see balance lugsails setting really badly, with a deep crease across the sail, or laden with unnecessary additional control lines. Rigged properly, the sail is simple and extremely efficient. It is popular on many modern designs of cruising dinghy, in particular the Scottish-influenced designs of Iain Oughtred. It is a particular favourite of the New Zealand dinghy designer John Welsford, who considers it the ideal cruising rig.

Gunter rig

The gunter rig originally evolved out of the lugsail, and this is why the spar at the head of a gunter sail is properly called the 'yard'

and should never be referred to as a 'gaff', even though it usually is. Gunter rig comes close to the Bermudan rig in windward performance, without requiring a lofty mast. Indeed, this is its main advantage over the Bermudan-rigged competition. The mast and spars are usually short enough to be stored in the boat when unstepped.

The disadvantage of the gunter rig is its complexity compared to a Bermudan dinghy. Unless the mainsail is to be lowered every time the sail is reefed, a gunter sail requires a separate peak and throat halyard, just like the gaff rig. Also, the long yard has a tendency to capsize and crash down on the crew's heads if the sail is lowered carelessly.

I sailed with the gunter rig for many years, and grew to love its many

A balance lug dinghy on the Norfolk Broads. Simple rigs are best for children.

eccentricities. Although it needs careful adaptation for efficient cruising, when properly set up it is perhaps the perfect rig for a cruising dinghy.

Yawl rig

The yawl rig was popularised by the Drascombe range, and has become increasingly popular among the cruising fraternity. Two masts may seem like an indulgence on a small boat, but the rig has many practical advantages. Traditional fishing boats often had two masts, and you can be sure that working fishermen would not have fitted the extra gear without a very good reason.

A yawl-rigged boat can create a snug 'storm rig' simply by lowering the mainsail and sailing on under a balanced rig of just mizzen and jib. The ability to reduce sail rapidly in this way is an extraordinarily useful feature in a cruising boat. Another advantage of a yawl is that, if the mizzen is left hoisted when the other sails have been lowered, it acts like a weathercock, holding the boat head to wind when lying at anchor or reefing. If I were looking for another cruising dinghy, I would seriously consider a yawl.

Spritsails

The sprit rig is a good choice for light craft that are mainly used under oars, but need to set a sail occasionally. Often the sail is not hoisted, but kept laced to the mast, which is set up when the crew want a rest from

A pretty yawl-rigged lugger. This is not a ketch, because the boat is too small. (Robert Hoffman)

A small spritsail dinghy. There is no way of reefing the sail – the whole rig is simply removed in strong winds.

rowing, and kept lashed down in the dinghy when not required. To set the sail, the mast is unlashed and lifted into a socket in a thwart. Then the peak of the sprit is pushed into a cringle in the peak of the sail and its lower end is attached to the mast by a short length of rope called a 'snotter'. Sometimes there is also a brailing line to enable the sail to be dowsed without lowering it. The spritsail is admirably simple, and spreads a lot of sail area on short spars. But it becomes rather more complex if you want a method of reefing it. Sometimes this is not even attempted.

Junk rig

The junk sail is the traditional sail of the China Sea, and was popularised in the West by the ex-commando Blondie Hasler, who used it with great success on his famous Folkboat *Jester* in the 1950s and 1960s.

Effectively a multi-battened lugsail, the junk sail has a complex multi-part sheet and an array of topping lifts that collect the sail when it is lowered. Its chief advantage is the ability to increase or reduce the area of sail simply by raising and lowering the halyard. The junk rig spreads out its stresses rather than concentrates them, like a conventional Western rig, and is readily made out of simple cheap materials. I have seen junk sails made from garden bamboos and plastic tarpaulin bought from a DIY shop which still perform extraordinarily well.

The junk rig is a rather specialised enthusiasm in the West, but it should not be rejected simply because it seems eccentric and quirky. The rig is much more clever and subtle than it may appear at first glance, and if you want to experiment with junk rig, it is worth making contact with other enthusiasts.

DINGHIES AND OUTBOARD MOTORS

If you intend to carry an engine and expect to use it regularly, ideally it should be mounted in a properly designed well, rather than just clamped to the transom. Few dinghies have an outboard well as good as the one on the Drascombe Lugger, a dinghy that is as effective under motor as under sail. Drascombe Luggers can be motor-sailed to windward without worrying about the possibility of getting the mainsheet wrapped around the outboard's powerhead or the propeller.

In stark contrast to the excellent arrangement on the Drascombe Lugger, many modern racing dinghies have no way of mounting an engine at all. When the wind drops, you must resort to paddles or try to cadge a tow. Older types of class dinghy can usually accommodate an outboard motor clamped onto the transom, but this is not an ideal location for an engine. An outboard hanging off the transom is prone to foul the mainsheet, and the propeller inevitably drags in the water when the motor is on the lee side. The outboard can also conflict with the rudder when the boat is under sail. This is why many experienced cruising sailors leave the motor at home and learn to row instead.

There is more about outboard motors in Chapter 4.

MY DINGHY

To illustrate the issues to be considered when buying a boat, I will tell you why I chose my own dinghy. I bought her just after I had sold my 6-ton cutter, when I had seen the light and decided to return to dinghy cruising. After many years of cruising in a traditional wooden 12ft (3.6m) Tideway dinghy, I was looking for more space while sleeping aboard, as well as the improved sea-keeping ability that comes with greater size, but I did not want to sacrifice the handiness of my old boat. The Tideway is a convenient size for handling ashore and remarkably easy to launch and recover. Consequently, I narrowed my search to vessels of some 15–16ft (4.5m) long. The extra length creates a much larger boat in cubic capacity, yet a family car can still tow this size of dinghy on an unbraked trailer, and it will fit in the average garage.

The classic British cruising dinghy of this length is the Wayfarer, and very capable boats they are too. But I wanted a boat with a simple and more robust rig, free from mass-produced fittings. She also had to be fast and weatherly, with good performance to windward. I selected the Ilur class dinghy when I saw large fleets of this popular French design at a Breton boat festival.

The Ilur is a modern design by François Vivier, based on the traditional inshore

Drascombe Luggers have very well designed accommodation for an outboard, just aft of their rudder.

fishing boats of the Breton coast, and little known outside its home waters. It is Vivier's most popular design, with nearly a thousand sets of plans sold, and many hundreds afloat in France. The Ilur's traditional fishing-boat lines and straightforward rig, beamy uncluttered hull and sturdy gear exuded an appealing feeling of self-assurance and all-round competence. She looked like the sort of boat you would not be afraid to take into the tough environment of a working harbour. When you stood up in the boat to handle long mooring warps, this dinghy would not threaten to tip you in. She looked like a boat you could rely on.

Ilurs are fully open, unencumbered by decking, which gives lots of room to work. The rig is a single lugsail, of a substantial 130sq ft (12sq m), set on an unstayed mast stepped well forward. The remarkably simple running rigging consists of a single halyard, sheet and tack downhaul. There is ample space for two to sleep aboard under the thwart on either side of the centreboard case, on flat floorboards well above any bilge water.

I have now owned *Avel Dro* for many years, and it is difficult to write dispassionately about a boat in which I have travelled so far. I find her full-bodied hull very stable and dry in a heavy sea. The clinker ply construction and alloy centreplate mean that she is lighter than she looks, and she is remarkably fast for her type and rig. After a first exciting sail in a fresh breeze, I bought two 50lb bags of sand from the local builders' merchant and put them under her bottom boards to calm her down a bit. Recently I have dispensed with extra ballast as my usual cruising gear provides enough weight, particularly the 12-volt battery and two heavy anchors and rodes.

Gybing *Avel Dro*'s big lugsail in a strong wind was also rather alarming at first. The

A Wayfarer dinghy sailing back down a creek after a secluded night afloat.

mainsheet block needs to be unhooked from one quarter and transferred rapidly to the other side. If this is not timed exactly, the wind simply rips the block out of your hand. I spent much time finding how to get the best from *Avel Dro*, and gearing her up for coastal cruising. Like any relationship, a new boat needs to be worked on. After a decade of ownership, I am still refining the arrangement of her rig and fittings.

Together, my boat and I have cruised past the granite cliffs of the Breton coast and braved the strong tides of the Bristol Channel. We have spent nights at anchor in the creeks and crannies of the English West Country and the rocky coves of Wales. The wood of her hull has absorbed all these memories, so that the moment I step aboard her, I leave behind the worries and troubles of my normal existence. The complexities of modern shore life are swept away, and I become immersed in the ways of the sea.

Avel Dro goes racing

There are two very different kinds of dinghies in the world. There are those with a mass of coloured control lines, which you will usually find going very fast, their crew dangling over the side covered in spray. These are racing dinghies. Then there are the simply rigged dinghies that you come across grovelling in muddy creeks. These are cruising dinghies, and this book is about them. But cruising dinghies sometimes go racing too.

Avel Dro often spends her summer holidays in France, visiting local boat festivals. French 'fêtes maritimes' tend to pass in a booze-fuddled blur, carousing with other enthusiasts. But there are invariably races as well. If you imagine that these are gentlemanly affairs, you couldn't be more wrong. The boats competing for the leading places take it very seriously indeed.

A delightful scene greeted Avel Dro as she emerged from the natural harbour of Ploumanac'h for the first race. The course had been laid out in a tidal lagoon surrounded by rose-red rocks and overlooked by the pretty Château de Costaérès, perched on a rocky island. But I was not interested in the scenery. There was a race to win, in which I was the only foreign competitor. The Red Ensign rippled out from the peak of my brown sail. I thought of Nelson and narrowed my eyes.

Two classes of small boats jockeyed for position at the start line. We all had reefs in our sails, and heeled viciously in the gusty wind. Most boats were carrying at least two people, which meant they had one person to read the race instructions and check their watch, as well as someone else to concentrate on the steering and avoiding the other boats. I was on my own in Avel Dro, one hand grappling with the tiller, the other trying to stop the race instruction sheets from blowing away. The tension was almost unbearable. Suddenly a gun was fired, the flags on the committee boat dropped like they had been shot, and we all thundered off on a reach towards the first mark.

I was not at all ready for the gun, but I accidentally started quite well. Avel Dro crossed the starting line about sixth. I took out two other boats on the first

Small boats dried out at low tide during the Ploumanac'h boat festival, on the northern coast of France.

downwind leg by cruelly pinching their wind, but then I got completely disorientated tacking among the rocks. By the time I worked out which buoy I should be heading for, another boat had overtaken me. I had just regained my composure when there was a great crash and Avel Dro stopped dead, throwing me onto the bottom boards. I had sailed full tilt into an underwater rock. This cost me at least one other place in the race and smashed the full bottle of malt whisky in my food locker.

The second lap went rather better. The wind began to die away and I wished I had not reefed. But I had learnt the course by now, so I did not get lost again or hit anything else. I even managed to overtake another competitor by a clever bit of tacking at the last mark. I was still gloating when I suddenly drifted into a calm patch. A little lugsail dinghy popped up out of nowhere, glided past and slipped over the line in front of me. Avel Dro returned to harbour determined to do better in the next day's race.

I moored alongside a pilot cutter from Carentec in the Bay of Morlaix. Her crew were so mortified by the news of the loss of my bottle of Laphroaig that they spent all afternoon singing me French sea shanties and pouring 'Paddy' down my throat, the Breton sailor's favourite Irish whiskey. Nor did I get to bed particularly early, as it was Bastille Day and there was a big dinner in a quayside marquee for all the boat crews, followed by live music far into the night.

The next morning I needed lots of black coffee to clear my head. The wind had moderated slightly, and I reckoned that Avel Dro was just capable of carrying full sail, even though most of the other dinghies were reefing. I had also figured out the meaning of all the flag signals, so I managed to start third in my class, at the best end of the line. Approaching the first mark, the leading dinghies left just enough room for me to slip between the buoy and the windward boat. Before they knew what was happening, Avel Dro had nipped neatly into their wind. Once the mark was abeam, I sheeted in and slid efficiently past two of the boats that had been ahead of me.

Hard on the wind, Avel Dro powered up to the next mark. The brisk breeze exactly suited her, laden with cruising gear, while lighter and faster boats were lurching about spilling wind. By the time she gybed round the windward mark, Avel Dro had established a commanding lead over the next boat in her class. This lead kept on growing for the remaining three circuits of the course. She was the third boat across the finishing line, but first in class by an embarrassing margin.

There is always a charming confusion at a French boat festival, and I turned up to the prize-giving with no idea how Avel Dro had done overall, when the results of the two races were put together. A host of notables were standing behind a table groaning with cups and prizes. They began to announce the places in reverse order. Boat name after boat name was called out. The third prize was awarded, then the second prize:

'Avel Dro de Bristol en Angleterre.'

I walked forward and my arms were laden with a huge cup, a book, a plaque and a boat model. Trying not to drop them, I shook hands with innumerable Frenchmen and kissed various Frenchwomen on both cheeks, and had my photograph taken by the local press. Racing, I thought, definitely has something going for it.

2 FITTING OUT FOR DAYSAILING

A summer's day on the river, drifting down with the current, fingers trailed over the side – a daysail down the estuary or a trip to a waterside pub for lunch – you needn't go far to have a great time in a dinghy. The aim is not to get somewhere as fast as possible, but to maximise the sheer enjoyment of being afloat, the joy of simply messing about in a boat. Venture just a little way up the lake, down the estuary, or around the corner from your usual launching site, and you will already be a world away from the anxieties of normal life.

A cruising dinghy rowing down a tidal creek. This is John Perry's own design, a very capable boat with many crossings of the western English Channel under her belt.

Rough and tumble

Cruising dinghies suffer many trials and tribulations. Their crews run them up onto rocky beaches, or moor them alongside high quay walls, where they crash and surge against rough stonework. They jump down into them from high quaysides, and expect their bottom boards to cope with the impact. A cruising dinghy has to be sturdily built to put up with all this punishment.

Even the best dinghy will probably need beefing up for the rough and tumble of the cruising life. The basic hull construction may be sound, but the quality of standard dinghy fittings is often woeful. This is why a seasoned cruising dinghy looks very different from a racing dinghy, even if they were both originally of the same class. Racing fittings have been exchanged for chunky, robust gear. The interior exudes an air of austere simplicity, clear of a racing dinghy's clutter of control lines. There is no mistaking the robust competence of a true sea boat.

Sorting out her rig

Racing dinghies need to have efficient rigs, or they would not win races. Cruising sailors like to have efficient rigs too, but their idea of efficiency is rather different from their racing brethren. A racing sailor demands a rig that is fast under sail and as close-winded as possible. Cruising dinghies have to go to windward as well, but their crews also have other priorities.

On a cruising boat it is essential that the sails can be set, handled and reefed easily when out on open water. Racing dinghies usually set their sails ashore in the dinghy park, and are launched already rigged, so it doesn't matter if it is a time-consuming business. The crew of a cruising dinghy do not have that luxury. They need to set sail smartly out on the water, in all conditions.

In the days of sail, working seamen were less interested in squeezing the last knot of speed to windward out of their boat than in their ability to hand sail rapidly in a squall. Traditional rigs were retained on working craft long after the Bermudan rig had been universally adopted by racing craft, not simply due to conservatism, but because the traditional ones were found to be more practical. They had evolved to cope with the tough life of the longshore mariner. Their technology was robust and easy to repair. Working sailing craft typically had low rigging stresses and spread their sail area longitudinally rather than vertically. Masts were low, and the rig was pushed out beyond the confines of the boat with additional spars, like bowsprits and bumpkins, to minimise capsizing forces.

Traditional rigs have many advantages on a cruising boat. Their short masts are easier to step than a tall Bermudan mast, and require the minimum of rigging. Just like the old working boatmen, cruising sailors also need their boats to be reliable and durable.

Simplifying and strengthening

The standing rigging of a cruising boat should be as simple as possible. Complex arrangements of spreaders and jumpers are best avoided. As stainless steel rigging is always prone to sudden failure, it could be worth replacing it with Dyneema rope, which is just as strong but more flexible and longer lasting – or you could choose a rig with no standing rigging at all, like mine.

THE DRASCOMBE OR DEVON LUGGER

Nearly 50 years after it was first designed, the Lugger remains the quintessential British cruising dinghy. While other contemporary designers concentrated on producing boats for the sailing club racing scene, which were also capable of being cruised, John Watkinson designed the Lugger as a pure cruising boat, sufficiently seaworthy for coastal passages. This is reflected in the her weight and robust construction. Although some were built of plywood, the design was popularised by the fibreglass versions produced for many years by Honnor Marine in Devon.

At present, the Lugger is built by a successor company to the original Honnor Marine and also by Churchouse Boats. The two designs are nearly identical, but during the sadly mismanaged liquidation of the original Honnor Marine in 1997, the trademark 'Drascombe' ended up being seperated from the company owning the production moulds. The upshot is that only Churchouse Boats can use the original name 'Drascombe Lugger', and the present Honnor Marine, who retain the original moulds, market theirs as the 'Original Devon Lugger'. Despite this sensitivity, elsewhere in this book I tend to use 'Drascombe Lugger' rather loosely to refer to both modern companies' boats, as well as those from the original production run. This is not intended to reflect a preference. If the divided production of the Lugger produces difficulties for writers attempting to be even-handed, it means that a customer for these boats is in an enviable position of being able to compare the products of two competing manufacturers.

The Lugger carries a boomless gunter sail, a jib and mizzen. All three sails are of modest area for this size of boat. In light winds it is common to see Luggers motoring, especially to windward. Given a good breeze they sail very well, however. Their slim hulls cut through a rough sea confidently and fluenlly. They are a safe family boat, happily accommodating up to seven people and very difficult to capsize. The hull incorporates ample built-in buoyancy, which makes it unsinkable.

These boats are very well made, of thick fibreglass with special bronze fittings. They are rugged enough to sit happily on a mooring, out in the weather all season. The Lugger also has one of the best outboard motor wells of any dinghy, which allows the motor to be cocked up out of the water when the boat is under sail, but keeps it protected from damage. The usual conflict between outboard motor and rudder is completely avoided by mounting the rudder in front of the outboard well. This means that the Lugger's rudder is rather idiosyncratic, however. It is dropped into a slot, rather like a daggerboard, and has to be retracted before sailing into shallow water, when the dinghy must be steered with an oar or with the outboard.

Although Luggers are designed to be effective under power, they also row very well, as long as you use sufficiently long oars. If you want to use the boat for camping aboard, there is space for a couple of people to bed down either side of the centreboard case on the flat bottom boards, well clear of any bilge water. There are small stowage lockers under the side benches and a very capacious one under the stern deck. Tent arrangements vary. A ridge tent can be set up between the masts or a standard hooped land tent can be bought off the shelf and simply dropped into the boat.

Extraordinarily well conceived, and still extremely well loved by large numbers of owners, the Lugger is the focus of a passionate community of people who organise regular rallies for Luggers and the other designs in Watkinson's original Drascombe range. These are also well worth looking at, in particular the larger Longboat and the smaller Dabber – as well as my favourite, the lovely little Scaffie, which Honnor Marine still produce.

(Didier Carion)

A simple lanyard is the best solution for tensioning standing rigging.

Although bottlescrews are the conventional method of tensioning standing rigging, they are best replaced by rope lanyards on a cruising boat. A lanyard can easily be replaced should it fail miles from the nearest chandlery, which certainly cannot be said of a bottlescrew. Lanyards also cope better with the unfair strains that can occur when shrouds come into conflict with dock walls.

Running rigging should also be simplified. Racing boats usually have a mass of very thin control lines running through tiny blocks, to reduce windage. Ropes on a cruising dinghy should be sized not for strength, but for ease of use – even when you are tired, your hands are cold, and night has fallen.

Halyards need to be of a decent diameter, so they are comfortable to use in all conditions. The original halyard cleats will probably also need to be swapped for larger ones. These should have horns large enough to hang a coiled halyard on. On my dinghy the halyards are made fast to simple wooden belaying pins, which take the rope turns more sweetly than any cleat. They may look rather 'retro', but they are still the business.

The rig of a cruising dinghy must allow good visibility all round. Low-cut headsails that sweep the foredeck should have at least a window, but it is probably better if they are re-cut with a raised foot so that the crew can see beneath. This may mean moving the jib fairleads so that the re-cut sail sets properly.

Modifying a Bermudan-rigged dinghy

The Bermudan rig relies on a tall mast, which creates a lot of weight aloft, even when the sail is lowered. There is a good case for replacing an old wooden mast with an aluminium extrusion or a carbon fibre mast. The resultant reduction in weight will make the dinghy markedly stiffer and more seaworthy. On the other hand, it is much easier to make a temporary repair in a wooden mast, should it get broken.

Bermudan-rigged dinghies often bring the falls of their halyards down inside the mast, to emerge through a turning block at the foot, from which they are brought up to a cleat. Halyards arranged this way can be difficult to tension properly as there is not enough distance between the turning block and the cleat to 'swig' them tight. Racing dinghies are often fitted with Highfield levers or similar devices to achieve a tight luff, but complex fittings like this can be a liability on a cruising boat. It is very difficult to repair specialised items of chandlery should they fail when on passage, so a spare must be carried, and they are also difficult to operate with cold, wet hands. The traditional method of bringing the halyard down the outside of the mast and straight to a cleat is hard to beat.

Gunter- and gaff-rigged dinghies

Small gunter-rigged dinghies usually have a single halyard on the mainsail. This arrangement is admirably straightforward, but once a reef has been put in the mainsail, the yard will inevitably sag away from the mast so that the sail does not set properly. The simplest solution is to lower the sail right down into the boat, unbend the halyard and then re-bend it onto the yard higher up, before re-hoisting the sail. More sophisticated gunter-rigged dinghies usually have two halyards: a peak and a throat. The peak halyard is attached to the yard by a wire span or a track on the front of

the yard, in order to allow the yard to slide down relative to the mast when the sail is reefed. Once the sail has been hoisted, the peak halyard does not need to be touched when reefing – only the throat halyard is adjusted.

As a gunter yard usually sets slightly away from the mast, the luff of the sail should be cut with a slight angle at the throat. This subtlety is often omitted on small boats, such as the Mirror dinghy. Instead, the luff is cut straight, so that the yard needs to be hoisted hard against the mast for maximum sailing efficiency. To achieve this you must adopt a single halyard rig or be very clever with the lead of the halyards.

Compared to the quite similar gaff rig, the gunter mainsail has the advantage that the two halyards can be hauled up separately, and this makes the rig easier for a singlehander. Usually the peak is hauled up first, followed by the throat halyard.

A traditional boat in the Baltic Sea. This sprit-rigged vessel has a mizzen mast, but she is sailing under just jib and mainsail.

Gaff sails also have separate peak and throat halyards, but both of them need to be hoisted at the same time. A gaff sail should be rigged with both halyards running down the same side of the mast, so that the halyards can be 'paired' in the hand, and both hoisted by the same person.

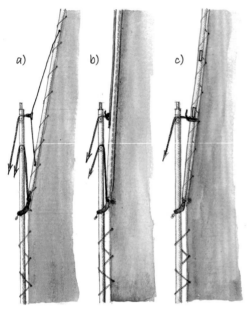

a)   b)   c)

There are various ways of setting up a gunter rig so that the mainsail can be reefed. Here are three common methods.

a) Wire span
The peak halyard is shackled to a saddle which slides along a wire span on the yard. it is hard to peak the yard up tight to the mast by this method.

b) Track
The peak halyard is made fast to the slider in a bronze or stainless steel track mounted on the face of the yard. A clove hitch is a suitably secure knot. The yard must have a groove for the head of the sail.

c) Traditional
The peak halyard is made fast to the mast with a fisherman's bend. There is no throat halyard. The sail must be lowered each time the sail is reefed and the halyard reattached to the yard at the correct position, where it is restrained by a wooded wedge.

On my old gunter-rigged dinghy, the mainsail halyards were taken down to turning blocks under the mast thwart and then led through a pair of cam cleats. These were used to grip the halyard temporarily after hoisting. This modification allowed me to make fast the halyards around the belaying pins one at a time. Some gaff-rigged dinghies use clam cleats to achieve the same result. You need to have some means of temporarily cleating one halyard while you make fast the other.

The mast tabernacle

It is very desirable to be able to raise and lower the mast while the boat is afloat. Only the very smallest mast can be lifted to the vertical and dropped into its mast step while the boat is bobbing about in the water. Raising a mast of any length is a tough job, even ashore. On some dinghies the mast has to be lifted into a shallow socket on the foredeck and then held vertical while the standing rigging is set up. This is impossible afloat.

Ideally, a cruising dinghy will step her mast in a tabernacle. The Wayfarer is an example where this is standard. On other dinghies it is a very desirable adaptation, allowing the mast to be raised and lowered under control. Tabernacles are often fabricated in galvanised mild steel or stainless steel.

On my old Tideway, I built a timber tabernacle by cutting a slot in the forward thwart and forming a three-sided wooden enclosure beneath it to take the foot of the mast. The mast was reinforced with side cheeks of oak, drilled for the stainless steel bolt on which the mast pivoted. I fitted a two-part tackle on the forestay, led back to a cleat on the foredeck. If I hauled on this tackle it would pull the mast up to the vertical, and also tension the

The view forward in my old Tideway dinghy, showing the mast stepped in a tabernacle. Just aft of the washboard is the cleat for the forestay tackle. The boom is held down by a fixed line and the sail luff is tensioned by a two-part purchase on the throat halyard, just visible to port of the mast. Notice the lack of kicking strap.

shrouds. Before I made this modification, raising *Baggywrinkle*'s mast was a frustrating process, and the rigging inevitably got tangled halfway through. Afterwards it became a one-handed operation.

Jib sheets

If your dinghy sets a jib, it must be possible to cleat and release the sheets when the dinghy is being sat out by the crew. This is sometimes difficult if the cam cleats are mounted low down. If the cleats are mounted on wedge-shaped blocks, the cleat can be operated remotely by someone sitting on the opposite gunwale. Getting the angle of the wedge right usually needs experimentation. On my Tideway, I found that if the fairleads were located so they were convenient for the crew, they were in the wrong place for the sail to set correctly. A short rope with a loop in the end was used to correct the lead of

the sheets and improve the set of the jib. I called this a 'lizard', but crewmembers with a racing background claimed it was a 'Barber Hauler'.

Mainsheet

Holding the mainsheet can become very tiring if a cruising dinghy is on the same tack for a long period. This problem can be mitigated if the rope for the mainsheet is substantial in thickness. 10mm or even 12mm in diameter is not excessive, as it is much more comfortable to hold a large diameter rope. You may need to increase the size of the sheet blocks to match.

Kicking straps

A powerful kicking strap is usually considered essential to get the best out of a Bermudan or gunter sail, but they are a confounded nuisance on a cruising boat. When you are working in the forward part

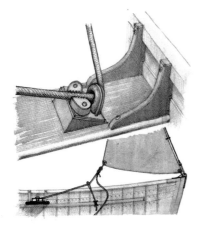

(LEFT) On my old Tideway, the cam cleats were mounted on timber wedges, so that they could be operated from the far side of the dinghy. The lead of the sheet was adjusted by a short rope that is either called a 'lizard' or a 'Barber Hauler'.

(BELOW) Instead of a kicking strap, many cruising dinghies set a preventer from the boom to the lee gunwale, to keep the sail flat when the sheet is eased.

of the dinghy, the boom inevitably swings over to your side of the boat and then the kicking strap pins you against the back of the foredeck, gasping for breath.

As a kicking strap is generally only really required when the sail is sheeted out, many cruising dinghies remove it altogether. When close-hauled, the sheet holds the boom

down and keeps twist out of the sail. If you are sailing with the wind free, a 'preventer' can be set up instead. This is a rope set up tight between the boom and the lee gunwale, which prevents sail twist and also an unexpected gybe.

Since the first edition of this book, various people have commented on my advice about kicking straps and reminded me that on performance dinghies a powerful kicking strap tackle is used to induce mast bend, which flattens the sail for strong winds. Although this is very much a racing technique, it can be appropriate on fast cruising dinghies. On this issue, as with other topics in the book, I try to give you my own personal view, but also to make you aware of other choices that are available. There is no one correct way to go dinghy cruising.

Reefing

If a normal class dinghy can be reefed at all, the usual method is to remove the boom from its gooseneck, then rotate the boom to roll some of the sail around it, before replacing it on the gooseneck. This is a relatively simple job ashore, but extraordinarily difficult afloat. It will be necessary to beach the dinghy to put in a reef, or perhaps pick up a vacant mooring. This is acceptable for a dinghy that is only used on daysails in sheltered waters, but a more effective system of mainsail reefing is vital for open-water cruising (see Chapter 6).

FITTING OUT HER HULL FOR DAYSAILING

The problem with centreboards

The usual method of preventing leeway is a pivoting centreboard. On heavier dinghies this is sometimes a galvanised steel plate. A metal plate is wonderful for sounding your way up a narrow creek with a shingle bottom, as it acts like a minimum depth alarm on an electronic echo sounder. When the plate starts clinking on the shingle, you know you have entered shallow water and it is time to tack.

A problem with all centreboards is that sand or mud can find its way up inside the centreboard case when you beach

This new wooden Tideway has a tackle on her galvanised centreboard and halyards belayed to cleats on the boom. She also has a kicking strap.

your dinghy, jamming the plate in place, so it refuses to budge when you want to lower it. The only solution is to hammer it back down again, by applying a judicious amount of force. If the top of the case is open throughout its length, you can press a piece of hardwood, shaped specially for this purpose, against the aft end of the centreboard and then hammer at the top of it to ease the board down again. Some centreboard cases are fully enclosed, and in these cases a hole should be drilled in the top of the case, stopped with a rubber bung when not in use, and large enough to introduce a wooden rod that can be pressed against the aft end of the plate, allowing it to be hammered down again in the same way. You will also need to carry a hammer or mallet in your dinghy's tool box.

Gritty beaches on granite coasts are a particular problem, as the rough sand can easily jam your plate rigid. This frequently happens to me when sailing on the Bristol Channel, where many of the harbours have dubious shelter and the boat often ends up pounding for a while as the tide ebbs. The centreplate can become so jammed that it is impossible to move it downwards, even with a cold chisel and a hammer, and the only solution is to take out all the stores and other gear, turn the boat over, knock out the pivot and hammer the plate upwards into the boat, away from the impacted sand.

To address this problem I have fitted a slot gasket to my dinghy. These are made for racing dinghies to diminish the water friction of the open slot, and hence give a slight increase in speed, but they also help to stop sand getting into it. This is not a total solution to a jammed plate, but it has greatly diminished the problem on *Avel Dro*. Some cruising dinghies are designed with an offset centreboard which does not emerge through the keel, to avoid this problem, in particular some of the designs of John Welsford.

Daggerboards

Although centreboards are the norm, small dinghies are sometimes fitted with a simple daggerboard instead. This is a wooden board that slides vertically in a short slot, and is usually lifted out completely in shallow water. Daggerboards have the benefit of simplicity, but in all other respects they are inferior to a centreboard. If they are not lowered right down in their slot, they are always in the way. When sailing into shallow water, a daggerboard does not lift automatically when it hits the bottom, but brings the boat to an abrupt stop instead. If the dinghy has a good tide under her, this could damage the hull. It is worth investigating the possibility of adapting the hull to accommodate a proper pivoting centreboard instead of a daggerboard. This alteration is often made to cruising Mirror dinghies.

Leeboards

Leeboards are pivoted wooden boards mounted externally on the topsides of the hull. The windward board is usually raised when sailing. They are very popular in the Netherlands, even on small boats. They have many advantages: they leave the centre of the dinghy unencumbered, they cannot get jammed by sand or gravel when pounding on a beach (a perennial problem with a centreboard, as we have seen), and they can be made so that the immersed leeboard creates lift to windward. The disadvantage is that leeboards are vulnerable to damage when the dinghy is moored alongside a quay.

Adding ballast to a light dinghy

As we have seen, heavier dinghies are generally more forgiving than light boats. Their motion is less rapid and less tiring for the crew, and they are less vulnerable to capsizing. In order to add ballast to a light dinghy, some owners remove their boat's original timber centreboard and replace it with a heavy galvanised steel plate.

Traditional dinghies were generally fitted with heavy metal centreplates as standard, but you should be cautious about fitting one to a modern dinghy. Retrofitting a heavy plate can have undesirable side effects. A case designed for a light timber centreboard will need reinforcing to cope with the stresses of a heavy plate and the added weight of the metal may also adversely affect the performance of the dinghy, transforming a previously dry dinghy into a wet boat when sailing to windward.

A heavy centreplate can also be a liability if the boat capsizes. If the dinghy turns turtle, it will drop back into the slot under its own weight, instantly negating any righting moment it may have provided. This makes it difficult to right the dinghy. A light wooden board, by contrast, usually remains sticking out of a capsized hull, and can be used to pull the boat upright. Dinghies with heavy plates sometimes have a pin or other device to hold it down when out at sea, preventing the plate from dropping back into its slot in capsize. This must always be released before sailing into shallow water, or the dinghy could be damaged if the plate were to hit the bottom at speed.

Instead of retrofitting a heavy centreplate, it is usually better to add ballast to an over-light dinghy by placing some pigs of lead under the floorboards, which can be moved fore and aft until the dinghy is trimmed correctly. Old lead water pipe folded into a long sausage is sometimes used. Lead ballast needs to be held in place in the hull, or it will inevitably shift when the boat heels over. An alternative solution is to put a couple of bags of sand under the bottom boards.

My 15ft (4.5m) dinghy has no added ballast apart from the coastal cruising gear carried aboard. This has the effect of changing her from a dinghy of moderate weight to a heavy one. Most of this gear remains on board even when I am daysailing. When laden with her cruising gear, my dinghy displaces over 880lbs (400kg).

Sitting out

Many dinghies benefit from being 'sat out' when working to windward, and should be fitted with toe straps and a tiller extension, just like in a racing boat. The straps should be adjusted so that your thighs sit comfortably on the side deck, and the tiller extension falls comfortably to hand, as you may be out there for many hours on a long windward leg. My old Tideway always needed sitting out to make decent progress to windward. Perching on the narrow gunwale became uncomfortable after a while, so I made two padded cushions out of closed-cell foam covered in nylon cloth, which I fastened to the side benches. These were only attached to the boat on their outer edge, so that they could be folded over the gunwale beneath me, for comfort when hiking to windward.

Rudder gear

As the rudder of a cruising boat is always vulnerable to damage, the dinghy should have an alternative system of steering if the rudder fails or becomes detached. If you have a transom rowlock or sculling notch, an oar can be pressed into service as a

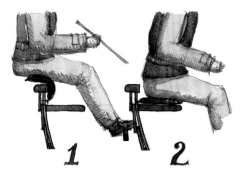

1   2

If a cushion is attached to the side seat along its rear edge only, it can be used both when sitting in the boat and when hiking out.

jury rudder. But the main rudder should be sufficiently strong that failure is a remote possibility. Pintles and gudgeons should be well sized, and through-bolted for strength.

A lifting rudder is always prone to failure in a cruising dinghy, and this is why traditional dinghies usually had a fixed rudder blade. In shallow water the whole rudder was simply lifted off the transom. My own dinghy is arranged like this. A lifting rudder is more convenient, but also a more complex piece of engineering, which must be robustly constructed. The simplest lifting rudders have a metal blade that falls under its own weight, so they only require an uphaul line. Rudders with a wooden rudder blade must be ballasted with lead, or they will need a downhaul as well. Shock cord is often used, but it is not really adequate. Only rope is resilient enough to prevent the blade bobbing up when sailing fast. The downhaul must also release itself instantly should the blade hit the bottom. Fortunately, a special clam cleat is available, designed especially for this purpose. It holds

(RIGHT) 'Clamcleat' make a special device for holding down a lifting rudder, which releases automatically if the blade hits an underwater obstruction.

a rope securely, but releases it instantly when the load exceeds a certain level. If your rudder blade is the type that floats up under its own buoyancy, this standard product is the best solution.

Another standard fitment on racing dinghies is a device to stop the rudder falling off the transom when the dinghy is inverted, and also prevent it from bouncing off if the rudder blade touches the bottom. I have not fitted one of these devices on my own dinghy, preferring the rudder to bounce off, as this prevents it from becoming damaged in shallow water. A lanyard made fast to the transom stops it floating away.

Stowage

There needs to be somewhere aboard a cruising boat to stow food and spare clothes. It is unseamanlike to leave loose gear strewn around the boat. One day you will trip over it and fall over the side, and that will teach you not to be so messy. If your boat does not have sufficient stowage lockers, you will need to devise places where you can lash down

Clamcleat®
rope cleats

SAVE YOUR STERN

4-6mm⌀
(³/₁₆"-¹/₄")

● Hold your rudder downhaul in a CL257 Auto-release Racing Mini.

● The cleat flips up to release the rope if the rudder blade hits an obstacle or the bottom.

● The CL257 is easily reset or adjusted for different release loads, even out on the water.

● Also suitable for centre boards

www.clamcleat.com

View looking forward on my present dinghy AVEL DRO, showing the stowage of gear. Notice the old-fashioned GPS in use on centreboard case. When I took this photograph there had been a problem with the chartplotter mounted below the thwart, so the spare had to be pressed into service.

your gear in waterproof bags, out of the way of the crew. Most of the gear in my dinghy is stowed in this way.

SELF-STEERING

Singlehanders cannot spend all their time at the helm. They need a way of fixing the tiller in position while they attend to other matters. Long ago, John Huntingford of the Dinghy Cruising Association created a device from sundry bits of chandlery that holds the tiller in any position, with variable friction. I have fitted the 'Huntingford Helm Impeder' to all my dinghies over the years. It can be decoupled from the tiller instantly, but I usually leave mine in place all the time while sailing. The helm impeder should never be set up so tight that the boat is prevented from luffing up when hit by a

squall, however, as this is a desirable safety feature.

One of the virtues of a traditional hull form is the boat's ability to sail herself. The external keel and skeg of a traditional dinghy helps her to track straight. When the tiller of my old Tideway was lashed and the mainsheet cleated, she would continue to sail in a straight line on virtually any point of sailing. I could aim her at the harbour mouth, fix the tiller and hoist the sails while she continued on her chosen course. She often sailed right out of the harbour without needing any further adjustment to the helm. The Ilur is less well balanced, as she only has a single sail, but still steers herself much of the time.

For all its elegant effectiveness, John Huntingford's device simply applies friction to the tiller. More sophisticated

Details of John Huntingford's Helm Impeder

Extremely simple to make, it allows locking pressure to be varied on the tiller but always allows instant movement of the tiller.

Infinitely variable on any tiller steered boat, it is useful to reduce 'sailing load' (weather helm) on cruising yachts.

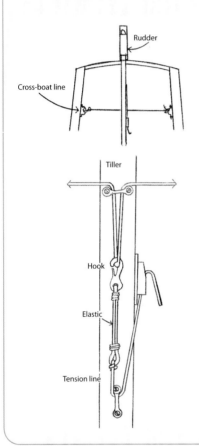

Rudder

Cross-boat line

Tiller

Hook

Elastic

Tension line

Practical
A cross-boat line is secured (usually) below the tiller. It is quite loose, but it can be varied according to securing method (ends tied, or hooked to fittings etc.). Once at the correct length it can be left in place permanently.

Form the centre of this line into an open loop and pass it through a deckloop fitted on the tiller, where it is secured with a hook.

The hook is attached to elastic that then connects to a tensioning line running to a cleat on the tiller, placed for easy access.

In use
Pulling the tension line increases the frictional grip of the cross-boat-line where it passes through the loop on the tiller. Friction is variable from 'nothing' (while sailing) to 'locked' (when going forward to pick up a mooring), or any degree in between.

The tiller can be placed at any steering angle and it will stay in place.

The system is tolerant of variations of fittings and a variety of fixing positions according to interpretation and circumstances.

The tiller can be totally released from the device by unhooking the tension line.

The rudder could be at either end of the diagram, but in general it would be at the lower end.

Many years ago, John Huntingford devised a way of applying variable friction to the tiller of a dinghy so that the helm did not need to be held continuously. This deceptively simple device remains popular among Dinghy Cruising Association members. (DCA)

self-steering systems, incorporating a wind vane or an electronic autohelm, will actively steer the boat. The autohelm is more convenient for a dinghy. Typically it is a piston-like device that clips between the tiller and the gunwale, and maintains

the boat on a specified compass heading. The device needs to be wired into 12-volt power, but is otherwise self-contained. An autohelm may be welcome aboard a stable dinghy used for long sea passages, but it is prudent to wear a safety harness when it is operating. The dinghy would certainly sail on without you if you were to fall over the side and become separated from the boat.

ANCHORS AND RODES

An anchor is vital in a cruising dinghy, and there are a wide variety of different types to choose from. The relative merits of different patterns of anchor is a perennial matter of debate among cruising sailors, and a popular topic when a sailing magazine needs to fill some empty pages. In fact any type of anchor will hold a dinghy as long as it is heavy enough and enough cable is veered. More modern forms of anchor are claimed to be effective at much lighter weights than traditional types, but their superior performance relies on them digging into a favourable bottom, such as mud or sand. If you want an anchor that is equally effective on difficult holding grounds, such as rocks and kelp, the traditional 'fisherman' pattern is still hard to beat.

On my 15ft dinghy I carry a plough anchor and a fisherman anchor, both 10lb (5kg) in weight. This is a good working size for most dinghies, but a larger dinghy may benefit from a 15lb (7kg) anchor instead. The Dinghy Cruising Association used to recommend that the weight of a fisherman anchor in pounds should be the same as the boat length in feet, but as fisherman pattern anchors are rare now, this advice has been removed from the current DCA boat recommendations. I still use a fishermen anchor, and although it is rather lighter than the old DCA recommendation, it is shackled to 10m of chain, which weighs it down somewhat. Beware of the seductive idea that a smaller dinghy needs a lighter anchor. Below a certain weight an anchor will not set reliably, and simply

Various dinghy anchors lined up on the beach. From the top, they are a fisherman pattern, a plough type, a Danford and a Bruce.

My fisherman anchor, stocked and lying in the bottom boards ready for use. Notice the clip for the stock to allow the anchor to fold, which has now been replaced by a permanent fixing.

skids across a hard bottom. Ten pounds is a good minimum weight for any pattern of anchor.

Fisherman anchors

The main disadvantage of the fisherman anchor is its upturned fluke, which can foul the cable if you are not careful when veering the anchor. It will also punch a neat hole in any hull that settles onto it at low tide. This is annoying if it is your own dinghy and embarrassing if it is someone else's. For this reason I also carry a plough anchor aboard my dinghy, which I use as my stern anchor whenever I am drying out on a beach close to other dinghies. The fisherman is used as the bow anchor and dug in above the high-water mark, where it cannot attack any dinghy hulls. I doubt that a plough anchor is the best choice of stockless anchor if you are buying new, but it is the anchor I have, and I have not seen any good reason to change it.

Fisherman anchors have a folding stock. When folded flat they are easier to stow

than most patent anchors, but a common failing is the wedge that holds the stock in place, which often fits poorly. On my fisherman, I replaced the wedge with a hairpin-shaped stainless steel clip, widely obtainable from chandleries. The anchor could then be stocked and unstocked easily, with no danger of the clip coming free when the anchor is on the bottom. The clip was securely lashed to the short length of chain that once connected the wedge to the anchor, so it cannot get lost.

Over the years I found I had got too lazy to fold my fisherman anchor and preferred to sail with it stocked and ready for use at all times, so I replaced the clip with a length of heavy gauge stainless steel wire, folded round the stock, so the anchor is always ready to deploy. This is because the fisherman has gradually become my preferred anchor if I need to get a hook down in a hurry, as it is much more pleasant to use than the plough.

Choice of rode

As I often sail in the seriously tidal waters of the Bristol Channel, I have very long anchor rodes. My anchors are both bent on 10m of chain, which is spliced to 40m of rope. (Modern charts have depths in metres, so I measure my warps in metres. The equivalent lengths in traditional measurements are 5 fathoms of chain and 22 fathoms of warp.) I do not mouse my anchor shackles. Instead I have galvanised shackles on my anchors and make them up tightly with a spanner. Unlike stainless-steel shackles, a tight galvanised shackle will not come undone when you are not looking.

The combination of chain and rope helps to keep the pull on the anchor horizontal. The chain also puts up with rubbing against a rocky bottom rather better

This cruising Wayfarer has a wooden reel for the anchor rode mounted under the foredeck.

than rope does. But some dinghy sailors prefer an all rope rode, as they dislike the damage that chain can wreak on their pristine paintwork. I do not have pristine paintwork. If there is no chain on your rode, I would recommend choosing an anchor the next size up in weight.

Pre-stretched terylene braid is often used for the anchor rode, and this has the advantage that the rope can be used for other purposes, such as hauling the dinghy up the beach on boat rollers using a block and tackle. I prefer to have nylon anchor rodes, however, as they are more springy and absorb shocks. I use 10mm diameter three-strand laid rope. This is oversize for the stresses involved, but allows for abrasion in use without the rope becoming too weak to hold the dinghy. It is also a comfortable size in the hands.

A friend recently showed me the all-rope rode on his cruising dinghy, which is a leaded anchor rope. I had not come across it before. It is a braided line weighted with lead internally and is specially designed for

kedge anchors on yachts. It comes in various diameters and weights, but as a guide 30m of the 10mm diameter warp weighs 5.6kg – so as much as the anchor again. By this means, you can have the weight of chain without battering your paintwork.

Stowing the anchor rode

You should never coil down an anchor rode as it will assuredly tangle. In some cruising dinghies the rode is wound onto a specially made reel. A simpler solution is simply to flake the rope down into a plastic bucket. If the bucket has a hole in the bottom, water will drain out and the bitter end of the cable can also emerge through it. Bitter ends should always be made fast securely to a strong point on the dinghy, or one day you will lose both anchor and rode over the side.

My present dinghy has wooden hatches in the bottom boards, one each side of the centreboard case, giving access to my chain lockers. The cables are flaked down straight into the lockers, first the nylon rode and then the chain on top. There is a cut-out in the corner of each locker lid, through which the chain can emerge when the lid is shut. The lids of the lockers have simple catches, to stop the rodes escaping in the event of a capsize.

KITTING OUT FOR SHELTERED-WATER SAILING

There are two types of boat that go out sailing. There are those equipped to deal with any conditions they are likely to meet, and those that expect someone else to rescue them if something goes wrong. The second approach is fine if you are racing, when there is always a rescue boat handy to come to your aid. But if you set out on your own in a cruising dinghy, even on a short voyage, it is your responsibility to look after yourself. You should not expect other people to risk their lives to rescue you. Your boat should be properly equipped to sail in safety, whatever the conditions.

Even a dinghy that never ventures beyond familiar waters should carry basic safety and navigational gear. It is usually more convenient to leave this equipment on board throughout the season. Alternatively, you could keep a 'grab bag' handy at home, and take it aboard whenever you go out sailing. In some countries there are national regulations governing the safety equipment to be carried by small boats, and these should be observed. Here in the UK, the equipping of a small pleasure boat is generally left to the judgement of the individual skipper, but with this precious freedom comes the responsibility to ensure that your boat is properly equipped.

Compass and chart

If you always sail in local waters, you may feel that carrying a chart and compass is overkill. The first time you are caught in a fog, you will be thankful you have them aboard. An orienteering compass is adequate for inshore waters. It will quickly re-establish a sense of direction, and the

chart will give you a safe course to steer.

In familiar waters, it is rarely necessary to plot an accurate position. Navigation is simply a matter of looking at the view to check that you really are where you think you are. But sometimes a compass bearing is necessary to remove any confusion. This can be done very effectively with an orienteering compass. Aim the compass at your chosen landmark and rotate the bezel so that the lines on the bottom of the compass bowl align with the compass needle. Make the appropriate allowance for variation and then place the compass on the chart and rotate the whole compass until the lines on the bowl align with the vertical (longitude) lines on the chart. This will give you a position line, without having to use a pencil or parallel rules. A single position line is usually sufficient to confirm your location in familiar waters.

Cruising dinghies often carry a large-scale map of the surrounding land as well as a chart. Countryside maps are usually more detailed than even the largest scale chart and tend to mark the lines of high water and low water more accurately. They are also very useful if you want to explore ashore. It is a poor dinghy cruise that does not include a landing and some exploration inland.

Logbook

Many people set sail without doing any formal passage planning at all, but ideally all cruising boats should carry a logbook, even on daysails, in which the skipper can note down the weather forecast and basic tidal information. These are the bare

A chart kept in a small waterproof case together with an orienteering compass form the basic navigational kit when daysailing.

rudiments of passage planning, now a legal requirement for passages outside sheltered waters. I use an A6 artist's sketchbook as my logbook, which is easily slipped into the pocket. The thick cartridge paper copes reasonably well with the inevitable dampness afloat.

Lead line

If you are caught out in fog, the best response is to sail into shallow water, away from large craft. In this situation a lead line will enable you to follow a depth contour across the shallows. Lead lines are also invaluable to ascertain the true depth of water when anchoring.

There are traditional ways to mark a lead line, so that the depth can be felt in the dark, but for our purposes a line some 10m long with a marking painted every metre will be sufficient (or 30 ft long and marked every fathom if you are using non-metric charts). Cheap lead lines can be purchased at most chandleries, and these will do the job perfectly adequately. Alternatively, you can make your own with a fishing weight and a length of thin line.

First aid

An adequate first aid kit should be kept aboard in a plastic waterproof box. Standard kits can be purchased from chemists or yacht chandlers. Typically they contain an array of special bandages, which seem never to come out of their wrappings. More frequently used are the treatments for minor cuts and abrasions. I carry a wide selection of self-adhesive plasters for this purpose, as well as plenty of antiseptic cream. The cloth-based self-adhesive plasters seem to adhere more readily to damp skin than the plastic ones, and also provide cushioned protection for the wound.

A simple lead line remains an effective way of ascertaining the depth of water under your dinghy.

Packets of any personal medicaments that you need to take regularly should also be kept permanently in the first aid kit, so you don't have to remember to pack them each time you go sailing. These might include contraceptive pills or heart medication. In my case I never venture far from a pack of migraine tablets. The first aid box is also a convenient place to keep a box of matches and some spare batteries.

Electric torch

A torch is vital should you end up sailing after dark. Indeed, a good torch is mandatory under international regulations, so that you can signal your presence to other craft. You may not intend to sail at night, but sailing boats have a distressing habit of getting delayed by calms or head winds. The torch should be waterproof and have a lanyard so it is not lost overboard. LED torches create a powerful light with very little battery power.

Even with modern electronic communications, I still carry a traditional flare pack.

Distress flares

Now that we all have mobile telephones and VHF radios, pyrotechnic distress flares may seem an antiquated method of calling for help. They are surprisingly expensive, difficult to keep dry, have a limited shelf life, and are not straightforward to dispose of legally. Nonetheless, they still have a vital place on a cruising boat. They are an unambiguous signal that you are in difficulties, clearly recognisable by any professional mariners in the vicinity. Two orange hand smokes for daylight and a couple of red hand flares for use after dark would be a good basic set for a boat sailing in sheltered waters. Keep the flares in a watertight box, somewhere you could still reach if you end up in the water and your boat is inverted. Just inside the transom is a good place, held in place with a loop of shock cord.

Although my dinghy has an EPIRB and a VHF I still carry a few hand flares, but I am considering replacing them with an LED flare. These cost rather more than a standard set of flares, but they can be run for a few hours and are less dangerous to operate than pyrotechnics.

Marine VHF

A handheld VHF set is a more effective method of calling for help than pyrotechnics. It enables you to specify the nature of your difficulty to the rescue services. It can also be used for communicating with other vessels in non-emergency situations and receiving the general safety warnings and weather forecasts that are broadcast by the coastguard at intervals. VHF sets are now so cheap there is no good reason not to carry one, and they should be considered part of the essential kit for any cruising dinghy. But you should ensure you have any necessary licences and that you are trained in the protocols of marine radiotelephony. (More information on marine VHF is contained in Chapter 6.)

Ship's papers

In some countries it is obligatory to carry registration documents and details of your insurance, and this applies even to foreign boats sailing in their waters. In the UK, small pleasure boats do not need to be registered, but proof of insurance is sometimes demanded at slipways and in some marinas. I keep copies of any necessary information in a waterproof bag, just in case. This includes not only my boat insurance details but also my VHF licence and the instruction books for the electronic equipment on board. Legally a UK vessel taken abroad, even on a road trailer, should be registered under the Small Ships Register and display her official registration number. It is always worth carrying proof of ownership, such as a purchase receipt (and a record of tax paid), if you have one.

A Wayfarer sailing in sunny weather. The crew are mostly well covered, but exposed skin is vulnerable to burning. (Mark Broadwith)

Sun cream

Sun cream may seem like an obvious item to take with you, but it is easily left behind if it is overcast when you set off from home, so keep a small bottle aboard, just in case. Do not underestimate the dangers of sunburn in a boat. The wind on the water keeps you cool, so you become badly burned before you realise. Choose a cream with a powerful protection factor.

Food and drink

If you always keep a selection of emergency food items in the dinghy, such as snack bars with a long shelf life, they will keep everyone happy should your voyage be prolonged for some unexpected reason. Also ensure there is always a decent amount of drinking water on board. People rarely feel sick in a dinghy, but if anyone is feeling a bit queasy, drinking plenty of water helps.

A sharp knife

Even if you always carry a knife on your person, there should also be a ship's knife on board. It should either have a fixed blade or one that can be securely locked into place. Unfortunately, knives with fixed or lockable blades are considered offensive weapons by some legislatures, such as here in the UK. They are permitted for specialist uses, like dinghy sailing, but you should avoid taking them off the boat. Safety knives can be obtained for marine use, specially designed so they can be used for cutting a rope but not for stabbing someone. These are fine if all you will ever need to do with a knife is cut some rope, rather than slice bread, cut cake, gut fish, whittle wood, or the myriad of other uses for a sharp knife on a cruising boat.

It is amazing how many people do not keep their knives sharp. The excuse is often given that a sharp knife is dangerous. Any knife is dangerous, and they should always be kept somewhere secure, but it is inevitably the blunt ones that slip and cut people. There is no point in keeping a knife aboard unless it is really sharp, and it will not remain so for very long unless you also carry a means of sharpening it.

I have sailed on boats where a ship's knife is kept in a scabbard near to the helmsman, instantly ready to cut a rope or perhaps to repel pirates. Maybe there are times when a knife so readily available comes into its own, but I have never known one. Prominently displayed knives are seen as provocative under UK law, so I keep my ship's knife in the stern locker, where it is close at hand but out of sight. You can pay lots of money for a good knife, but I use the excellent and inexpensive Opinel knives. These have a folding blade with a well-engineered collar to fix them in the open position, so that they cannot fold shut on your hand.

Spare clothes

It is prudent always to take a full set of wet-weather gear with you, even if the day is fine and sunny when you set off. Perhaps you will be spared the rain, but you may still need your 'oilies' for a wet beat to windward. Also carry some spare warm clothing, just in case your return is delayed and the evening is a cold one.

GPS navigation

GPS is not essential for daysailing, and should not be considered a replacement for the traditional tools of a chart, compass and lead line. But a GPS device is an extremely useful bit of kit nonetheless. The speed readout is particularly helpful. Unless you buy a chartplotter, you will have to plot your GPS positions onto a paper chart by referring to the latitude and longitude scales in the margins. If you take the trouble to grid up your charts with pencil lines at close centres before you set off from home, aligned with major divisions of lat and long, this task becomes much easier. Some yacht charts are already gridded in this way. (I will discuss GPS at much greater length in Chapter 6.)

A basic handheld GPS device mounted on Avel Dro's centreboard case. As she now has a chartplotter, this is used as a spare.

Living off the sea

The design of my dinghy is based closely on the small sailing boats that fished the inshore waters of north-western France until just after the Second World War. This is why she is often mistaken for a fishing vessel, particularly in France, where everyone trails a line over the side of their boat to catch something tasty for dinner.

So integrated are sailing and fishing in France that their yacht chandleries contain long racks of fishing gear, with a bewildering array of lures, lines, weights and floats. Once when I was browsing in a French chandlery, I became seduced by the notion of a self-sufficient existence – living off the sea, hauling wet glistening fish over the side onto the bottom boards of my boat, frying them fresh and serving them with herbs gathered on the foreshore. I asked the shopkeeper what was the best gear for the local coastline. He sold me a hand line with a number of extremely sharp feathered hooks and a lead weight on the end. We dragged this tackle behind us all the way round the Breton coast, but the only fish we saw came out of tins.

I decided to call in expert advice. My mate Colin comes from the far west of Ireland, where Atlantic gales batter the rain-swept fields, and there is nothing to do but drink Guinness, sing Republican songs and fish from small boats. He'd know how to get the blighters to bite at my hooks. Fortunately he now lives not far away from me in England, so I did not need to go to his native Killybegs in County Donegal to learn sea fishing. We could do it at Weymouth instead.

So it was that Colin and I stood on the balcony of the Weymouth and Portland National Sailing Academy, looking out across the huge abandoned harbour to the distant breakwater, built to shelter the anchored dreadnoughts of Britain's lost naval might.

'What do you reckon is the best place to catch fish around here?' I asked.

'Utterly no idea,' said Colin. 'I only ever fish in Ireland. But you'll be wanting to look where other boats are already fishing.'

We peered hard at the deserted expanse of the harbour, looking for fishing boats. A few racing dinghies zipped about, like flies in an empty room, but no one was fishing anywhere. We decided to sail over to the cliffs of the Dorset shore, and try some casts in the shallow water at their feet.

There was no one else fishing there either. Colin reckoned it was still worth a try, so we lowered our sail and Avel Dro drifted a cable or so off the shore. Colin made some experimental casts with his rod and I brought out my French hand line. Colin examined it critically.

'Good. They've given you a decent weight on the end of that. I was worried it would be a bit light.'

I told Colin how I had towed the line all round Brittany and not caught anything.

'No wonder,' said Colin. 'You can't just tow it. You've got to jiggle it the whole time, to make the big fish think that the lures are tasty little fish that they want to eat. And you need to keep altering the depth. When you catch a fish, you must remember how much line you had out, so that you can let it out again to the same depth and catch another fish from the same shoal.'

We drifted along for a couple of hours or so, while I patiently fished with the hand line, and Colin cast with his rod. There were no bites at all, other than the ones we took out of our sandwiches. Colin was hunched over his rod like an ivory Buddha, and utterly content.

'This is the whole point of fishing,' he said. 'It's an excuse for a peaceful day out without needing to do anything.'

'But where are all the fish?' I asked.

'Don't worry, there are plenty of fish in the sea. But fish are pretty small and the sea is really huge, so there may be a few gaps between them.'

It was coming towards evening, so we abandoned our drift along the coast. We hoisted the lugsail and set off back across the bay towards Portland Harbour, dribbling across the silky sea at a couple of knots. This was exactly the right sort of speed to catch fish, according to Colin, so we trailed the hand line behind us, and took turns to jiggle it at various depths.

Eventually we arrived back at the breakwater of the old Naval anchorage. As I rowed Avel Dro through one of the gaps, Colin gave out a cry and hauled in the line smartly. A silvery mackerel was dancing on one of the hooks. He removed it with practised nonchalance, chucked it in a bucket and rapidly let the line out again to the same depth, but no other fish took our line that day.

The Sailing Academy was dark by the time we arrived back at the slipway. A solitary man was wandering on the foreshore and he watched us recover Avel Dro in the dusk.

'That looks like a good workmanlike boat,' he said. 'Do you use her for fishing?'

'We did today,' we said.

'You can't beat it,' he said, 'whether you catch anything or not.'

You know what? He was dead right. But it was still good to have caught a fish.

Colin catches a mackerel on Avel Dro.

3 DAYSAILING ON ALL WATERS

You can be taught the basics of dinghy sailing in just a few days, and yet spend a lifetime refining your boat-handling techniques. Dinghy sailing never becomes routine. There is always something new to learn and somewhere new to explore. So far in this book, we have discussed how to find a good boat and equip her for cruising in sheltered waters. This chapter is about the basic skills you need to take her out cruising. There will be hints and rumours of more ambitious voyages that can be undertaken in little boats, but the main aim of this chapter is to encourage you to see a sailing dinghy as a tool for independent sailing, not as a beach toy or a racing machine. It does not matter if you never venture out of sheltered waters or wander far from your starting place, as long as your days afloat are enjoyable and refreshing ones. If you are itching to take your dinghy out to sea, the more extensive equipment and advanced skills required for voyaging in open waters will be addressed later, but the basic skills of boatmanship in the following three chapters are vital for everyone.

These Wayfarer sailors are packing their boats for a day's sailing.
(Mark Broadwith)

GAINING EXPERIENCE

Skills learnt while racing are invaluable to a cruising sailor. There is nothing like competing with similar dinghies to teach you how to read the wind and the subtle feedback from the tiller. But the proficiency needed to cruise an open boat effectively is greater than a racing sailor can possibly imagine.

A good skipper and crew develop a deep empathy with their boat. After many hours afloat they feel comfortable aboard their dinghy and confident in her ability to look after them. This is not something that can be learnt from a book. Not even this one. The instinctive skills of a true boatman or woman are only acquired with experience, and experience can only be obtained in real-life situations. Ideally you will build up your experience in a measured way, in increasingly testing situations, never going too far beyond your existing abilities. But it is inevitable that you will be 'caught out' one day – suddenly immersed in a situation far beyond anything you have experienced before. This happens to everyone. When it happens to you, do not panic. Dinghies are more seaworthy than their diminutive size may imply. Your boat is capable of coping with conditions far more severe than anything you are likely to be out in.

HOME WATERS

Happy are those people who live on the coast and keep their dinghy on a mooring close by, ready to sail whenever the weather is fair. Confident in their knowledge of their local waters, of the pattern of currents and winds, they instinctively work the tides to a favourite waterside pub or a sheltered beach for a picnic in the warm dusk, without having to worry too much about passage planning. This is a very relaxing way to sail.

If you keep your dinghy at home, and trail her to the water every time you go sailing, you will often use the same launching sites time after time. Sailing in familiar waters needs so much less preparation than venturing somewhere new. When you just want a relaxing time on the water, it is easier to go somewhere you already know well.

VENTURING INTO THE UNKNOWN

Eventually, though, your home waters begin to feel prosaic and predictable. You begin to hanker after fresh experiences. In looking for somewhere new to sail, try to find an area with interest on land as well as on the water. The joy of dinghy sailing is being able to get close inshore – to venture up creeks and land on islands, and explore the fine detail of the coastline.

If you own a trailable dinghy, finding new sailing waters also means finding a new launching site. The planning of a daysail inevitably begins with choosing a slipway. The ideal launching site should offer a choice of places to visit, whatever the wind direction. I like to use slipways that are accessible at all states of the tide, so I do not need to worry about finding the slipway dried out if I get back late.

When taking a trailable boat away for a few days' holiday, it is usually more convenient to leave the dinghy afloat overnight, rather than pull her out of the water each evening. Marinas are depressing places, chock-full of ostentatious little-used yachts, yet they do provide secure places to leave a dinghy unattended overnight. A marina pontoon is much more convenient than leaving her lying at anchor unattended.

Avel Dro visits a chateau in the Bay of Morlaix.

Another advantage is the handiness of the marina bar, which will feed your hungry crew after a long day out on the water, before they get too mutinous.

PLANNING A DAYSAIL

If you have followed the guidance in the preceding chapters, your dinghy will be reliable and robust, and decently equipped for daysailing. But a safe and enjoyable day out means giving some thought to the peculiarities of the waters on which you have chosen to sail. Even sheltered waters are not completely free from challenges. A good skipper is always aware that mishaps can occur even on placid waters.

A relaxing daysail requires good planning. The skipper will study the charts, check the weather forecast, make notes about the tides, and obtain local information about the slipway. Even the availability of car parking should be considered.

Sailing boats have a knack of showing up your shortcomings at the most inconvenient moments, particularly if you are trying to impress a romantic date. It is when you are at your most relaxed that a sudden emergency is most likely to happen. The crisis may not be life threatening, but anything that spoils a pleasant day out sailing is regrettable.

PLACES TO SAIL

Lakes

Lake sailing has its own special pleasures. I spent much of my childhood in the Lake District of north-west England, where great mountains enclose wooded valleys and lake water laps against rocky shorelines and washes softly on shingle beaches. On these lovely lakes and meres, a small dinghy can delve into the nooks and crannies of the shoreline – reed-fringed bays, sheltered

inlets and little rocky islands. The Cumbrian Lakeland has hardly changed in the passing of years. It is still just as delightful as it was in my youth, and freely accessible to anyone with a small boat.

Lakes are gloriously free from many of the perils and worries of the sea, and are good places to sail in winter, when the sea is uninviting. But the winds are often fluky, particularly if the lake is surrounded by trees or high ground. If you are sailing among mountains, katabatic gusts can strike down from the heights, threatening to invert the dinghy. The level of lake water can also change rapidly in periods of heavy rain. Be

(LEFT) A spritsail dinghy drifts gently across a small lake.

(BELOW) A Kittywake dinghy sailing on Rudyard Lake in winter. At the helm is her builder Roger Wilkinson, who has brought his dog along. (Andy Morley)

careful of this if you leave your boat pulled up on the beach unattended overnight.

Lakes also suffer from the grave problem of private shorelines. In tidal waters you are usually free to land on any beach below the high-water mark. The shores of lakes tend to be privately owned, however, and landing may be forbidden.

Rivers and canals

Rivers are some of the most fascinating places to explore in a dinghy: ancient trade routes lined with interesting towns and flowing with history. Unless you have enough width to tack, river sailing is often a case of blowing along with the wind in one direction and then rowing or motoring back. Alternatively, you might sail downstream and then use public transport or a taxi to return to your car. Some rivers have locks and weirs, and are properly called 'river navigations'. These have similar characteristics to canals – a controlled water level and clearly identified mooring places. Others, such as the River Loire in France, are still essentially wild, and must be navigated with more circumspection.

If there are trees close to the bank, they can have a surprisingly large effect on the wind, and make sailing very frustrating. In these conditions it is often quicker to tow the boat from the bank. If there are two or more crewmembers, one should stay on board to steer the dinghy, while the rest haul on a long rope tied to the end of a halyard leading from the masthead. This lifts it over any waterside vegetation, and also makes steering easier, as the dinghy is pulled from its pivot point, rather than the bow. Do not try this on a very tippy dinghy, however, or you may pull her over.

If you are sailing on your own, and you need to tow your dinghy from the bank,

John and Josephine raise their gunter mast after passing under a low bridge. (Pierre Roulet)

take both the painter and stern warp ashore with you, then adjust their relative lengths so that the dinghy is pulled along parallel to the bank.

Large rivers and canals often have opening bridges, but on smaller waterways bridges are usually fixed and you will probably need to lower your dinghy's mast to pass under them. This is easier if it is stepped in a tabernacle. Practised river sailors enjoy 'shooting' fixed bridges without stopping. This means sailing up to the bridge at full speed, lowering the sail and mast just before the span, gliding through with the mast down, and then raising the rig again once clear of the bridge, all without stopping. It is very fulfilling to do this smoothly and

A group of dinghies lock into the River Aulne navigation in western Brittany, during a raid.

competently, and very entertaining for onlookers if you get it wrong.

On tidal rivers the flood tide takes some time to flow upstream against the river current, so high water is later the further up the river you go. Because of this, a boat sailing upriver with the flood is able to 'carry her tide' deep into the hinterland, while a boat coming down with the ebb will encounter a foul tide rather sooner than she may have expected. You have more time to sail up a river with the flood than to return on the ebb.

The strongest tides and currents are generally found on the outsides of the river bends. A dinghy attempting to 'beat the tide', or make progress against the current, should keep in the slacker water on the insides of the bends, but be careful not to run aground in the shallower water also found there.

Estuaries

Estuaries combine the excitement of sea sailing with greater shelter. They vary in character. Some are peaceful havens rich in wildlife, while others are bustling places full of shipping. A wide expanse of open water provides a clear fetch on which the waves can grow steep and high in a fresh breeze, so choose one without large areas of open water if you are looking for sheltered sailing.

LAUNCHING AND RECOVERY

Once you have chosen a place to go sailing, with a convenient slipway, you can plan your day in detail. Allow sufficient time to launch your boat and to recover her at the end of the day. The rigging of the boat and putting her to bed is as much a part of your day out as the sailing itself.

Avel Dro being towed from the bank on a canal in western France. An oar has been set up in the bow to carry the tow rope over the bankside vegetation.

Rigging and de-rigging a dinghy should not be long, involved chores. A cruising dinghy should take no more than half an hour to rig and launch, and the same length of time at the end of the day. Some dinghies seem to need over an hour. If this is the case with yours, I would consider radically altering the rig or even changing your boat. The best rigs for daysailing are simple and uncomplicated ones.

To speed up launching and recovery, cruising sails are usually left on the spars all season, rather than stripping them off and packing them in sail bags, which is the normal racing dinghy practice. If you have a stout flat cover that you can put over the whole dinghy, you will not have to pack away every small item in case it blows away when being towed, or be afraid of attracting petty thieves when you stop for fuel on the way home.

There is much more about launching and recovering a dinghy in Chapter 11.

Slipways

One of the great advantages of a cruising dinghy is the ability to trail her to a wide choice of different waters behind a car. This remarkable freedom is often spoilt by mediocre slipways. In the UK, slipway provision is generally deplorable. Often slipways are badly maintained, with nowhere to moor the boat while the car and trailer are being parked, and frustratingly distant from the nearest car park. Sometimes the car and trailer must even be parked in two different places, which is particularly inconvenient if you are launching your dinghy singlehanded. Perversely it is often the most expensive slipways that are the worst to use. Other countries seem to do this better.

THE NESS YAWL

The Ness Yawl is a fine example of the contemporary movement to update traditional craft for modern uses. The Ness Yawl is based on the traditional vessels of the Orkney islands, and a Viking influence can be clearly seen in her long, lean clinker hull. These beautiful craft sit prettily on the water and look ravishing under sail. Designed by the prolific Iain Oughtred, they are fast boats, particularly in light airs.

The Ness Yawl is not as capacious as its great length implies, as much of it is taken up by the two pointed ends. Although the boat can accommodate up to four people under sail, the Ness Yawl is ideal for a crew of two, and is not too large to be cruised singlehanded. Ness Yawls perform very well under oars, but they cannot carry an outboard motor except in a well. This intrudes on their lovely lines, so many have been built without one. They are best considered as a 'sail and oar' boat, rather than a motorsailer. The length of their hull can present a storage problem ashore, as it is far too long for a normal garage, but on the water the long, lean hull rides lightly over the seas, the prow slicing the waves apart and the waters closing quietly behind her without fuss.

The hull can take a variety of rigs. The most popular option is a balance lug on an unstayed main mast, stepped well forward, and a small Bermudan mizzen on a second mast near the stern. The mizzen will hold the boat quietly head to wind if the mainsail is lowered while reefing, or for anchoring. Both sails are self-tacking, which is handy for a singlehander. As the mizzen mast is mounted amidships in the pointed stern, the tiller has a large hoop so that the rudder can be operated past the mast.

(Jacob Glanville)

The Ness Yawl's modern construction makes her very light indeed. Sailed singlehanded, she is a fiery steed, and particularly fast on a reach. New ones can be built from plans by skilled amateurs or ordered from specialist boatbuilders, but they also turn up fairly regularly on the second-hand market. In 2012 Giacomo de Stefano completed a voyage from London to the Black Sea in a Ness Yawl – all without an engine – via river and canal.

If your dinghy is launched and recovered with the sails kept bent onto the spars, it simplifies and speeds up the process. (The white dinghy is a Seil.)

If the car park is some distance from the slipway and there is nowhere convenient to moor the boat, a crewmember has to stand on the slipway holding the boat. This is impossible if you are sailing singlehanded, and is one reason why it is important to research a slipway before using it for the first time.

Lists of slipways can be consulted in pilot books, found on the internet or located by using smartphone apps. A marina slipway is often a good choice if you are sailing somewhere new. Not all marinas have a slipway, but when they do it is usually more sheltered and better maintained than most public hards. Marinas also usually provide a pontoon where you can moor the boat adjacent to the slipway. Marinas are relatively expensive in the UK, but the extra outlay is worthwhile if it makes your day more pleasurable.

Sometimes you arrive at a normally sheltered slipway to find it exposed to an onshore wind, and waves are breaking on the ramp. In these trying circumstances, your techniques of launching and recovery must be slick, or the boat could easily be damaged. It is best to choose slipways that are sheltered in all wind directions.

TIDAL PLANNING

In tidal waters, take the tide into consideration when choosing the date to go sailing. Days that have high water around midday are usually ideal. The coastline looks better at high water, and you will be able to explore right to the head of remote and secluded creeks. But dates when low water is in the middle of the day have advantages too. You can sail to a beach in the morning, allow the boat to dry out as the tide ebbs away, then go for a walk and return to your dinghy just before she floats off again. This is a neat trick that really impresses your sailing guests. But it is always wise to put out an anchor, in case you are delayed. Your guests

These Wayfarers have just been launched on a slipway without a pontoon. A crewmember is looking after them while the cars are parked. (Iain McRobbie)

won't be quite so impressed if they return to find that the boat has drifted away.

Plan the day around the tidal streams rather than the wind. The weather is fickle, but tides are predictable years in advance. I always like to have a fair tide on the way out as well as on the way back, perhaps by taking the flood tide up the estuary in the morning and then dropping back with the ebb. There will inevitably be a head wind in one direction, but beating with a fair tide is much less frustrating than tacking against the tide. Avoid locations with strong tides at certain times of the day, as a swift stream running against the wind can kick up unpleasant waves.

USE OF THE LOGBOOK

As a successful daysail inevitably involves some pre-planning, get into the habit of noting the salient information in a logbook, such as target times for getting to your destination and back again in the evening. I generally record the latest time that I need to turn round and sail for home, or start motoring back to base. Getting home in

good time makes a lot of difference to the success of a day afloat.

Passage planning notes can be very brief, such as:

Aim to be at the island by 12pm.
Set off home by 2pm.

Information on local tidal flows should be simplified and distilled into something clear and concise, like:

N tide until 3pm – then S.

If there are any important local 'tidal gates', I like to write these down too:

Return over the bar before 4pm, before ebb sets in.

I also usually write down the local weather forecast for the day.

This is not full-scale passage planning, such as you might do for a sea passage. These are just simple reminders for a daysail. They may seem so simple that they would be impossible to forget, but when things start going wrong, it is easy to get flustered and confused about the exact time of the tide, or what exactly the weather forecast said. It only takes a few seconds to note these things down, so you have a clear record that you can refer to at any time.

If you have a smartphone, as most of us now do, it is tempting to refer to it for the tide times and the marine weather forecast whenever you need to, rather than go to the trouble of recording this information in the logbook at the beginning of the day. We have all got into the habit of constantly looking at our phones for all sorts of information, with the casual assumption that they will be able to give us whatever information we want, whenever we want it. However, out in the wilds this cannot be relied upon as a signal will inevitably not be available when you need it, or you will find you have inadvertently drained the battery. Best to keep the phone stowed somewhere secure for emergencies, and not to keep referring to it. Look about you at the scenery instead. I carry two smartphones on my boat, so I know I will always have one that is charged, but another alternative would be to carry a portable power bank.

Sailing techniques

Setting sail and then getting the boat clear of the slipway is often the most stressful part of a daysail, particularly for novices. Slipways are often located in busy corners of harbours, and you have to hoist sail while the dinghy is bouncing about in the chop caused by passing power craft. The best launching sites are in quiet, sheltered locations with a convenient pontoon to moor the dinghy, where the sails can be hoisted in calm water. These are often in marinas.

Setting sail

It has become the normal practice on modern yachts to hoist the sails while motoring to windward, but this is unwise in a sailing dinghy. The motion is atrocious in anything of a chop, and there is always the risk of a spare rope getting flicked over the side, wrapping itself around the propeller and bringing you to a sudden stop.

It is better to row or motor your boat into a patch of clear water, and then hoist the sails while the dinghy is drifting. A drifting dinghy will tend to lie broadside onto the wind, so the sails must be hoisted while they are squared off over the side. Traditional rigs are designed to cope with this. Everyone used to hoist sail this way, before the easy availability of auxiliary power started to erode traditional sailing skills. By contrast, many modern rigs seem to be designed with the expectation that the sail will only be hoisted while the boat is lying head to wind, otherwise the luff jams

Hoisting sail while drifting on my Avel Dro. This is best done when the sail is on the other side of the boat, so the person at the halyard is not buried under the sail.

This Wayfarer has picked up a spare mooring in order to hoist sail.

in its track or the mainsail headboard gets caught under the spreaders. This is why yachts usually motor to windward when they raise their sails and racing dinghies have got into the habit of hoisting their sails ashore in the dinghy park. Neither of these options is suitable for a cruising dinghy. It is vital that her sails can be hoisted and lowered when the wind is on the beam.

If there are some convenient buoys near to the slipway, it is tempting to pick up a mooring in order to hoist sail. In non-tidal waters the dinghy will lie happily head to wind while you do so. Once the sails are hoisted, a dinghy with a conventional sloop rig should have her jib backed as she casts off from the buoy. The dinghy will make gentle sternway, spin slowly on her heel, and then pay off onto the desired tack. Once the mainsail is drawing, the jib can be brought across onto the correct side.

In tidal waters, hoisting sail on a mooring is much more complicated, as you need to consider the effect of any tidal stream on your moored dinghy. If the wind and tide are running in the same direction, she will lie comfortably head to wind while you hoist the sails. If the wind and tide are opposed, however, your dinghy will not lie quietly head to wind, and hoisting sail becomes problematic. As soon as you start to raise sail, your dinghy will start moving, even though she is still made fast to the buoy. This rarely ends happily. She will start sailing around the mooring out of control and probably wrap the mainsheet round your neck.

The importance of tight halyards

A good crew should be able to hoist sail smartly, without fuss. Halyards that are led straight down the outside of the mast and directly to a cleat are much more seamanlike

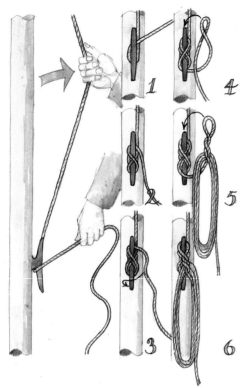

Swigging tight a halyard and then cleating it, finishing with a locking turn (4). The fall is then coiled and hung on the cleat.

than more complex arrangements as they can be 'swigged' tight in the traditional way, without the need for tackles or winches. To swig a halyard, take a turn around the base of the cleat and hold tight onto the free end. Then grasp the fall of the halyard with your other hand at about eye level and pull it away from the mast. This will gain you an extra few inches of slack, which can be eased around the bottom of the cleat with the other hand. This process should be repeated a few times, until the halyard is tight and the sail luff is bar taught.

Belaying a halyard

It is amazing how much inventiveness you find in the cleating of halyards. There really

is no need for all this innovation. The right way to belay a halyard is to take one full turn under both arms of the cleat and then lay a couple of figures of eight on top. All the other methods were only invented to confuse and frustrate people who know how it should be done properly.

If you are ever offered the chance to ship before the mast on a big square-rigger, never finish the final figure of eight on a cleat with a locking turn. This is practically a keelhauling offence on a windjammer. On a sailing dinghy rigged with synthetic ropes, the locking turn has an honoured place, however, as it stops the halyard from being accidentally knocked off the cleat by a flailing sheet.

Once the halyard has been belayed, the remainder of the rope should be coiled and then hung on the cleat. A laid rope should always be coiled clockwise, 'with the sun', and you should always start the coil from the 'bight', where it comes off the cleat. If you throw back your other arm to its full extent when making the coil, each loop will end up the same diameter, and the resulting coil will be neat and tidy.

To hang the completed coil on the cleat, reach through the coil with one hand, grasp the bight and then pull it through the coil, forming a small loop. Twist this loop a few times and then drop it over the top horn of the cleat, so that the coil of rope hangs neatly from it. Never tuck the coil behind the standing part of the halyard. This slovenly practice may be common on yachts, but it is a serious infraction on a cruising dinghy where traditional standards of boatcraft are still maintained.

Cleating the mainsheet

It is often stated that you should never cleat the mainsheet of a sailing dinghy, in case a sudden squall causes the boat to capsize. But the crew of a cruising dinghy have too many other things to do other than hold onto ropes all the time, so we often cleat the mainsheet in light airs. Doubtless this would be foolish on more tippy boats, but a stable dinghy is safe with cleated sheets in fair weather.

In strong and gusty winds the mainsheet should never be cleated, no matter how stable your boat, but the pull of the rope may numb your hand if you are on the same tack for a long time. A half turn around a cleat can take some of the strain. Keep hold of the free end though, so that the sheet can be released instantly and run out freely in an emergency. Some cruising dinghies use a ratchet block to take some of the tension out of a tugging sheet.

Racing dinghies like to sail as close to the wind as possible, sheets pinned in tight and bearing up into every gust, but a different technique is required if you are trying to make progress in rough water. In these conditions you need to keep sufficient way on the boat to punch through the waves, so it is best to dump wind by easing the sheet slightly in the gusts, rather than luffing up and losing power.

Tacking in rough water

When tacking in steep waves there is a tendency for a dinghy to get stuck 'in irons', head to wind. If this happens, you must reverse the helm as she starts to make sternway, so that she comes off the wind onto the correct tack: otherwise she will fall back onto the original tack.

To avoid this problem, try to ensure that the dinghy is moving as fast as possible before you bring her head up into the wind, and that the plate is fully down. Wait for a smooth patch of water and then sail her

The pull of the mainsheet becomes tiring on a long passage. Some of the strain can be taken out of the rope by taking a turn around a cleat.

round gently, without any sudden motion of the tiller, so that the rudder does not create turbulence and stop her. On dinghies with jibs, it helps to bring her head round onto the correct tack if you allow the headsail to back slightly before you sheet it across to the other side.

Gybing

On yachts it is normal to sheet in before gybing. In a dinghy it is usually best to keep the mainsheet right out, and then sail more and more by the lee until the sail blows straight across. You might think that the dinghy will lurch dangerously as the sail slams across. In fact the sail comes to rest very gently, stopped by the wind on the other side of the sail. This is the best way to gybe a dinghy, and safe even in strong winds. You must ensure that the mainsheet cannot get wrapped round the rudderhead or the outboard motor, however.

A Wayfarer close tacking in rough water. (Mark Broadwith)

In very strong winds it is prudent to avoid a gybe by bringing the boat up into the wind and tacking instead. If your plate has been lifted for running off the wind, you must lower it before trying to tack, or she will certainly fail to come about. It is easy to forget this in the heat of the moment. Tacking in big waves is always problematic, as it is easy to get stuck in stays. Gybing is usually a more reliable way to bring her round.

Boomless mainsails tend to gybe gently, as there is no boom to fly across. But if the sail has a pulley block shacked to its clew, this could hit someone's head when it is blowing across. My dinghy has a light brass loop on the clew rather than a block, so that there is little danger of hurting someone when gybing.

It is difficult to generalise about sailing techniques, as every dinghy is different in her behaviour. My present boat cannot be gybed with the sheet eased, as I have described, because sometimes the top of her lugsail lifts over the top of the mast and becomes jammed there. Instead I have to gybe her by sheeting the sail in and then allowing it to run out when the sail has moved across. Whatever general advice you may read, each boat is different and prefers to be sailed in a different way. You must become the expert on your own boat.

Heaving-to

Heaving-to is an invaluable technique for slowing your boat and putting her into a stable position. A boat lying hove-to is a comfortable place to carry out chart work, pull in a reef, and carry out any activity that needs to be done calmly, while the boat

A sloop-rigged dinghy hove-to, with her jib sheeted to windward and helm a-lee.

is not leaping around. The contrast between punching vigorously through the seas and a boat lying quietly hove-to is profound.

Different boats will heave-to in different ways, and you must experiment with your own dinghy to discover how she prefers to lie. A Bermudan sloop will normally heave-to comfortably if the jib is backed to windward, the tiller put hard down and the mainsheet eased right out. The dinghy will come to rest with the forces in the sails balanced out, the jib acting against the mainsail.

Once hove-to, the dinghy should lie with her bows at about 45 degrees to the wind direction. She will drift slowly downwind, leaving a slick of smooth water to windward. Ideally the boat will be almost stationary in the water, protected from breaking waves by her slick. Some dinghies may keep moving slowly forward, leaving their protective slick astern. If yours does this, experiment with lifting the plate so she makes more leeway.

I have described the process of heaving-to in a sloop-rigged dinghy, as these are the most common type. Boats with other rigs require different techniques. A two-masted dinghy will usually heave-to if her mizzen is sheeted tight amidships, the other sheets are released and the tiller is left to its own devices. My own dinghy has only a single sail, but she will usually heave-to if the centre place is raised, the sail sheeted half out and cleated, and the tiller put to leeward. If the wind is too strong for her to lie comfortably like that, I lower the sail and raise the plate. She then sits with her stern at about 45 degrees to the wind, being pushed downwind under the windage of her bare mast.

Running dead before a strong wind. I am keeping a wary eye on the burgee to ensure that I do not gybe accidentally. (Ronan Coquil)

The hull of a traditional dinghy helps her to heave-to in a stable and predictable fashion. A modern dinghy, with her smooth underbelly and no skeg, can range about rather more. Her crew will need to experiment to find how much plate she needs, and how she likes her sails to be sheeted.

Winter in Poole Harbour

Winter sailing can be utterly delightful or utterly miserable. The weather lurches between moods – clear and cold one day, morose and damp the next. On sunny days the limpid light brings the scenery into crisp relief, so still and perfect it is like sailing across a painting. But the high pressure that brings the winter sun also means dribbling about in a flat calm. For a decent sailing wind, you need to go out when the once green landscape has turned harsh and drab, and bitter showers bluster across the sullen waters. This is also the sort of day that gives winter a bad name.

Chris and Caroline had wanted to come sailing for months, but always demanded good weather, which is impossible to guarantee in the UK. But the sky looked promising that winter Saturday, so we set off for the coast. I looked forward to pottering past wooded islands bathed in winter sunlight and having Poole Harbour completely to ourselves.

During the summer months, a sailing school operates from Rockley Point, the slipway is busy with boats and a little kiosk serves hot drinks to parched sailors. We arrived to find the café battened shut against the blustery wind, and that no one was out sailing.

We launched Avel Dro, tied a prudent reef in her sail and then tacked smartly out of the narrow creek. Soon the channel curved round to the south-east. We eased the sheet, Avel Dro picked up her skirts and swept out into the Wareham Channel, the water chattering along the sides of her clinker hull and flowing into a lengthening wake behind her.

Poole Harbour is a place of contrasts. A deep shipping channel runs across the northern side of the harbour, and the shoreline is built-up with houses, a Ro-Ro terminal and various marinas. The southern half of the harbour is a maze of shoals and pockmarked by wooded islands. Narrow swatchways cut across the shallows, marked with lines of wooden posts. The shoreline is remote countryside with innumerable drying channels winding deep into the heathland beyond. The largest island in the harbour is called Brownsea – picturesque and well wooded, it was our planned destination for the day.

Chris and Caroline sailing AVEL DRO in Poole harbour, little knowing what is in store.

An east cardinal beacon indicated the helpful shortcut through the shallows to the Upper Wych Channel, which brought us to Long Island. In those days it was not covered in 'private' signs, so we landed on the beach and walked through a narrow wood to the saltings on the far side. The wind ruffled the marsh grasses and rustled in the trees. Birds piped at each other on the foreshore and poked at the mud with their beaks.

The wind had strengthened in the brief time we were ashore. Back on board, with Avel Dro snoring along, we munched our lunch as she devoured the waves. Soon a line of posts came into sight marking a swatchway running off to starboard, which led us into a narrow strait between one of the islands and the mainland shore. At that moment the VHF crackled into life:

'Sécurité, Sécurité, this is Portland Coastguard ...'

I switched to the Working Channel. The coastguard read out the shipping forecast for the local sea area, beginning with a warning of westerly gales 'imminent'.

'Perhaps we should head back now,' I said – trying to adopt a measured, skipper-like tone. 'We don't want to be caught out by bad weather in the dark.'

I gave the helm to Chris and studied the chart. The sky rapidly darkened and the water became dark and sullen. Soon rain began to fall.

The tides in Poole Harbour are bizarre. Most of the time the water hangs around just bobbing up and down a little. About an hour before low water it suddenly decides to rush out to sea. Two hours later, it all comes rushing back. It was now just entering the rushing out phase of its cycle, and I made a tactical mistake. I allowed the tidal stream to slide us into the deep Wareham Channel, when I should have kept in the shallows close to the shore, where the ebb stream was weaker.

The wind, rain and tide grew stronger. Avel Dro was battling against all three of them. Rain squalls lashed at us as we tacked frantically back and forth, hauling in the sodden lugsail on each tack. Out to starboard was a rake of landing craft in drab camouflage colours, moored to the Royal Marine base at Hamworthy. Avel Dro heeled to the gusts and the water coursed powerfully past her sides, but the landing craft resolutely refused to slip away astern. The tide was defeating us. A longer tack, another squall, and we managed to slip into a muddy bay, just beyond the far perimeter fence of the Marine's base.

Chris and Caroline splashed ashore. I waded back deep into the waves, pushing Avel Dro back afloat before the ebbing tide grounded her immovably in the mud. I scrambled back aboard and rowed out to an empty mooring, just offshore. We were under half a mile from Rockley Point, but we could get no further until the tide turned, much later in the night. The rain was pouring down, the tide was racing past, it was getting dark and I was stuck out on a mooring with two-thirds of my crew marooned on the beach.

On the other side of the security fence I could see a big concrete slipway, where the elite marines of the Special Boat Squadron launched their assault craft and amphibious vehicles. I cupped my hands to hail Chris, and suggested that he went into the base to ask if we could haul out our boat there. He waved his agreement, and then disappeared. Caroline stood forlornly on the beach in the rain, looking at me. I stood in the boat and looked at her. Nothing else happened for a long time, except we both got a lot wetter.

Eventually a car drew up. Caroline told the driver about our predicament. He offered us a lift back to Rockley to collect our car and trailer. She accepted, and shouted the news to me in the boat. But until we could use the slipway, I had no choice but to stay on the mooring, and there was still no news from Chris. The man got into his car and Caroline joined him. Now there was only me standing in the pouring rain. Floodlights came on in the base, illuminating rows of chunky military vehicles lined up on the glistening hard, under a damply flapping white ensign. Then a marine came out and lowered the flag. Otherwise you would have thought that the base was deserted.

Eventually Chris appeared on the slipway, accompanied by a young man in battle-dress and a green beret. I left the mooring, sculled around the end of the perimeter fence and grounded on the concrete just in front of the marine. Although undoubtedly highly trained for secret and potentially deadly missions, he looked friendly.

Chris explained why he had taken so long. When he arrived at the main entrance of the base, the guard at the barrier responded by pointing his machine gun at him. Chris explained what we wanted, and was promptly marched off to see the commanding officer. Only after a stressful interview, with many searching questions about our motives and plans, was he finally given permission to use the slipway.

The unpredictable can happen at any time when you are dinghy sailing. That is part of its fascination. Our brief potter in Poole Harbour had ended in a minor adventure with the commandos. But cruising dinghy sailors often have tall tales like that to tell when they get back to work on Monday.

AVEL DRO meets the Special Boat Squadron. (Chris Madin)

4 BOATCRAFT UNDER ENGINE AND OAR

Learning how to handle your dinghy effectively under oars and engine is as important as developing your sailing techniques. I use the word 'boatcraft' to describe the all-encompassing skills needed to handle a small boat in all waters, under sail, under oars or under engine. Some of these old skills are almost forgotten in the impatient modern world, but dinghy cruising sailors will find that their usefulness still endures.

A Drascombe Lugger motoring with just her mizzen set. This particular Lugger has been painted in traditional Breton colours and has had a bowsprit added. (Didier Cariou)

OUTBOARD MOTORS

If an outboard motor is carried aboard a cruising dinghy, it often comes into its own towards the end of a daysail, when everyone on board is beginning to feel tired. With an outboard motor available, you can keep sailing all day without worrying about getting back to base should the wind drop at dusk, as it so often does.

There is no shame in using an outboard to make a passage quicker or to keep the crew's spirits up, but it is unwise to think of it as your last reef. Engines should not be relied on to save your bacon in really tough conditions. There is a huge difference between the easy sway of a vessel under sail and the violent motion of one being bludgeoned along by an engine. If the wind is very strong, it will become difficult to power into the seas. The boat will pound viciously into the waves, the propeller lifting out of the water as she lurches over the crests. Motoring downwind in heavy weather is even worse, when the following seas threaten to swamp the engine.

Compared to sailing or rowing, an outboard motor is a brutal way to move your dinghy along. The instant a small petrol engine is fired up, you are cut off from your surroundings by the noise. But you forgive the brute when it gets you back to base in bad conditions, or makes a voyage possible in a flat calm. I remember many evenings motoring back in the dusk over a flat sea, watching the lights on the buoys slipping past, the purposeful throb of my engine a comforting sound in the still of the evening, hurrying me back home.

Choice of outboard motor

Due to recent changes in legislation, four-stroke outboard motors have become the norm for small boats. These are frugal, robust and relatively quiet units. Many old two-stroke engines still survive, however, and remain legal to use at the date of writing. Electric outboards are also available. Their technology is improving all the time, and although they are still generally less powerful and have a shorter range than petrol models, they are clearly the future. Quite apart from their environmental advantages, the lack of need to carry cans of fuel and oil makes them very appealing. They are also almost silent in use.

Dinghies do not need particularly large outboard engines. Usually the smallest size is adequate. If we are talking about petrol outboards, most dinghies are quite happy with a 2hp outboard, but the larger 3hp and 4hp engines can be helpful if you need to push a heavier dinghy to windward in heavy weather.

It is important to ensure that the outboard motor's shaft is the correct length for your dinghy's transom, and the propeller is not too deep in the water

Peter Small's Mirror dinghy has an additional timber transom a few inches astern of her original, so that an outboard can be mounted clear of her rudder and mainsheet. (Peter Small)

nor too shallow. Cruising dinghies tend to have deep transoms and may need an outboard with a longer shaft. Alternatively, the engine can be clamped to a separate bracket securely bolted to the transom at the correct height, which also helps to keep the engine well clear of the rudder and the mainsheet.

Recent changes in legislation have made four-stroke outboard motors the norm for small boats. These are frugal, robust and relatively quiet units. Many old two-stroke engines still survive, however, and are still legal to use at the time of writing.

A remote tank carries much more fuel than a petrol motor's integral tank and is better for extended use.

Electric outboards are also available, which are almost completely silent. Their technology is improving all the time, but they are still generally less powerful and have a shorter range than petrol models.

Fitting an outboard

A small engine can often be clamped straight onto the transom of a dinghy, so dinghies with flat transoms are much more outboard-friendly than those with pointed sterns. Double-ended dinghies usually need an outboard well, for an engine to be fitted properly. A transom-hung outboard is simple and straightforward, but the motor is always rather vulnerable in a seaway or when mooring alongside. A motor mounted in a dedicated well is a more seamanlike arrangement.

Transom mounted outboards should have a security lanyard between the engine and a strong point on the dinghy, so that the motor cannot plummet to the bottom of the sea if you fumble while doing up the clamps. An outboard left on the transom of an unattended dinghy inevitably risks

Another view of the additional transom on the stern of Peter's Mirror, here lashed down on her road trailer. (Peter Small)

being stolen, so it should be padlocked in place.

Although many people sail around with the outboard motor permanently mounted on their dinghy's transom, it is more seamanlike to remove it for extended passages, and lash it down under the thwarts alongside the centreboard case, with its power head covered by a canvas bag. Some dinghies have a dedicated stowage locker, with chocks to keep the engine at the correct angle. This is particularly important for some four-stroke engines, which must be laid down in the correct orientation for their gearbox oil.

Manoeuvring with an engine

It is best practice to steer with the dinghy's rudder rather than the outboard motor as this allows the person at the helm to sit well forward in the boat. Ensure that the outboard is mounted where it cannot take chunks out of the rudder when it is put hard over, however.

THE SEIL

The Seil was designed to be used to cruise on the Loire River in France, the last great 'wild river' of Europe. François Vivier was asked to produce a robust and simple vessel for use by youth groups and associations on the river and its tributaries. Influenced by Scandinavian 'pram' dinghies, Seils are light, stable and fast. They are capable of planing off the wind, and have won many competitive raids against other cruising dinghies. Designed to be rowed by two to four people, they have a fairly narrow hull for their length. But despite their speed under sail, Seils are excellent family boats – tough, unsinkable and very well thought through. They also make admirable camp-cruisers. I once met a group of four French teenagers all sleeping aboard a Seil under a boom tent.

François Vivier writes: 'The Seil is a large pram I initially designed for a group of yachtsmen from Nantes area. The full fore and aft hull lines make the Seil a very seaworthy and stable boat.

'Of moderate width, the Seil is easily pulled under oars and is a very good compromise between sail and oar abilities. A Seil was victorious in the 2004 "Sail Caledonia" raid in Scotland.

'The Seil has the capacity to take up to six crewmembers, which makes this boat well adapted to family or collective uses such as sailing schools and youth organisations. She is rigged with a high aspect standing lugsail. Two rowing thwarts are provided. With a crew of young people or children, it is possible to row with two oarsmen per thwart.

'The Seil was produced in GRP for many years by "Canotage de France", and these fibreglass Seils remain the most common today. But the wooden version of the Seil is particularly easy to build, and also has the advantage of a greater lightness. The latest version includes many improvements. Plans are available for home-builders together with a very detailed building handbook.'

(François Vivier)

This Wayfarer is about to moor to a
buoy, and the person on the foredeck
has the painter ready. Notice that the
helmsman is steering using the rudder,
not the outboard. (Mark Broadwith)

Most modern outboards have gear levers
with forward and neutral, and sometimes
also a reverse gear. This means the engine
can be started when the dinghy is still
moored up, and need only be put into gear
after the shorelines have been cast off.
Engines without gearboxes must only be
started after the dinghy has been rowed into
clear water, as the dinghy will inevitably lurch
forward when they suddenly leap into life.

Manoeuvres under power should be
carried out gently, with judicious use of the
throttle and gear lever. If there is more than
one of you aboard, put the less experienced
crewmember on the helm. The more
experienced person should concentrate
on navigation and keep a good lookout all
around. A novice can steer a dinghy under
power if they have learnt simple helm
orders, and these only take a couple of

minutes to explain. A skipper's place is not
at the helm, but in a position where they
can deal with any unexpected incidents that
arise. A vessel can be 'conned' with clear
directions from the skipper. This is standard
practice on naval ships, and dinghy sailors
should emulate them.

Before casting off from the mooring, the
helmsman should be shown how to engage
forward and reverse gears and to use the
throttle. In addition to the vital 'stop', only
three speed settings need to be defined:
'slow ahead', 'half ahead' and 'full ahead' (as
well as the same settings in reverse, if this is
available). You only need four helm orders:
'amidships', 10 degrees, 20 degrees and 30
degrees of helm. I always ask my crew to
repeat the order back to me. The ritual of
repeating helm orders may seem fussy, but
it makes the process more professional and
confirms that the person at the helm has
heard correctly. On naval ships they would
always add 'sir', but you do not need to
insist on this level of formality, unless you
really want to.

When leaving harbour, the skipper can
deal with the difficult tasks of casting off,
fending off and coiling down the ropes,
while calmly giving the helmsman a series
of orders:

'Midships,' says the skipper, pushing off
the dinghy's bow with an oar.

'*Midships*,' repeats the helmsman.

'Slow ahead.' – '*Slow ahead.*'

'Port ten, half ahead.' – '*Port ten, half
ahead.*'

The dinghy moves away from the quay
wall and out into open water.

'Midships, full ahead.' – '*Midships, full
ahead.*'

'What's your head?' asks the skipper.

'*One two zero,*' replies the helmsman,
looking at the compass.

'Turn to starboard and steer 160,' says the skipper.

'*One six zero*,' repeats the crew.

When giving courses to steer, it is always clearer to give a compass course rather than saying something like 'steer for the white house', as the helmsman may not be able to see the particular white house you meant and ends up steering for another one instead.

You rarely see a pleasure boat being 'conned' in this calm and professional way. Usually the boat owner remains rooted at the helm and barks increasingly frantic orders at the other unfortunate crewmembers, who do not have much experience and cannot understand what he wants them to do. The wise dinghy sailor will not be so arrogant or autocratic.

Rowing

Racing dinghies often have no alterna-tive method of propulsion should the wind drop except for paddles. This is fine if you never venture far from a sailing club, where there is usually someone prepared to give you a tow home, but a dinghy venturing further afield must have an efficient form of auxiliary propulsion. Paddles are a woeful way to propel a boat any distance. Even if you carry an outboard motor, your dinghy should also have oars.

Rowing has a reputation of being difficult, uncomfortable and inefficient. In British waters you rarely see anyone rowing other than in gigs or skiffs, where it is basically treated as a means of exercise rather than a way of going somewhere new. Rowing does not need to be a chore, however. The

reason so many people believe it is hard work is because they use oars that are far too short. If a sailing dinghy carries oars at all, they are usually cheap mass-produced items, short enough to stow easily on the bottom boards. Dinghy sailors will happily find space for an outboard motor, spare fuel can and tools, but not for a pair of decent oars. Using an outboard is commonplace, but rowing a dinghy any distance is considered weird.

This is sad, as rowing a dinghy with a pair of well-proportioned, well-balanced oars is nothing like the gruesome experience of doing it with poor ones. Proper sea oars are sophisticated tools, perfected through hundreds of years of refinement. Poetic in their fitness for purpose, they unleash their force smoothly into the water. Once you have rowed a dinghy with a good pair of oars, you wince at the unsubtle brutality of outboard power and resort to it as rarely as possible.

Some cruising dinghy sailors never carry an engine, preferring the purity of navigation under just sail and oar. They take pride in

Even a child can row a small dinghy.
(Nick Vowles)

This modern French-built plywood Ness Yawl has three pairs of oars.

moving quietly and ecologically, burning no fuel and making no unnecessary noise – gliding over the waves as quietly as the water birds, in harmony with the sea around them.

Proper oars

If you want oars for realistic use, they must be of a decent size. In old photographs of small working craft in the days of sail, the oars dominate the interior of the boat – huge things almost as long as the hull. My own dinghy has a beam of 5'6" or 66 inches. According to Collars' formula, she should have oars 10'5" (3.2m) long. These are large objects to stow in a boat only some 15ft (4.5m) long overall.

Oars are traditionally made of either spruce or ash, with a straight knot-free

Calculating the correct oar length

Collars of Oxford, celebrated oar makers and the experts on the subject, use the following formula to calculate the correct oar length in inches:

1. Outboard length of the oar

Beam of boat in inches: _____

Add 8.5 _____

Divide by 2 _____

Multiply by 2.45 _____ = *outboard length*

2. Inboard length of the oar

Beam of boat in inches _____

Divide by 2 _____

Add 2.25 _____ = *inboard length*

Adding figure 1 to figure 2 gives the total length of oar.

(1.) _____ + (2.) _____ = _____ *inches*

(One inch = 2.54 centimetres.)

For efficient rowing, you need oars of a decent length. (Amy Edelman)

grain. Spruce oars are lighter and more flexible, but rather less robust than ash ones. Modern racing skiffs use carbon fibre oars, but these are still often called 'oar leathers', even though they are increasingly made from synthetic rubber rather than the traditional leather. Synthetic sleeves for flat water tend to have spoon blades, whereas sea oars traditionally have long thin blades, symmetrical on both sides. Sea oars can also be used for sculling over the stern with a single oar, which is a vital part of boatcraft.

Oars in cruising dinghies are used for all sorts of purposes other than just rowing: punting along the bottom, fending off from quaysides, levering the boat over soft mud, or poling out a boomless sail. This is why it is a good idea to reinforce the blade tips of wooden oars with fibreglass. I cut off the ends of my oar blades and replaced the last few inches with a piece of plywood, grooved into the remaining blade of the oar. Then I wrapped fibreglass round the whole assembly, and finally sanded it all down to a smooth section.

The collars that protect the oar from being scuffed by the rowlock are called 'oar leathers', even if they are made from synthetic rubber rather than the traditional leather. Synthetic ones are more practical, but real leather collars are a nice touch on a traditional dinghy. They should be glued and then laced in place, rather than nailed, as a row of nail holes can cause rot at a vulnerable place on the oar shaft.

Stowing oars

Many mass-produced dinghies cannot accommodate oars much over 8ft (2.4m) long. These are just about adequate for a 12-footer, but woefully undersized for a beamy dinghy like a Wayfarer, and this is probably one reason why Wayfarers have

Rowing Avel Dro. As I am trying to make progress against wind and current, I am keeping close to the bank. (Ronan Coquil)

acquired a reputation for being hard to row, rather than there being any intrinsic problem with their excellent hull design.

Oars are often stowed on the bottom boards, either side of the centreboard case, but it can be difficult to remove them from this position if they are wanted in a hurry. A better location is to stow them along the front edge of the side benches. Dinghies with open foreparts sometimes stow the oars with their blades against the inside of the prow and their handles pushed against the gunwale on each side. On traditional

(ABOVE) With two people rowing, a small dinghy can really be speeded along – as on this Youkou Lili dinghy, designed by François Vivier. (François Vivier)

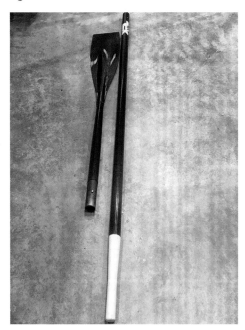

small working craft, oars were often stowed with their blades sticking out over the stern of the boat, and this remains a perfectly seamanlike solution to the problem

Some cruising dinghies carry two-piece oars, which can be dismantled for stowage. These need well-engineered couplings to be effective, but they are a good solution if you do not have the stowage space for full-length oars. Duckworks in the USA have recently introduced some well engineered two-piece carbon fibre oars to the market, that can be purchased in various lengths up to 9'6" (2.9m). They also have a joining ferrule that can be used for longer oars. Lack of stowage space is no longer a reason not to carry a good sized pair of oars.

(LEFT) Two-piece carbon fibre oars from Duckworks – ideal for a boat with little stowage space. (Duckworks)

Rowing position

It is important to have a proper rowing position. Either a fixed thwart is required, as in a traditional dinghy, or a movable seat that can be fixed at the right height for rowing, perhaps on top of the centreboard case. The rowing seat should be at least 7" (18cm) below the rowlock sockets and its after edge about 11–14" (27–35cm) forward of them. If you can fit a foot brace, it will be a great help in extended rowing. This should be about 7" (18cm) below the top of the rowing seat, and its fore and aft position should be adjustable to the length of the oarsman's legs. It greatly improves comfort if you put padding under the rower's bottom. A piece of closed-cell foam is ideal. This can either be permanently fixed to the rowing thwart or kept somewhere handy and placed in position for rowing.

Some dinghies have two rowing positions, one on a forward thwart and another on the midships thwart. The forward position should be used when you are rowing with another crewman at the helm, so that the boat's stern does not cause drag. The amidships rowing position is for when you are alone on board, or if there are crewmembers sitting in both bow and stern, so that the boat is trimmed level fore and aft.

Some keen 'sail and oar' dinghies carry two sets of oars aboard. Rowing with two oarsmen and four oars you can really lift a dinghy along, making a huge difference to her speed. If you have stowage space for an extra pair of oars, they will prove a good investment.

Rowlocks

A cruising dinghy must have proper rowlocks. (The Royal Navy insists on calling them 'crutches'. Doubtless they are right, but everyone else knows them as 'rowlocks'.) The cheap plastic rowlocks often provided are hopeless. They should be removed straight away and replaced with more practical fittings. At the other end of the price spectrum, brass or bronze rowlocks look very smart and shiny, but these metals are really too soft for extended rowing. Best for sea use are traditional galvanised iron rowlocks. They look tough and workmanlike because that is what they are. Choose the even-headed ones, which also hold the oar securely when you are backwatering. Rowlocks come in a number of sizes. You may want

Rowlocks often need to be mounted on timber packs so that the oars do not foul the gunwale. They should also have a lanyard to attach them to the boat.

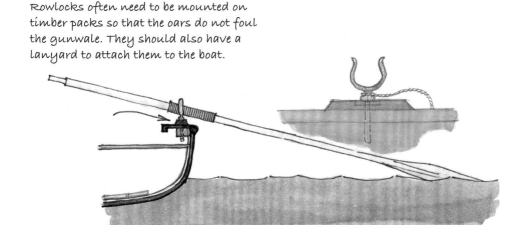

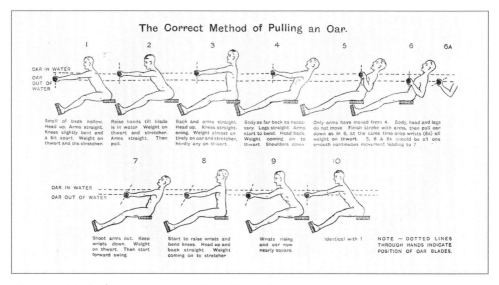

The correct technique to row a sea boat (from the ADMIRALTY MANUAL OF SEAMANSHIP 1937).

to go for a larger size for a seagoing dinghy, so that the oar does not jump out of the socket in rough water.

Dinghies with modern carbon fibre oars often also have modern captive rowlocks, incorporating a hinged stainless steel bar which folds over the oar and locks it in place. If you are that serious about your rowing it is also worth looking into fitting a sliding seat and a proper foot rest. With this sort of set up, rowing becomes a pleasure not a chore.

Rowlocks impart a great force on the gunwale, which should be reinforced to take the strain. So few people do any real rowing nowadays that this is often forgotten, even on otherwise well-designed dinghies. It may also be necessary to take off the rowlock plate and fit a wooden pack beneath it, so that the rowlock is raised sufficiently that the oar does not foul the rubbing strip or the side deck.

Traditional dinghies always had a sculling notch in the transom so they could be propelled by sculling over the stern. On a dinghy not so blessed, an additional rowlock can be fitted on the transom, mounted off centre, so that you can scull without having to remove the rudder. This should be fitted with a leather gaiter, to prevent damage to the oar, as the sleeve or oar leather will be in the wrong place.

Iron rowlocks sink rapidly if they get dropped in the drink so they must be fastened to the boat with thin lanyards. If you provide a separate rowlock for every socket, you will never need to detach the lanyards and so you will never lose a rowlock over the side. Ensure that the lanyards are of such a length that it is impossible for anyone to place a spare rowlock near the steering compass, or one day you will find yourself following a seriously misleading heading.

If you really cannot stow a pair of oars long enough for efficient rowing, consider shipping just one oar for sculling over the stern. This oar can usually be left in the sculling notch or stern rowlock while sailing, with its blade projecting astern of the dinghy. I tend to sail with one oar poking out over the stern most of the time, ready for a quick bit of sculling, but have recently got into the habit of sliding the oar into the boat when sailing in congested waters, after a dinghy passed too close under my stern and broke the oar in half. Breton boatmen propel sizeable working craft with a single sculling oar, and this is an excellent solution for a beamy boat that cannot be rowed easily.

Manoeuvring under oars

Oars should be the first choice for close-quarters manoeuvring. A boat under power is difficult to control at low speed, as there is insufficient water flow over the rudder for it to work effectively. Oars give more precise control, which can be deployed more accurately and subtly. A boat under oars can be turned round in her own length, and she can ferry-glide sideways into the narrowest berth by judicious use of wind and tide.

Rowing may seem a primitive way to propel a boat, but it is actually very subtle and capable of much refinement. Rather than tugging hard at the oars, allow your trunk and hips to do the work. Rowing should feel like walking rather than running – a smooth and measured activity that you should be able to sustain for a long period. An experienced oarsman uses the power in the back and thigh muscles rather than the arms, which should remain straight for much of the power stroke, like pieces of string linking the shoulders to the oars.

If you have two rowing positions in your dinghy, it is more effective to row with two people on the oars, even if you have only one pair of oars aboard. One crewmember should use the forward rowing position, while the other sits on the midships bench and rows on the opposite side of the boat. Two people and two oars will put much more power into the water than just one person rowing. You may need a third crewmember at the helm, however, as two rowers will not maintain a straight course unless they are experienced.

If you want to try rowing with two people, without someone also on the helm, the technique is for the person in the aft rowing position to concentrate simply on maintaining an even regular stroke. Meanwhile, the rower in the bow needs to concentrate on keeping in time, but also to manage the steering – taking a stronger or weaker stroke as appropriate to keep the boat tracking straight, and looking over their shoulder from time to time to check the heading.

SCULLING OVER THE STERN

Sculling over the stern is an essential part of boatcraft. It is difficult to describe the technique, however. Rather like riding a bicycle, it is best learnt by practising. You will struggle for ages, getting nowhere. You will become hot, flustered and frustrated. Then, just when it feels totally hopeless, you will acquire the knack. I am reluctant to explain the technique, as too much thinking about it makes it harder to learn. But there is so much misunderstanding about the subject that a little laying down the law is probably called for.

When you row with two oars they behave like paddlewheels, but when you scull over the stern the single oar operates more like a propeller. The blade of the oar moves through the water at an angle, producing forward motion in the boat. Propellers are a very efficient method of propulsion, and so too is sculling. Once you have learnt the skill, you will use it most of the time in preference to rowing. An experienced

Fanny learning to scull at the île de Sein.

Learning to scull

The best way to learn sculling is to go out in the dinghy and just practise. In crowded waters, take a crewmate along with you to sit in the stern, and to keep a lookout for other vessels. A friend of mine has a more brutal suggestion, which either works or removes you from the statistics entirely. He recommends setting off alone in your boat with no sail, no engine, only one oar and crucially an offshore wind. If you get back you'll be able to scull, he says.

I suggest you start learning to scull by using both hands. The delights of one-armed sculling can come later. Stand in the middle of the boat with your feet apart, facing the stern. Lift the oar into the sculling notch and raise the loom of the oar until the blade is dipped into the water. The blade should be horizontal and the handle of the oar should be at eye level. As you do this, the oar will try to float out of the sculling notch, and your crewmate may need to hold it down for you.

When the oar is in the correct position for sculling, the blade should be fully immersed behind the transom, piercing the water surface at an angle of some 30 degrees. Your arms should hold the

sculler can propel a dinghy almost as fast as by rowing.

The great advantage of sculling is that it is done standing up and looking forward. This makes it invaluable for close-quarters work in harbours – bringing the boat alongside a quay wall or picking up a mooring.

How to scull a dinghy over the stern, showing the motion of the wrist. For clarity only one hand is shown, but it is easier to learn with two hands.

(ABOVE) Nautical gear is not compulsory when sculling. This oar is a little short for maximum efficiency, but this is not really a problem in such a small tender.

(BELOW) An Ilur dinghy being sculled across a French harbour. Notice the relaxed posture of an experienced 'godilleur'. (François Vivier)

handle of the oar from below, elbows bent at about 90 degrees, wrists and forearms in line, perpendicular to the axis of the oar.

Now make a gentle stroke. Do not try to propel the boat with this first stroke. Just watch what happens. Push the handle of the oar gently to one side, with your wrists slightly relaxed so that they are 'left behind' by the movement of your forearms. Your wrists should cock to about 15 degrees. One of your wrists will now be bent back as far as it can go. Continue pushing sideways until your body weight is almost on one leg, and then reverse the stroke and start pushing the other way, allowing your wrists to cock in the other direction. Once again they will be 'left behind' by the motion of your forearms. You will see that the angle of the oar blade has reversed.

The process is as simple as that. The oar blade is pushed from side to side through the water at an angle of some 15 degrees, reversing at the end of each stroke. The same side of the blade is always uppermost. Steering is achieved by pushing harder in one direction than the other.

The trick is to maintain pressure on the oar, even through the change of angle, as this prevents the oar floating out of its socket. It is a matter of discovering the correct rhythm. Each boat needs a different sculling rate, depending on the length and weight of the sculling oar. Using a new oar on a new boat can disconcert even the most experienced of scullers.

All you need now is practice. Eventually you will find it easier to scull with only one hand, standing sideways on to the sculling oar, so that you can look forward and propel your dinghy with competent nonchalance. Right-handed people tend to scull with the right hand, so they will find it more convenient to have the sculling notch on the starboard side of the transom.

Drifting up the Dart

Night has fallen, and we still have not reached the narrows. The fitful wind is dropping away and we have been rowing for some time. High above our limp sail, a half moon rides in the dark sky, flecked with winter stars and framed by the silhouettes of the hills around us. We have left Dartmouth's gaily illuminated quaysides far behind, and the black shores are as featureless as the water we glide across.

The tide is flooding, thrusting us into the darkness ahead. Boats on moorings loom out of the gloom and rush past. We are the only boat moving in this primeval night, silent but for the steady beat of our oar strokes. Hunched over the helm, I shine the torch ahead, trying to penetrate the mist steaming from the water. Somewhere in the clinging murk ahead is the Anchor Stone, a large rock right out in the centre of the channel.

The square topmark of a perch rears up against the night sky, but the Anchor Stone remains just a sinister shadow, half imagined against the black of the bank. I alter course to leave the rock well to starboard. As we turn, the lights of the village of Dittisham come into view beyond the narrows, clambering up the port bank.

Avel Dro moored to the pontoon at Dittisham, handy for the pub.

We can hear the tide rippling against the ferry pontoon long before we capture it in the circle of torchlight. The pontoon sweeps towards us with dreadful inexorability, and we suddenly realise how fast the tide is hustling us along, far too quickly to step ashore with a line. We cannot risk anyone falling into the water in the darkness.

Letting the pontoon slip away astern, we turn into the tidal shadow behind it and drop the sail into the boat. I reach for the sculling oar and propel Avel Dro into the gap between two moored dinghies. The torch reveals some lettering on the pontoon edge:

'Reserved for Berth Holders.'

We make fast nonetheless. This late in the year, hopefully no one will mind.

Hurrying along the pontoon, we come to the Ferry Boat Inn, a pink-rendered building hard against Dittisham's short quayside. Its door opens into light and homely chatter. There is a snug throng of people inside and a promising rake of hand pumps. We remove our damp oilies, pile them on a chair, then sit back and let the cosy conviviality of the bar soak into us.

Boats have an almost alchemical power over pubs. They transform even the most ordinary boozer into pure gold. It seems such a simple formula for contentment – go sailing and then go to the pub – but it works every time for me.

5 MOORING AND ANCHORING

It is a poor daysail that does not involve landing somewhere for a run ashore. If you are sailing in non-tidal waters, beaching the boat is a simple matter. Pull the bow of the dinghy up the beach a little way, then tie the painter to a convenient tree, or dig an anchor into the sand. In tidal water it is rather more complicated. Either the tide will be ebbing when you arrive at the beach, so your boat will rapidly end up hard aground, or it will be flooding and she will soon float away.

A flotilla of Minahouet dinghies pulled up on the beach. (François Vivier)

LANDING ON A BEACH

A light dinghy can be carried up the beach above the high-water mark. But most cruising dinghies are too heavy for this. The alternative is to anchor your dinghy in deep water while you go ashore. In warm climates you could simply swim ashore after anchoring the dinghy, but this is not a popular pastime in the water temperatures where I usually sail.

A surprisingly effective technique is to tie a length of rope to the crown of the boat's anchor, then take the other end of this rope up the beach and tie it to a tree or a rock. Balance the anchor on the stern of the dinghy, and carefully flake out a reasonable length of anchor cable in the bottom of the dinghy. Now give the dinghy a hard shove into deep water. When she is far enough out, tug on the shore rope, which will yank the anchor off your dinghy's stern and into the water. Hopefully the anchor cable runs out freely without getting snarled up, and your dinghy ends up lying happily to her cable, clear of the beach. When you want your boat back, just haul on the shoreline, which trips the anchor and drags it up the beach, pulling your dinghy towards the shore.

Security

There is little that can be done to secure a beached sailing dinghy against the attentions of the light-fingered, apart from hoping that they will steal a more impressive-looking boat instead. I rarely worry too much about the possibility that my dinghy will be stolen, but a dinghy left afloat is more secure than one left lying on a beach, so I tend to anchor off if I have any doubts about the place. Alternatively, I remove the oars and carry them with me when going ashore, which makes stealing the boat rather more

difficult. Shoreside pubs seem quite pleased when you arrive and prop your oars up outside the door, as it adds to the nautical decoration.

The pilfering of small objects out of the boat is a different problem. If you are intending to leave your dinghy on the beach while you go to the pub for lunch, cover up or remove anything expensive and easily detachable, such as the steering compass. Ideally there will be a locker aboard for small valuable items, which can be secured with a padlock. Do not use a padlock that is too large, however, as you do not want to give the impression that the locker contains anything expensive that would make it worth smashing open for. Your aim is simply to deter the casual thief.

ANCHORING

There are many reasons for dropping anchor. You might anchor to hoist sail or to reef, or drop the hook for a lunch stop. Anchoring is also a good way of leaving the boat afloat overnight in tidal waters.

When choosing somewhere to anchor, pick a location away from strong tidal streams and sheltered from the wind. Try to anchor over sand or mud rather than rocks, as the holding will be better. Ideally you will be able to see down through the clear water and pick a nice piece of sea floor for your anchor to land on. If you are sailing somewhere where the water is muddy, you will need to come to a judgement about the sea bottom from the chart and indications on the foreshore.

Only drop anchor under sail if there is no tide or current. Otherwise it is best to lower sail and then to approach your chosen anchorage under oars. Lower the anchor with sufficient scope for the depth of water,

AVEL DRO lying quietly at anchor at the Île Ilur on the Golfe du Morbihan, after which her class of dinghy was named.

then row the dinghy downwind until she is brought up short by the anchor rode, to ensure that the anchor is well dug in.

Veering cable

The more cable you veer, the more securely your dinghy will lie at anchor. Six times the depth at high water is advisable for a rope rode, but a dinghy anchored in a narrow creek often does not have the swinging room for this amount of cable. A good rule of thumb is 3 x depth + 10m, for example:

Measured depth	=	5m
Additional depth at HW	=	3m
Add: 5 + 3	=	8m
Multiply by three: × 3	=	24m
Add 10m + 10	=	34m

Although this is rather less than the 48m that would be veered in this depth of water

using the '6 x depth' formula, the dinghy will still swing through a circle of nearly 70m.

In practice, I almost invariably anchor in about this depth of water and veer some 30m of cable.

There are times when substantially more cable needs to be veered. When I am sailing in the Bristol Channel, which has a tidal range of 12m, I often need to veer my full 50m of rode with an additional 30m attached to the end of it, making a total length of 80m (44 fathoms). A common problem when veering this amount of cable is another boat arriving later in the day and anchoring in your swinging circle. If they cannot be persuaded to move, you must either maintain an anchor watch or re-anchor further away.

There are various ways of marking an anchor rode. I use plastic cable ties, which are easy to see and can be felt in the dark.

My anchor warps are stowed under the bottom boards either side of the centreboard case. The rodes are marked every 10m with a cable tie. I have 40m of nylon rope and 5m of chain on each anchor.

I have one tie for 10m, two for 20m and so on. My standard technique is to drop the anchor on 20m of scope, which is marked by two cable ties. Then I check the actual depth of water with my lead line and work out the right amount of additional cable to veer, based on the depth of water at high tide. Then I almost invariably end up veering another 10m.

Lying to two anchors

If you need to stop your boat swinging around her anchor in a wide arc, perhaps because you are anchored in a narrow creek, you should put out two anchors. Usually a stern anchor is put out first, and the dinghy continues forwards oars or under her own momentum before lowering a bow anchor. The warps are then adjusted so that the dinghy lies midway between the two anchors. This is also a good way to ensure that your boat dries out in a particular spot on a tidal beach. I often anchor this way, and dry out over perhaps half of the tide, but it needs to be somewhere sheltered, as a dinghy with her tent up sitting broadside onto the wind creates a lot of windage, and can cause even the best dug in anchor to drag.

In less sheltered waters, both anchors should be put out over the bow. This still keeps the boat in more or less the same place, but allows her to swing head to wind. If the aim is to reduce the swinging circle of the dinghy, the two anchor warps should make an angle of at least 120 degrees with each other. One anchor is dropped conventionally and then the boat is allowed to drop back to the full extent of the rode. The dinghy is rowed at an angle to the line of the first anchor warp and the second anchor is lowered.

THE NORSEBOAT 17.5

The Norseboat comes from North America, and was purpose-designed for cruising. She is part of a family of three similar designs ranging from 12'6" to 21'6" long (3.8–6.5m), the Norseboat 17.5 being the middle one in the range. Her narrow hull is designed to be efficient under oars, but also effective under sail. The rig is a fully battened mainsail with a curved yard and a furling jib. The hull is very beautiful. It has a high bow flowing back to a wineglass transom. Inside are two rowing positions and space for up to four people under sail, or two when camp cruising, for which the boat is specifically designed. There is ample stowage for cruising gear and even space for a portable toilet. A bed can be formed at thwart level by lifting the bottom boards. A folding dodger provides shelter when sailing, and the tent cover clips onto the back of this. A bimini can also be set up to provide shade when sailing in hot climates.

In 2010, two British Royal Marine officers called Kevin Oliver and Tony Lancashire took a Norseboat 17.5 through the Northwest Passage in Arctic Canada under sail and oar, sleeping on board at night in sub-zero temperatures. Trapped by pack ice, they had to pull the boat across the ice using a block and tackle for many days before they regained open water. At night they usually hauled the boat ashore on inflatable boat rollers, and had to keep a look out for bears. Photographs from this trip are shown here.

A dinghy lying to two anchors. If the anchors are veered on separate rodes set at an angle to each other, the dinghy will not swing around such a large circle. For security in rough weather the two anchors should be in tandem on the same rode (right).

Once both anchors are well dug in, the length of each rode should be adjusted so that each anchor is lying to the same length of cable. This is a very secure method of anchoring and useful if you are leaving the boat unattended overnight, but the two warps will inevitably twist around each other as the boat swings to her anchor, so you should not leave her like that for too many days.

If you have to anchor your dinghy in very deep water, a very secure method is to attach the end of the first anchor cable to the crown of the second anchor, and then lower that to the end of its scope as well, so that the two anchors operate in tandem, one behind the other. The anchors will need to be reset when the tide turns. I don't do this very often, but if you find your anchor is dragging in a strong wind, it is a good way to address the problem without having to raise the first anchor and reset it.

Sheltered anchorages

Take care in choosing an anchorage. High land to windward will create shelter in its lee, but beware of the strange winds under rocky cliffs that can strike your dinghy from all directions. The best shelter is found close to a wooded shoreline, as trees dampen the wind. Beware of midges though if you are in an area that is prone to them, such as the west coast of Scotland. In such places it is better to anchor further out.

An anchorage that is sheltered when the wind is coming from one direction may become uncomfortably exposed if the wind changes. The fetch of a strong wind blowing over just half a mile of water will produce pronounced waves, making the anchorage uncomfortable for a dinghy.

The best dinghy anchorages are completely sheltered on all sides. Often the most sheltered anchorages are in narrow drying creeks, so you must not be afraid of allowing your dinghy to dry out. If you need to get ashore and are worried about getting trapped aboard at low tide by the mud, the solution is to anchor directly over the channel, which usually has a pebble bottom. This is generally firm enough to walk on, even when the rest of the mud is soft.

Always be careful when crossing soft mud to get back to your dinghy. If in doubt, take an oar with you and prod the mud in front of you. Your seaboots must also fit tightly or they will be sucked off. If you do happen to get trapped, soft mud will not 'drag you down' as long as you do not struggle. Lie flat on it, as if swimming, and it will keep you afloat. You should then be able to slither your way to safety. You will get very muddy though.

Rigging an outhaul

Where I live in Brittany, and also where I used to live in the English West Country, large numbers of small boats are kept on outhauls throughout the season. An outhaul is an excellent method of keeping a boat afloat in tidal water, and allows you to bring her into the shore whenever you want.

Begin by removing the rode from your anchor and shackle a spare pulley block to it instead (keep a spare block in your tool kit specially for this purpose). Pass a long rope through the block, at least 30m (17 fathoms) long, but preferably double that. Then row out from the beach and drop this anchor in deep water, beyond the low-tide mark if possible. Tie the ends of the rope together and then row back to the shore with them.

You now have an endless rope stretching from the shore out into the water. The dinghy should be made fast to this rope, one end at the bow and the other at the stern. She can now be pulled into deep water by hauling on one part of the rope, and hauled back onto the beach by pulling on the other part. In order to keep the dinghy in place when it is out in deep water, the loop of rope on the shore must be made fast to another anchor dug into the beach, or tied to a convenient tree.

Outhauls are very simple in principle, but they take a surprising amount of time and tremendous lengths of rope to set them up. They can also fail to work at embarrassing moments, perhaps because the rope has picked up seaweed or got itself wrapped round a rock underwater. To ensure trouble-free use of your outhaul, you need to remove any seaweed from the path of the rope and drag any large rocks out of the way. Outhauls are not worth the trouble for a brief stop, but they are worth considering if you are on holiday somewhere with your dinghy, want to leave her afloat for a few days, and have

An outhaul mooring. This enables the dinghy to lie afloat in deep water but still be able to be brought into the beach at all states of the tide.

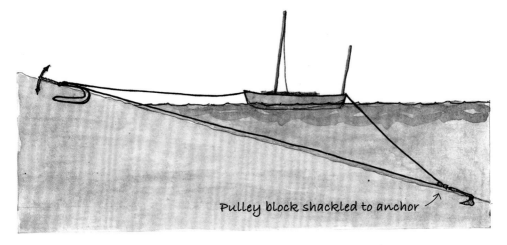

Pulley block shackled to anchor

(ABOVE) Wayfarer dinghies on outhauls in a tidal inlet. (Mark Broadwith)

(LEFT) Three Wayfarers using outhauls to moor to a quayside, where their crews are camping ashore. (Mark Broadwith)

enough spare time to wander around the beach with two anchors and many fathoms of rope.

The Pythagorean mooring

Here is another clever rope trick using ancient Greek trigonometry, and particularly handy in places with a modest tidal range. Perhaps Pythagoras invented it while dinghy cruising. Begin by laying out a single anchor in deep water, with just enough cable veered so that the dinghy can reach the beach. Imagine that this anchor cable forms one side of a right-angled triangle, and the second side of the triangle is formed by the shoreline. Now walk along the beach with a second anchor, parallel to the shoreline, so that its anchor cable pulls the dinghy

away from the beach at an angle until she lies in deep water, midway between the two anchors. When both anchor warps are tight, dig this second anchor into the sand, just above the high-water mark. The two anchor warps form the hypotenuse of a right-angled triangle, with the dinghy lying halfway along it.

Carrying a tender

Another way to anchor a dinghy in deep water and yet still be able to get ashore to the pub is to carry a tender. Larger dinghies like the Drascombe Lugger sometimes tow a small rigid tender, at the loss of some speed. Or you could stow a little inflatable tender aboard your dinghy and inflate it only when needed. Proper inflatable yacht

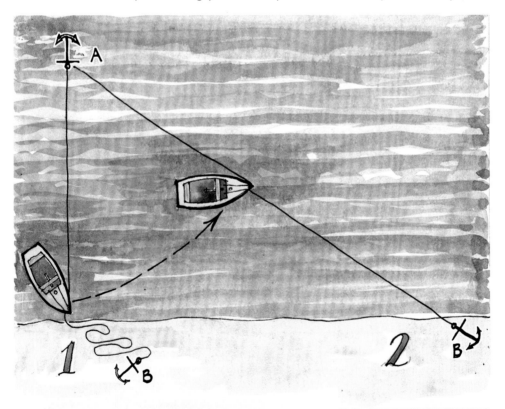

The Pythagorean mooring is an ingenious way of keeping a dinghy afloat without going to all the trouble of setting up an outhaul.

A toy dinghy can be used to communicate with the shore. John Perry propels his with two table tennis rackets rather than oars, as they are easier to stow.

tenders are usually too bulky to be carried aboard a dinghy, so some people carry a beach inflatable instead, which is adequate for use over a short distance. A tender only needs to accommodate one person, as you can offload the rest of your crew onto the beach before rowing off to anchor the dinghy in deep water. Once this has been done, you return to shore on your own in the toy tender.

Considering they are just toys, beach inflatables are surprisingly robust. Their chief flaw is usually their poor quality air valves. Spending rather more money will obtain you a better quality boat, but usually at the expense of greater weight and pack size. Rather more expensive, but also much more robust, are the boats produced for the modern sport of packrafting. Packrafts are single person boats designed to fit in a rucksack. They are designed to be propelled by a double paddle, like a kayak. One day I will probably get one of these, but in the meantime I paddle around in my beach toy.

MOORING BUOYS

If you keep your dinghy on a mooring, you will already know everything there is to know about them, particularly the importance of checking them regularly. For the rest of us, other people's mooring buoys are handy places to secure our dinghies temporarily in deep water. Everyone picks up spare moorings, but it is polite to remain aboard if you are using someone else's buoy, in case the owner returns and wants to moor up.

Some harbours have visitors' buoys that you can use (but you may have to pay for the privilege). All other buoys are owned by someone, who may come along at an inconvenient moment and ask you to move somewhere else.

The best way to pick up a mooring is to drop your sails in clear water and then row or motor the dinghy up to the buoy. Picking up a mooring under sail is more complicated, as you need to consider the relative directions of the wind and tide.

Making fast to a buoy

On sailing dinghies with long foredecks, the crew may be unable to reach a buoy lying under the bows without climbing on the foredeck. It is better to come alongside a buoy amidships, attach the painter to it and then allow their boat to drop back so the buoy lies in front of the bows. Some cruising dinghies carry a special mooring rope with a big snap hook on the other end of it. They clip this onto the loop on the top of the buoy, to hold their dinghy in place while they make her fast more permanently.

As I can stand right up in the prow of my dinghy, I usually pick up a buoy by leaning over and grabbing it when it arrives just under the bow. Then I push the painter through the loop in the top of the buoy and bring it back on board as a temporary attachment.

Many buoys have a 'pick-up rope' attached to their base, which should be used for more permanent mooring. The pick-up rope often has a small 'pick-up buoy' at the end of it. Bring the little buoy aboard your boat, and then make the pick-up rope fast around a cleat or belaying pin. Pick-up ropes are often thick and slimy with weed, so you need a big cleat for this. The loop in the top of a plastic buoy is strong enough to hold a dinghy temporarily, but must not be relied on for long-term mooring.

If the pick-up rope is too thick to be brought aboard, or there is no pick-up rope on the buoy, you must use your own rope instead. On small plastic buoys, your mooring rope should be passed through the shackle on the bottom of the buoy. Only the large buoys fitted with stout metal loops in the top are designed to take the strain of a mooring rope attached directly to the buoy.

When using your own rope to moor to a buoy, it is tempting to push the rope through a loop on the buoy and then bring it straight back to your boat, as this makes it much easier to cast off the mooring. This is acceptable for a brief stop, but it is not a secure way to moor if you will be leaving your boat unattended. Always push the mooring rope through the loop twice, to form a full round turn, as this greatly reduces chafe.

If you leave your dinghy on an exposed buoy in bad weather, your boat will inevitably snatch and worry at the mooring, and there will be a risk of her mooring rope chafing through, even if there is a round turn on the warp. Small boats often come free from moorings in rough conditions. If bad weather is expected, a very secure way

of making fast is to shackle your anchor chain to the buoy. If you let out a couple of metres of chain, its weight will also reduce snatching.

QUAYSIDES

Increasingly, even commercial fishing harbours are equipped with floating pontoons, and it is becoming rare to need to moor to a high quayside in tidal waters. We are becoming spoilt, and the techniques of proper alongside mooring are being forgotten. While short lines are all that is needed to make fast to the cleats on pontoons, mooring a sailing dinghy to the quay wall involves serious lengths of warp. Perhaps you need to make fast to a tall, slimy quayside intended for big steel trawlers, not fragile little dinghies, and you must be able to secure your boat properly, even in a large tidal range. If the waves start breaking against the quay wall your dinghy could easily be damaged if she is not properly made fast.

A cruising dinghy should have substantial mooring cleats on each bow and each quarter. These will come under huge snatching forces if the boat is set surging backwards and forwards by the wash of a passing fishing vessel, so they should be glued and fixed with the very largest screws, or through-bolted to generous backing plates.

Entering a strange harbour for the first time, be prudent and lower the sails while you have plenty of sea room. Come in under oars or engine, put the fenders out and make ready the warps. It is a good idea to have at least two really big fenders, of dimensions that would not embarrass a 40ft yacht. If you keep them lashed down low in the hull, they will also double as buoyancy

Alongside the quay at Clovelly in North Devon. The timber ladder is convenient for access while we refill the jerrycans with water, but could foul our gunwale when the tide rises.

bags, and can even be used as boat rollers if you ever need to haul the boat up a beach.

The quayside may be far over your head, reached by a steel ladder let into the quay wall. Come in slowly until you are alongside the ladder, and then make fast temporarily to one of the rungs, while you prepare your mooring warps. Then clamber up the ladder with the rope ends. When climbing, it is best to grasp the rungs of the ladder rather than the uprights. This is not only safer, but they are less likely to be covered in barnacles that may cut your hands, as peoples' feet will have rubbed them off.

Throwing a mooring warp

Sometimes a helpful person high up on the quayside will offer to catch a thrown warp. Unless they look like they know what they are doing, it is best to refuse politely, rather than put your trust in the skills of an unknown quayside loiterer.

If you do decide to throw a rope, re-coil it immediately before throwing, to ensure that it is not tangled. Split the coil, taking a third of it into your throwing hand, and leave the remainder of the coil in the other hand. Then throw the smaller coil with a wide swinging motion of your arm. As the thrown part of the rope flies through the air, the remainder should follow it, uncoiling neatly from your other hand. If you miss first time, just haul in the rope, calmly re-coiling it, and try again. Learn how to coil and to throw a warp smartly and you will stand out in any harbour as a true expert in boatcraft.

Making fast to a quay

On traditional quaysides, the mooring rings or bollards are usually a long way apart and judging the correct length of mooring warp can be difficult. You can easily spend half an hour ensuring that all your warps are set up correctly in a tidal harbour. If the mooring warps are too short, you could return from a run ashore to find your boat dangling from them. If they are too slack, she will range around uncontrollably at high water and may get damaged.

A dinghy should be made fast to a quay with at least three mooring lines: a bow warp, a stern warp and also a 'spring' running from her aft quarter forward to

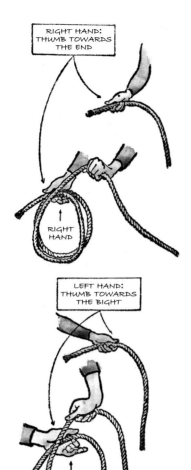

Throwing a rope (from A Seaman's Pocket Book, HMSO 1943)

Coiling a rope. (from A Seaman's Pocket Book, HMSO 1943)

the quayside. A second spring running aft from the bow is not usually necessary for a dinghy with a transom, but may be needed for a double-ender. The length of each mooring warp should be at least three times the maximum height of the quayside at low water, so that they make an angle of about 30 degrees with the horizontal. This means carrying some seriously long ropes. My standard mooring warps are fairly short these days, only some 15ft (5m) long, as

these are more convenient when coming alongside pontoons, but I carry a number of 50 ft (15m) mooring warps too. As well as these, one or two warps of 100ft (30m) in length are not excessive, and I often need to use all these against a high quayside.

Make fast the bow and stern warps while your boat is still held in place by the temporary lashing at the foot of the ladder. Best practice is to tie the very end of the warp to the bollard or ring and then adjust the length of the warp from within the boat. This is not essential, but you must be able to be cast off your warps from inside the boat in an emergency, even when they are loaded. Once your mooring warps are set up to your satisfaction, remove the temporary lashing to the ladder, or a falling tide will leave her hanging in the air, and a rising tide will sink her.

If a larger vessel is already alongside the quay, it is convenient to moor your dinghy alongside her, as this means you do not need to worry about the tidal range. It is polite to ask permission first before treating another boat like a pontoon, however. A

30°

Making fast to a quayside.

AVEL DRO drying out while moored alongside on Lundy Island. At high water springs this breakwater is completely covered.

cruising dinghy is usually made welcome in this situation, even though a yacht would be discouraged from doing the same thing. When you cross the decks of the other boat to go ashore, remember that it is the 'done thing' to walk forward of the mast, not clomp straight across her cockpit.

Drying quaysides

Many quaysides dry at low water, and all sorts of rubbish is chucked over them, which your dinghy could end up sitting on at low tide. If the water is clear, you may be able to peer down and inspect the seabed beneath. If the water is murky, make local enquiries about the state of the seabed at the foot of the quay. A well-used quay will probably be safe, but long-abandoned quaysides are often foul with debris.

MOORING TO A PONTOON

Mooring to a pontoon is much more straightforward than making fast to a tidal quayside, and is increasingly the norm even in commercial harbours. A pontoon is more or less at the same height as your dinghy, and will stay in that relative position at all states of the tide. Unfortunately, the gunwale of a sailing dinghy is usually at just the right height to slide under the pontoon deck. If the wash of a passing powerboat disturbs the pontoon, its deck can come crashing down onto your dinghy, seriously damaging her. The solution is to moor alongside one of the floats under the pontoon, and set your fenders up against it, so that the dinghy is prevented from sliding underneath. You may have to be rather choosy about your pontoon berth to achieve this.

Even when moored in the comparative safety of a marina, a dinghy should have a

Avel Dro moored to a pontoon, with bow and stern lines as well as a spring. The sail has been temporarily laid in the rowlocks out of the way of the crew, but it will not be left there while the boat is unattended.

bow warp and stern warp, as well as a spring running forward from the quarter. Mooring ropes should be properly cleated or tied off, not just passed through a ring or round a cleat and brought back to the boat, as they may chafe through. You see many slovenly practices in marinas, but there is no reason for cruising dinghies to adopt them too.

Marinas often set aside a special pontoon for small boats. These sometimes dry at low water, and your dinghy could end up lying at an uncomfortable angle. Before you leave your boat unattended, prod about with an oar and spare a moment to think what will happen to your dinghy when she is sitting on the bottom. Also ensure that you have raised the plate and the rudder. Marinas seem such safe places that it is easy to become complacent, but they have their perils, just like any mooring place.

SCAMP

Probably the cutest, most perky boat about, SCAMP is an acronym for Small Craft Advisor Magazine Project. The American magazine commissioned the design in 2010 from New Zealand's John Welsford, with the brief to produce the smallest possible boat that it was capable to cruise in, while still being seaworthy enough for exposed passages.

The dinghy is full of clever, innovative ideas. She has a shelter rather than a cabin, which is designed to be used to sit in out of the wind and rain, to make a brew and also to stow gear you want to keep out of the rain. The idea is that you sleep on the floor of the cockpit under a boom tent. SCAMP carries water ballast and is designed for easy righting in the event of a capsize. The high bow and stern make her very resistant to turning turtle and she can be righted with very little water retained inside.

Typical for a Welsford design, SCAMP is designed for easy home construction in plywood, but in the USA a GRP version is also available from Gig Harbour Boat Works. The single balance lugsail has three deep reefs and is designed to be efficient and easy to use. There are large lockers for all your gear and although the boat is designed to be rowed, an outboard motor can also be carried.

When adventure sailor Howard Rice was looking for a dinghy to visit Tierra del Fuego and Cape Horn, he chose the SCAMP as the basis for his specially built SOUTHERN CROSS. This is a huge boat for her diminutive length, as suitable for taking a family afloat for a leisurely picnic as for singlehanded adventure sailing in the Southern Ocean. And despite her endearing snubnosed beaminess, she is surprisingly fast under sail.

(Debra Colvin)

Mudlarks

When you drive over the great bridges that link England to south Wales and look down on the Severn Estuary beneath, it seems a grim and forlorn place. But the sport of sailing is remarkably tenacious. No matter how dangerous the coast and how unprepossessing the surroundings, wherever there is navigable water someone will have found a way to go sailing on it.

A few miles upstream of the bridges, the Lydney Yacht Club occupies a whitewashed building at the mouth of an almost forgotten ship canal, and is home to a fleet of cruising Wayfarers. I joined them in Avel Dro for a cruise in company. It was late in the season and the weather forecast was talking of Force 6–8 winds. The word 'rough' had also been bandied about. Only three boats had decided to go out sailing, and maybe this had something to do with it. Our plan was to make a quick dash downstream to the next haven. After a run ashore, we would then catch the flood back up the estuary to a creek on the opposite bank, where we would spend the night. The organiser, Annabel, was embarrassed about the modesty of this proposition. I thought we were ambitious to set off at all.

Annabel and Dave launched the Wayfarer Clubbar, and the swift brown stream swept them rapidly away. I followed more tentatively in Avel Dro. This was my first time sailing my own boat on the notorious Severn Estuary and I was rather apprehensive. A third member of the club assured us that he would come along later in a vintage motor cruiser to 'pick up the pieces'.

Our initial destination was St Pierre Pill on the Welsh bank of the Severn. This dubious drying creek is squeezed between the two huge suspension bridges that span the estuary. It was a beat all the way there against the sou-westerly wind, but the ebb was so strong that the ten-mile sail took us less than three hours.

St Pierre Pill is inviting enough, as long as you like mud. Deep inside the creek, was a cluster of miscellaneous yachts lying to homemade buoys. A dinghy pontoon extended from one bank. By the time Avel Dro arrived, Clubbar was already moored alongside and Annabel and Dave were standing on the pontoon, talking to a man who proudly introduced himself as Commodore of the Chepstow and District Yacht Club. He offered us the freedom of their clubhouse to eat our lunch in.

St Pierre Pill at low water, looking towards the new Severn Bridge. Avel Dro and Clubbar are alongside the pontoon.

The Commodore led us up the slippy bank and round behind some stunted thorn bushes. Out on the bleak flats beside the Severn stood a building that had clearly started life as a prefabricated domestic garage. Inside was a storeroom full of old pots of paint, a toilet, and a small kitchen area furnished with a rough table and mismatched chairs that looked like they had been found floating in the river. This was the clubhouse of the Chepstow and District Yacht Club.

We spread our food out on the table and fired up the gas stove for a hot drink. Outside the wind rose and rain lashed at the lonely little building. The Met Office had not exaggerated when they talked of gales. We wondered how long the deluge would last and if we would need to spend the night on the floor of the clubhouse.

By the time the evening tide had refilled the creek and refloated our dinghies, the weather had moderated, but there was still a stiff breeze into the pill. While close-tacking through the moorings, Clubbar's mainsheet became wrapped around one of the yachts. She heeled sharply and came to an abrupt halt. Annabel and Dave struggled to free her. Finally Dave flicked the mainsheet clear and she swung free, straight across my bows.

I swerved sharply to avoid them. With little room for manoeuvre, I slipped inside the line of withies marking the edge of the channel. I raised my plate, and Avel Dro glided smoothly across the shallows and back into the deep water beyond. But when I tried to lower the plate again, I found that it was stuck in its slot, jammed by the mud that had been forced up into it while we were aground.

Meanwhile I had managed to clear the creek. Avel Dro was now in the main river sailing very fast towards the great suspension bridge. Dangerously close under her lee was a small island at the confluence of the River Wye and the Severn. I brought her as close to the wind as I could, but she simply slipped sideways. When I compared the GPS COG readout with her compass course, I could see she was making a massive 30 degrees of leeway.

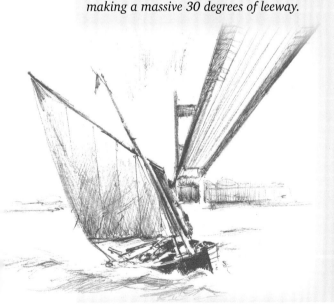

Avel Dro slid ever closer to the island, the great bridge towering above. It was nail-bitingly close, but she just grazed past and then plunged straight into a mass of white water. Avel Dro swept through the breakers, picking water up over her side and crashing from one wave to the next. It was wet, furious sailing, but we sailed clear and into the soaring shadow of the suspension bridge.

AVEL DRO passes under the old Severn Bridge with her centre plate jammed up. (David Summerville)

Anyone watching on the great bridge must have wondered at the little boat passing far below. The solitary crewmember seemed to be hammering at his boat with an anchor. But even this desperate measure failed to move the plate, and Avel Dro continued to slip sideways, hopelessly off course. She finally reached the English side of the Severn estuary, a quarter of a mile beyond her intended destination of Thornbury Pill, with no hope of sailing back against the wind and tide. Meanwhile Clubbar neatly tacked into the creek and vanished. I radioed them on the VHF:

'I'll be fine,' I said. 'I'll just anchor here, cook my supper and join you when the tide turns.'

The brown water rushed swiftly past the hull of my anchored dinghy, and onwards towards the great bulk of the nuclear power station that loomed portentously just beyond her stern. A large coaster appeared, bound upriver to Sharpness, but I was well out of the channel and she did not trouble me. Eventually it began to get dark, and lights began to illuminate the bridges and the navigation buoys.

Eventually the tide turned and I could raise the anchor and sail back downstream. Inside Thornbury Pill, I found Annabel and Dave's deserted Wayfarer moored to a pontoon. They had disappeared inside the cabin of Vanity, the little wooden motorboat owned by the fourth member of our cruise. I made fast to the pontoon and joined them aboard the motor cruiser. There was a convivial fug in her snug little cabin. We spent the evening swapping sailing stories. Vanity's elderly owner told us about the life of the great river, of the wooden sailing boats that once plied the wide tideway, and the busy ferryboats that took traffic between England and Wales before the building of the great bridges.

Our three boats departed at dawn to catch the last of the flood upriver to Lydney. It was a lovely morning. The low sun spread a golden light across the River Severn. The Cotswold Hills broke the skyline way out to starboard, while the green hills of the Forest of Dean glided slowly past beyond the other bank. As we approached the quay at Lydney, a row of small figures appeared on it and waved, like fishwives welcoming their husbands home from the sea.

The mouth of the River Severn may seem a strange and unglamorous place to sail a dinghy, but contentment can be found in the most unexpected places. The muddy creeks and the swift brown waters of the Severn estuary have a fascination and a haunting beauty of their own. In choosing to make these challenging and difficult waters their home, and learning to live with their fierce tides and great mud banks, perhaps the local sailors have found the secret of true happiness.

Avel Dro at Lydney Yacht Club's slipway, on the tidal River Severn.

6 PREPARING FOR OPEN WATER

Messing about in a little boat in sheltered waters is undoubtedly the most wonderful way to pass the time. But the wide horizon is beckoning. You are impatient to go out to sea, to experience the wonders of the deep in all its wild beauty.

A dinghy at sea is a working environment, a machine for sailing in. Out there, you cannot land on a sheltered beach if you want to make adjustments to your rig, or pick up a spare mooring to sort yourself out. The sea is the last great desert of the world, and it does not give small boats any quarter.

A dinghy that is to be used for unsupported sea passages must be equipped more thoroughly than one only used for sailing in sheltered waters. Lightly equipped racing dinghies occasionally make offshore passages, but a powered safety boat inevitably accompanies them. A cruising dinghy must be completely self-reliant, and carry everything she needs to navigate efficiently and safely on open waters.

A cruising Wayfarer off the Dorset coast, making good progress to windward with one reef in the sail. The loose bunt of her sail has been tidied up with a row of shockcorded reef points.

ASSESSING THE SAFETY OF YOUR BOAT

Once your dinghy clears the harbour and sets out along the coast, you are no longer 'messing about in boats'. Your modest vessel has become a true seagoing ship, and with this change in status comes greater responsibility.

In the UK, pleasure-boat owners have traditionally enjoyed extraordinarily light regulation, but British Common Law puts a *duty of care* on every skipper. In judging whether this duty has been properly discharged a Court would give weight to the advisory lists of equipment provided by organisations like the Royal Yacht Association or the Royal National Lifeboat Institution. The combination of non-mandatory recommendations and a general duty of care is a particularly Anglo-Saxon approach to regulation. Countries with other legal traditions take a more prescriptive approach.

The best place to consult the current regulations and recommendations affecting your vessel is an up-to-date nautical almanac. Not all international accords apply to small pleasure craft, and national regulations vary between countries, but a yachtsman's almanac will have selected the rules that apply to you. Also be aware that a boat taken abroad may be required to comply with foreign regulations as well.

In France and much of Europe, there are mandatory regulations for the equipment that a vessel should carry, depending on its CE category from A to D. This will be marked on the builders' plaque of a modern dinghy. Most dinghies find themselves in category C: 'boats operating in coastal

A Drascombe Lugger setting out to sea from Solva in West Wales.

waters and large bays and lakes with winds to Force 6, up to 27 knots, and significant seas 7 feet high'.

Compliance with the regulations is vital, but you should also take a practical approach to safety at sea. Safe navigation is not achieved by mindlessly following a checklist of rules. You must think for yourself, and work out what is best for your boat and the waters you sail in.

REEFING AT SEA

Working to windward in any sort of sea, a dinghy soon starts to pound heavily into the waves. Wise sailors reef early to ease the motion of their boats. The transformation is dramatic. The flogging sails and crashing spray suddenly vanish. No longer pressed

down by her rig, the dinghy lifts lightly over the seas, often with little reduction in speed.

Reefing techniques vary between different types of dinghy, but various general principles apply. You will need to stop sailing in order to pull down a reef, and this means that the dinghy will be lying broadside on to the wind when reefing. Most dinghies sit fairly happily in this position without ranging around too much, but it will ease her motion if you raise the centreboard, so that she can slide sideways if she is hit by a large sea.

Reefing methods that require the vessel to be lying head to wind are useless, and this includes most systems of mainsail roller reefing. Experienced cruising sailors usually have traditional points reefing or the modern system of 'slab reefing' that has evolved from it. The sail area is reduced by pulling down on reefing lines rove through cringles in the sail.

Reefing Bermudan and gunter sails

Triangular mainsails can normally be reefed without lowering them completely. The halyard is eased a little and then the reef is pulled home. It is convenient to have permanent reefing lines rove through the reefing cringles, but if they are fitted only at the leech, it will reduce the amount of rope draped along the boom. Instead, the luff cringle should be held down by a 'reefing hook' permanently fixed to the gooseneck. The luff of the sail is pulled down by hand and the appropriate cringle simply hooked into place.

Reefs in a cruising dinghy should be deep, a minimum of about 2ft (60cm). Normally the first reef is at the level of the lower batten on a Bermudan or gunter sail. If this batten is orientated parallel to the boom, it will not need to be removed when the second reef is pulled down.

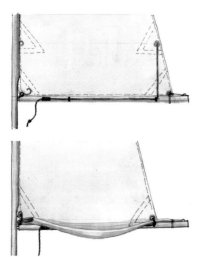

There are various ways of arranging slab reefing in a dinghy. This is one of the simplest and most effective, using a line to pull down the leech and a hook at the luff. Although only one reef is shown, most cruising dinghies should have at least two.

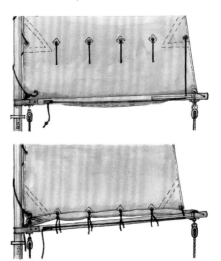

Traditional points reefing is very similar to slab reefing. Ideally, the sail should be loose-footed, so that the reef points can be tied above the boom.

AveL Dro with one reef in the sail. (Ronan Coquil)

Cruising sails often do not have sail battens, as they are a dreadful nuisance on a cruising boat. They prevent the sail from being rolled up into a neat bundle, and are forever popping out of their pockets. Removing the battens from an existing sail is very tempting, but it will mean cutting off the roach, which may destroy the balance of your dinghy. In all such matters, it is best to put yourself in the capable hands of a sailmaker who is used to the demands of cruising.

The process of reefing soon becomes familiar. The reefing line at the leech is pulled home first, which lifts the aft end of the boom and stops it banging you on the head. Then the halyard is eased and the luff cringle hooked down. All that remains is to retighten the halyard and the job is done. Tensioning the halyard tensions the foot of the sail at the same time, as it lifts the reefing hook to the vertical. It becomes a matter of pride to pull down a reef and get sailing again in a couple of minutes. On my Tideway, I spliced the two reefing lines together so that when the first reef was

pulled down, it also took in the slack on the second reefing line. This saved a few seconds each time I reefed.

It is not essential to tie down the fold of sail along the boom with reef points, but it does make for a less untidy reef. A smart way of doing this is to have a length of shock cord running through a line of cringles across the sail, with a series of small plastic hooks threaded on to it. Bights of shock cord from the other side of the sail are passed under the boom and hooked in place, holding the loose bunt of the sail tight against the boom.

Traditional reefing

Sails using traditional 'points reefing' generally need to be lowered into the boat for reefing and then re-hoisted, and you must allow yourself sufficient sea room to leeward to complete the operation. My dinghy is like this. She has a very traditional boomless lugsail with three rows of reef points, which must be tied in the old-fashioned way. After the sail has been lowered into the boat, I

A roller genoa on a Wayfarer. The smaller jib is set flying and is furled on the foredeck. (Trevor Thompson)

in a big sea. Some dinghies sail happily under a reefed mainsail only. If the jib is fitted with a downhaul line led from the head of the sail, down through a small block at the tack, then aft to a cleat, it can be dowsed without anyone needing to go forward.

Storm sails

A Bermudan sail can be reefed right down to a small triangle in high winds. More traditionally rigged dinghies sometimes carry a separate storm sail instead. The working sail is lowered into the boat and lashed down, and then the storm sail set in its place. On my llur I use an old jib as a trysail. Under this rig she has no windward performance whatsoever, but can run off in high winds without fear of gybing.

detach the tack downhaul and move it up to the next luff cringle. Then the mainsheet also needs to be moved up to a new cringle on the leech of the sail. Having done that, I carefully roll up the foot of the sail, pulling it tight and tying down the points with a series of reef knots. Finally the sail is re-hoisted and the tack downhaul re-tensioned. This process is nowhere near as fast as slab reefing, but I am prepared to put up with the relative inconvenience because of the other advantages of my rig.

Headsail reefing

On dinghies that set a jib, it is helpful if its area can be reduced in proportion with reefs taken in the mainsail. Fitting a roller on the jib luff is a convenient way to achieve this, as the sail can simply be rolled down to the desired size. Alternatively, the sail can be lowered and a smaller one set in its place, but this will be a wet business in rough weather. Crawling out onto a slippy foredeck could also be dangerous when the dinghy is bouncing about

GEAR STOWAGE AT SEA

Proper consideration must be given to stowage aboard. A sailing dinghy is a dynamic creation, designed to survive in a fluid habitat. Her bow must lift lightly to breaking seas, and it won't do that if you have stashed all your heavy cruising gear under her conveniently long foredeck.

Well-designed dinghies often have lockers for gear stowage, but these may not be large enough to take all the gear required for coastal cruising. If this is the case, you will need to find other places for the rest of your gear. Anything fragile should be stowed in tough containers, so it cannot get trampled underfoot. Waterproof plastic tubs are good for stowing smaller items of gear, but you will probably also have to make some special plywood boxes that fit snugly into the available space. Clothes are best stowed in waterproof bags such as the robust ones from Ortlieb. These not only keep the water out but also trap air inside, so they will provide positive buoyancy in the event of a swamping, if they are securely lashed down.

It usually takes a number of experimental passages before you find the best place to stow everything, so that nothing gets in the way of rowing, reefing, or any of the other activities that happen in a small dinghy. Remember that anything that is not securely lashed down or secured by a lanyard will be lost over the side in the event of a capsize or swamping.

MASTHEAD BUOYANCY

A capsize at sea should be avoided if at all possible. Heavy cruising dinghies are highly resistant to capsizing, but it can never be completely ruled out. Very beamy dinghies may become 'stable inverted': their internal buoyancy supports them in an inverted position and makes them difficult to right. Such dinghies should be fitted with masthead buoyancy to prevent them from turning right over. One way to do this is to incorporate buoyancy into the apex of the sail. Ask your sailmaker to form a pocket at the head of the sail some 35" (1m) tall, sealed by a strip of Velcro along the leech. Into this pocket is placed a triangular sheet of closed-cell foam.

Sail buoyancy provides less 'righting moment' when the sail is reefed down, and its effectiveness in resisting inversion is reduced, but it is often fitted to cruising Wayfarers, and is reported to be effective at preventing these dinghies from turning turtle, even with two reefs in the sail.

Another way of introducing masthead buoyancy is to fit an automatic floatation device that is triggered in the same way as a self-inflating lifejacket. 'Secumar' make a product especially for this purpose incorporating 20 or 40 litres of buoyancy, depending on the model. The device inflates

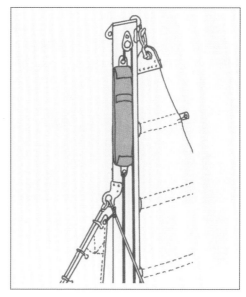

The Secumar masthead float (manufacturer's drawing).

automatically if the masthead dips below the water, preventing total inversion. When uninflated it is a thin sausage measuring approximately 19" x 4" (50 x 11cm), so it does not introduce too much windage aloft. These buoyancy devices should not be secured permanently to the masthead, but hoisted on a dedicated halyard, so that they can be rearmed and re-hoisted if they have been triggered.

PREPARATIONS FOR NIGHT SAILING

Legally, a small dinghy sailing is only required to carry a torch to make her presence visible to other craft at night, but if it is possible to show an all-round white light at the masthead, this is much more effective for indicating her presence to other vessels. The light could be permanently wired to a 12-volt circuit aboard, just like on a yacht. Alternatively, a self-contained battery light should be hoisted to the masthead using

Avel Dro's masthead light is an all-round LED. I have mounted it on a wooden pole so it can be hauled up the mast instead of my burgee.

the burgee halyard. This is the method I use. All round LED battery masthead lights have been developed which are light and waterproof, and ideal for a cruising dinghy.

A headtorch is also very useful when sailing at night. Pick a model with a dim red light mode as well as the standard bright white light, as this saves your night vision when sailing in the dark.

Fog horn

In these days of noisy engines and enclosed wheelhouses, one wonders how effective a puny fog horn can possibly be. These gloomy thoughts intensify when you are sailing in fog.

Small fog horns either have to be blown by the crew or they are push-button devices with an aerosol canister. Fog horns vary widely in noise output, and it is worth testing a selection before purchase. The better designs direct the sound away from your ears, so you are not temporarily deafened each time they are sounded.

A loud whistle is also worth its space aboard. Like anything small and easily losable, it needs to be secured with a lanyard.

Sea anchors and drogues

A sea anchor put out over a dinghy's bow will bring her head up into the wind, so that she stops in the water with the sails flapping. It can also be dragged behind the boat as a drogue, holding the stern perpendicular to the seas when crossing a bar.

Conical sea anchors can be purchased from chandleries or made up specially. A good size for the average dinghy would be 1'6" (45cm) wide in the mouth. Traditionally, a 'stout bucket' was used for this purpose, but maybe buckets are less stout than they used to be, as I find they have a tendency to split open under the water pressure of being dragged, so that they become useless for anything else you might want to use them for. (We will discuss the use of sea anchors in the next chapter.)

Pumps, bailers and buckets

Even the driest and most seaworthy open boat will ship water in rough conditions, and you must have a way of getting rid of it. Modern racing dinghies have a simple solution: many of them have no transom, and any water that comes aboard simply slides out of the stern straight back into the sea. But such dinghies are very vulnerable to being 'pooped' in a following sea, and are not ideal for cruising. Older racing dinghies are often fitted with 'self-bailers', which rapidly suck out the water after a swamping, but these devices are problematic on a cruising dinghy. They are prone to leak when you are lying at anchor, and can get damaged when you beach your boat. My objection to them is more philosophical. I dislike the idea of cutting a large hole in my hull below the waterline, as it introduces an obvious vulnerability into a sea-going boat.

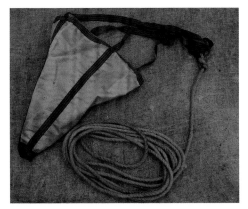

A drogue is useful to slow the dinghy down in a following sea and can also be used as a sea anchor.

Cruising dinghies usually prefer to rely on bailers or pumps. It is often said that the most efficient way to get water out of a boat is 'a frightened man with a bucket', but I suspect that a frightened man with a decent pump may be faster. I have two hand pumps on my dinghy, one on each side of the boat, and designed to be operated from the windward side bench, each pump sucking from the opposite bilge.

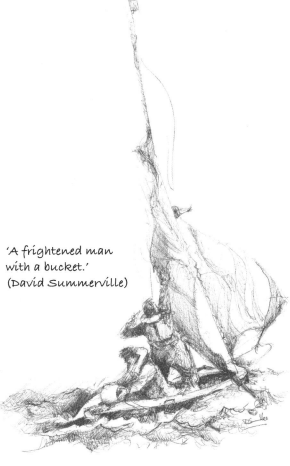

'A frightened man with a bucket.' (David Summerville)

AVEL DRO has hand pumps mounted on both sides, each sucking from the opposite side of the boat. Also shown is one of her steering compasses, which are mounted at each end of the main thwart.

Uses for a 'stout bucket'

Traditional equipment lists always include a 'stout bucket'. A bucket is one of the simplest pieces of equipment on board, but it has an amazing multiplicity of uses.

If your boat is full of water and there is already a frightened person tending every available pump, a bucket can be given to any crewmembers you have spare. When my dinghy is drying out on the mud, I fill the bucket with water so that I can wash my sea boots and other gear in it when I return to the boat after a walk ashore. It is also useful as a toilet.

THE BAYRAIDER

Swallow Boats design and build a series of cruising dinghies and small cabin yachts with many innovative features, and their designs are constantly being tweaked to achieve greater efficiency and practicality. The BayRaider 20 is rigged as a yawl and designed for performance, but also to be safe and stable. All the sails are self-tending when tacking, and their rig is designed to remain balanced when the mainsail is lowered, so that the boat can be sailed in high winds under just the jib and mizzen.

The well is simply arranged, wide and capacious, with an uninterrupted flat sole that is self-draining. Large lockers are provided to take your dunnage. There is an inboard mounting for an outboard motor at the stern, designed so that the motor can be cocked up out of the water when not in use.

The cleverest feature of the BayRaider design is the water ballast system. When the ballast tank is empty, the BayRaider has a sporty performance. When the tank is full, the weight of the boat is doubled and she is transformed into a stable family cruiser. The system also allows the boat to be lightened in weight for towing.

Swallow Boats take a great deal of care to ensure that their designs are easy to rig and quick to set up. The masts are stepped in tabernacles and the rigging is quite simple. The BayRaider 20 is ideal for family sailing and more ambitious coastal cruises. A huge asymmetric can be set from a running bowsprit to increase speed off the wind.

THE MIRROR

The Mirror dinghy was unveiled in 1962 as a 'people's boat' for home construction, sponsored by the DAILY MIRROR newspaper. It has proved to be an extraordinarily successful and long-lived design. Originally built of plywood and gunter-rigged, Mirrors are now commonly constructed from GRP and carry a Bermudan rig. These inexpensive boats make excellent cruising dinghies. They are light to launch and recover from the water, and can even be carried on a car roof rack. The Mirror was designed to be sailed, rowed or propelled with an outboard clamped on the transom, and remains equally effective in all these roles. I owned a Mirror dinghy for many years and was impressed by her ability to weather the most prodigious waves without taking much water aboard.

More capacious than her short overall length would imply, the Mirror was designed as a family boat and can carry two adults and two children when being rowed or propelled with an outboard. Under sail she is best sailed by a maximum of two adults or an adult and two children. An old wooden Mirror can be picked up for a few hundred pounds and converted to an excellent cruising dinghy very cheaply.

The Mirror can be converted into a very effective camp cruiser by carrying a number of pieces of plywood to create a bed at seat level and erecting a hooped tent on it. In this role she is an ideal size for one person, and has proved to be as effective as larger cruising boats.

(Andrew Richards)

Most of the time I use the bucket as a place for stowing rubbish. When it is in this use it is called the 'gash bucket'. The 'gash' itself is kept in a plastic bag, which is used as a liner within the bucket. This makes it easier to empty the bucket if you need to use it for any other purpose. Supermarket shopping bags used to make excellent gash bucket liners. They were just the right size, and you could use their handles to tie them closed when they were full. Unfortunately, these are no longer free from supermarkets and the 'bags for life' that have replaced them are rather too posh for this purpose.

STEERING COMPASS

Despite the recent advances in electronic technology, a traditional magnetic compass and a paper chart are still essential tools for navigation at sea. A fixed steering compass should be sited within easy sight of the helmsman, and properly gimballed. Mounting a compass is not straightforward, however. It must be kept away from any ferrous metal aboard your boat. Marine-grade stainless steel does not affect a compass, but a multitude of other items will do so, such as the anchor and outboard motor, galvanised rowlocks, flares and tools. A compass must also be mounted a good distance from other items of electronic equipment, like a GPS or chartplotter. Electronic equipment designed for marine use will specify a 'compass safe distance', but a crewmember's mobile phone will not.

The most convenient location for a steering compass is often the aft end of the centreboard case, but this is hopeless if your boat has a mild steel centreplate. An alternative is to fit twin compasses on each side bench, so that one or the other is

clearly in view on each tack. But beware of sitting too close to the windward compass if you habitually carry a knife in your pocket, as you could seriously affect its reading.

Ideally, the steering compass should be sited where it reads true on all headings, so you do not need a deviation table. A steering compass can be checked for accuracy by putting the boat on a series of headings, and comparing its readings with another compass sited a distance away. This is called 'swinging the compass', and is most easily carried out with the boat on the trailer at home.

The main compass should also be lit for night use. This can be achieved by fitting 12-volt power to your dinghy and wiring the compass into it. A simpler alternative is to purchase a compass with self-contained illumination. It is best to take this type of compass off the dinghy when not in use and keep it somewhere warm, or the batteries will corrode due to condensation within the battery compartment.

THE USE OF GPS

The Global Positioning System has revolutionised dinghy navigation. GPS receivers use a network of American satellites, originally put in place for military operations. Rare and expensive only a few decades ago, GPS sets are now available for very modest sums. The real revolution occurred when the Americans turned off 'selective availability' on 1 May 2000, which had hitherto degraded the signal available to civilians. GPS now produces a constantly updated position accurate to within 20m and perhaps as little as 3m in good conditions. This is a breathtaking level of accuracy. For anyone who has navigated over miles of featureless sea with only traditional dead reckoning to keep track of their position, modern GPS is little short of miraculous.

Occasional panics used to sweep the sailing community that America could turn off the whole system, but this is very unlikely now that so many rely on it. A competing European system called 'Galileo' is being put in place, which will work on similar equipment.

GPS as a main system of navigation

In the days before GPS, I navigated using only a chart, Walker log, tidal atlas and handbearing compass. However desirable it may be to keep these old skills alive, once you have fitted GPS in your boat, it instantly becomes your main means of navigation, and you rely on it almost completely.

The simplest GPS sets are small handheld units, and these have the advantage of being self-contained. They normally use AA batteries, and do not need wiring into an external power source. Their battery life is improving, but they will still devour a set of batteries every day or so, and you need to carry lots of spares.

GPS is so staggeringly accurate it is easy to become complacent. Nonetheless, it is still wise to keep a check on your GPS position by conventional means, just in case. Always keep a critical eye on your surroundings, and make sure that you really are where the GPS says you are.

Chartplotters

A basic GPS gives a simple latitude and longitude readout, which must be plotted manually on a paper chart. More advanced GPS receivers are preprogrammed with a full set of charts and show your boat's position pictorially. These are usually

referred to as 'chartplotters' and are available as fixed or handheld units. The chart is constantly refreshed and scrolls across the screen as you sail along.

It is possible to navigate by steering the symbol of your vessel across the digital chart on the screen of a chartplotter, just like playing a video game. To a sailor who has spent the time acquiring traditional pilotage skills of compass, lead line and chart, this is a travesty.

Positioning a GPS on board

A GPS or chartplotter should be fitted in clear view of the steering position, and also near enough so that it can be operated from there. Handheld sets have purpose-designed holders, adjustable for visibility, while fixed sets are mounted on rotatable brackets. Inevitably, the location of the GPS will conflict with the dinghy's steering compass, and you must give thought to the best mounting position for each device.

On my own dinghy, the chartplotter is permanently mounted on the back of my centreboard case, where it can be seen from the helm. It is wired into my dinghy's simple 12-volt system and uses its own internal

AVEL DRO's chartplotter.

aerial, which still works through the wooden thwart. I prefer a fixed chartplotter rather than a handheld unit, because of its big illuminated buttons. I found that the small buttons on my previous handheld set were rather difficult to operate when the boat was bouncing around in rough conditions, so it is now kept aboard as a spare.

SOLAS

Outside sheltered waters, even dinghies come under the remit of the international accords that regulate the navigation of vessels at sea. The International Convention for the Safety of Life at Sea (SOLAS) dates from the loss of the RMS *Titanic* in 1912. Originally the Convention did not apply to vessels of less than 150GT, but since 1 July 2002 SOLAS Chapter V has applied to 'all ships on all voyages', with exceptions for inland and sheltered waters. The following sections apply to small pleasure craft:

Regulation 19 – RADAR REFLECTORS
Regulation 29 – LIFESAVING SIGNALS
Regulation 34 – VOYAGE/PASSAGE
　　　　　　　　PLANNING
Regulation 35 – MISUSE OF DISTRESS
　　　　　　　　SIGNALS

Regulation 19: Radar Reflectors

All ships irrespective of size shall have if practicable … a radar reflector or other means, to enable detection by ships navigating by radar at both 9 and 3 GHz.

'If practicable' means that if it is possible to rig a radar reflector on your boat, then you should do so. You could probably wriggle out of the regulation by arguing that a radar reflector is 'not practicable' on your dinghy, but remember that she is the vessel that will come off worse in a collision with a big ship navigating on radar.

Fitting a decent radar reflector is difficult. The performance of the smaller reflectors has been discredited and the more effective ones are bulky and often heavy. Fortunately the traditional octahedral reflector comes out well in the tests: it consists of a series of aluminium squares, which slot together to form an octahedral form. To be effective it should be at least 1'6" (45cm) across. Ideally a radar reflector should be kept aloft at all times, but it is often difficult to find somewhere suitable in a dinghy's rigging, where it will not chafe the sails. You could copy the usual practice on small inshore fishing craft and rig a small mizzenmast to carry the radar reflector, navigation lights and VHF aerial, but this creates additional windage. On my dinghy I normally keep my reflector folded down and hoist it only in poor visibility.

Another solution would be to fit an active reflector. These devices detect when your boat is being scanned by radar and transmit a radar signal back. They consist of a short fat aerial, about half a metre long, which should be mounted at the masthead and wired into a 12-volt system. They are smaller than an effective passive reflector, but they are still heavy objects to have aloft on a dinghy.

Fitting a radar reflector of a decent size is so problematic that many dinghies do not bother. If you avoid entering shipping lanes and never sail in poor visibility, the risk of being run down by a large vessel is probably very low. But we must not be complacent about this issue. Large ships are increasingly reliant on electronic systems. For them, a vessel that has no visible radar signature simply does not exist. Perhaps the ideal solution is for a dinghy to detect any ships that may be a hazard, and keep well out of their way. This is not a fantasy, and I will suggest a way it could be achieved later in this chapter.

Regulation 29: Lifesaving Signals

An illustrated table describing the life-saving signals shall be readily available to the officer of the watch of every ship … The signals shall be used by ships or persons in distress when communicating with lifesaving stations, maritime rescue units and aircraft engaged in search and rescue operations.

Avel Dro's previous compact (and doubtless ineffectual) tubular radar reflector has recently been replaced by this larger octahedral model. In poor visibility it is hoisted aloft on the burgee halyard, in the correct 'catch water' aspect.

The requirement for an 'illustrated table' can be met by carrying a nautical almanac containing a list of the relevant symbols, which most of us do anyway. But there is a good reason for this regulation. It is very easy to forget the correct protocol when you are in a panic, and it is helpful to have an aide-memoire ready to hand, rather than leafing through the almanac in an emergency. I carry a heat-sealed sheet on my dinghy describing the visual signals, as well as instructions about sending a distress message over the radio.

Even though the main means of signalling distress at sea are now electronic, flares still have their place aboard a seagoing dinghy: perhaps a basic set of red hand flares and a few white flares to warn shipping of your presence at night. Flares should be kept in a waterproof container, fastened somewhere that you could still reach if the dinghy is inverted after a capsize.

Flares are explosive pyrotechnics and must be handled with care. A burning flare is an alarmingly powerful object. The first time you set one off you may drop it in shock. Handheld flares burn red hot, giving out a prodigious amount of heat. They are so bright they are hard to look at. Parachute flares (sometimes called 'maroons') fire a burning projectile high into the sky, which slowly falls to the ground, supported by a small parachute. They need to be launched at an angle into the wind so that they rise vertically into the night sky. This is harder than it sounds, and is worth practising.

I have recently reduced the number of pyrotechnic flares I carry on my boat, as they are problematic for all sorts of reasons, and when my current flares expire I will replace them with one of the new breed of electronic flare instead.

Regulation 34: Voyage/ Passage Planning

Prior to proceeding to sea, the master shall ensure that the intended voyage has been planned using the appropriate nautical charts and nautical publications for the area concerned.

This regulation makes formal passage planning a legal requirement for all vessels 'proceeding to sea' – which means leaving 'sheltered waters'. The precise limits of 'sheltered waters' are expressly defined and listed as 'categorised waters'. The full list of these waters is available from your local coastguard, but I believe that every vessel should do some basic passage planning, wherever she is sailing.

Regulation 35: Misuse of Distress Signals

The use of an international distress signal, except for the purpose of indicating that a person or persons are in distress, and the use of any signal which may be confused with an international distress signal are prohibited.

Despite the proscription in SOLAS, sailors who have just won a yacht race habitually let off flares in celebration and flares can often be seen illuminating the crowd at outdoor music festivals. Many yachtsmen fire off their out-of-date flares at home, in order to practise their use. If you are tempted to do this, it is best to pick a night when fireworks are common, such as New Year's Eve, and to do it well away from the coast, to avoid triggering a false alarm. Parachute flares should never be discharged near habitation, or where there is a risk of alarming farm animals.

COMMUNICATIONS AT SEA

Once upon a time, the coastguard constantly watched the sea from cliff-top lookouts all around the coast and every lighthouse had a watchman constantly on duty. But this has all been swept away. Lighthouses now operate unmanned and most coastguard lookouts are empty shells. Along many miles of empty coastline there is no one left to witness a visual signal from a vessel in distress. In these modern times, the traditional flare pack begins to feel

rather ineffectual. If you were to fire off a distress flare, would anyone see it or know what it was?

Flares are less vital than they were, and are no longer the primary means of alerting the rescue services, but they remain useful to help a helicopter or lifeboat pinpoint your exact location after you have signalled your distress by a 'Mayday' call on the VHF, or set off an EPIRB.

For a modern dinghy, a VHF set is now the primary means of sending a distress message. VHF is more than simply a means of calling for help, however, it is an integral part of your dinghy's navigational gear. Every commercial vessel uses radio communication, and a dinghy with VHF is plugged into the community of professional seamen. She can receive safety weather information broadcasts by the local coastguard, monitor R/T traffic between other ships and harbour VTS, and gain a good picture of what is happening in the waters around her. Every seagoing dinghy should have the means of transmitting and receiving VHF messages.

Some dinghies have a permanently mounted VHF transceiver, connected to a 12V battery, but a decent waterproof handheld VHF meets all the requirements for dinghy communications. It should be clipped to your clothing or kept conveniently to hand in the boat and secured by a lanyard.

The ideal VHF set should be simple and easy to use. You need a dedicated Channel 16 button for initial calling and distress messages, a button to select Dual Watch, a button to select the transmission power, a channel selector, volume control and squelch knob. Unfortunately, manufacturers have a mania for adding extra features to their radios, which create potential confusion.

A useful feature on some handheld sets is the ability to slide out the rechargeable batteries and substitute standard AA dry cells. This is invaluable if you find yourself far from mains power with a flat battery in your VHF.

GMDSS

The Global Maritime Distress and Safety System (GMDSS) is an international agreement on maritime safety procedures, equipment and communication protocols. Compliance with GMDSS is now mandatory on larger vessels, and is considered good practice even on small pleasure craft. The system is based on the following three electronic technologies:

- VHF communication at sea using Digital Selective Calling (DSC).
- Distress messages transmitted by DSC and Radio Beacons.
- Navigational warnings transmitted by Navtext.

Not so long ago, a book like this would have barely mentioned electronics at all. The only electronic devices you would have found aboard a typical cruising dinghy were an electric torch and a transistor radio. Safety at sea meant having a well-found vessel with an experienced crew aboard, using technologies that had been known for centuries. The sea has not changed much since then. Safe navigation on its wide and sometimes tempestuous waters still means having a good boat, a good crew and the right basic equipment.

Every year, people go to sea in wildly inappropriate vessels, without proper experience. When they run into more weather than they can cope with, they get

My VHF is stowed in the stern of the dinghy next to the flares (in the cylindrical tub). It is attached to the boat by a lanyard.

scared and seasick, and then they deploy an electronic device to call for help. Soon a helicopter or a lifeboat arrives, and plucks them to safety. Back on shore, they tell everyone how prudent they were to have carried the latest 'safety gear', even though they would not have got into trouble in the first place if they had had the right experience and well-found boat. The miracles of modern electronic technology should be seen as an additional level of security, not as a substitute for traditional good sailing practice.

Digital Selective Calling

Digital Selective Calling has superseded voice-only VHF on large ships, and is increasingly the norm on yachts. This technology comes into its own in an emergency. If you press the dedicated distress button on a DSC VHF set, it will automatically transmit a digital Mayday signal, giving information about your boat and your latest position. The VHF will continue to transmit until a receiving station acknowledges the Mayday call.

As aerial height is vital for the transmission efficiency of marine VHF, a seamanlike system would be an aerial mounted as high as possible and a fixed DSC VHF tranceiver, hard wired to a 12-volt battery. This would be an excellent set-up for normal communications aboard a dinghy, and more effective in normal use than a handheld unit. Handheld sets have a fifth of the transmitting power of a fixed set, and a much lower aerial height. You would still need to carry a handheld unit for emergencies, however, because your fixed set would be ineffective after a capsize, as its aerial would be pointing at the bottom of the sea.

Most handheld VHF sets still have no DSC capability and so cannot transmit a DSC distress message. Instead you must transmit a verbal distress message on Channel 16, which is less reliable in adverse conditions. Recently, however, a few handheld sets with DSC capability have come onto the market.

These have a GPS unit built into them, so they will automatically include your position in an electronic distress message. DSC technology is undoubtedly the future, and should be seriously considered if you are intending to buy a new VHF set.

There is however a problem with handheld DSC sets. Their integral GPS uses a lot of battery power, even when they are simply on standby listening, and they need frequent recharging. This should be borne in mind. For this reason I still use an ordinary H/H VHF, but then I also carry an EPIRB, which is covered in the next section.

Distress radio beacons

These are radio beacons that interface with COSPAS/SARSAT, the international satellite system for search and rescue (SAR). They are commonly known as **emergency beacons**, **PLBs** or **EPIRBs**. When activated, the beacon sends out a distress signal that is detected by a network of satellites. Beacons for marine use divide into two types:

- **EPIRBs** (Emergency Position-Indicating Radio Beacons) for a vessel in distress.
- **PLBs** (Personal Locator Beacons), primarily to indicate a person in distress.

Modern EPIRBs transmit on both 406 MHz and 121.5 MHz, and automatically trigger a rescue when the Coastguard receives their signal. Small buoy-like objects with an aerial sticking out of the top, once activated they float in the water upright, attached to your swamped or capsized vessel by a light line. No further action is required after the EPIRB has been turned on.

A fixed DSC VHF is a useful addition to the dinghy sailor's armoury, but it needs a permanent antenna.

THE DEBEN LUGGER

The Deben Lugger is a rare example of a commercial dinghy thoroughly designed for camp cruising, in which all the equipment necessary for days of happy, safe sailing and comfortable nights under canvas can be bought as a package from the same company. It is a striking design with a powerful carbon fibre rig on two masts: a large balance lug mainsail with three deep reefs and a smaller mizzen. This modern adaption of the classic small fishing boat rig is ideal for a cruising dinghy.

There is a folding pram hood to shelter the crew either sailing or at anchor, which becomes the front of the hooped camping tent to cover the well. There are lockers galore for your cruising gear, an outboard well, well planned storage slots for special two-part oars, and even anchor stowage has been considered.

The hull started off as the Drascombe Driver, in happier times when the Honnor Marine and Drascombe names both applied to the same company. John Watkinson conceived the design as an auxilary sailing dinghy fitted with an inboard engine, of a similar size to the original Honnor Marine Drascombe Lugger, but very few were sold as the idea was probably too radical for its time.

Now the old Driver design has been revisited, refreshed and completely rerigged by Alex Haig of Anglia Yacht Brokerage in Suffolk, to emerge as a truly original and special vessel. If you are looking for a new cruising dinghy for the Deben Lugger's home waters of East Anglia as well as further afield, this is well worth a look.

(Anglia Yacht Brokerage)

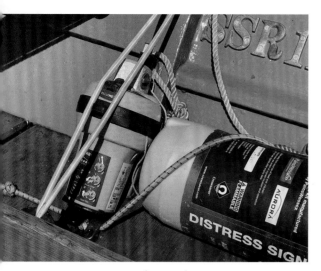

My EPIRB is kept in the stern. The rubber bungee is to protect it from being hooked off by flying ropes.

PLBs are like smaller versions of an EPIRB, and designed to be kept in a pocket or clipped to your clothing. They will not operate when floating free in the sea, and some of them do not even float. Instead they rely on being held in the correct orientation by the person wanting assistance. They are rather cheaper than a fully specified EPIRB, but the better ones are as effective in most situations. As they are more compact, they are perhaps the better choice for a cruising dinghy.

Distress radio beacons are expensive pieces of kit, and are of no use at all in normal safe navigation. They have one purpose only, and that is to call for help when all other means have failed. They are the ultimate backstop, but do not replace traditional skills of safe navigation.

Navtext

GMDSS is also concerned with the transmission of safety and weather information to vessels at sea, through a system called Navtext. A typical Navtext

set is a small unit with an LCD screen. It receives text messages transmitted by the Coastguard and stores them in its electronic memory. Modern yachts are commonly fitted with this technology. The principle of receiving weather forecasts as text is a good one. It means you always have a clear written record of the current meteorological predictions and safety warnings to refer back to. There is no easy way to fit Navtext in a dinghy at present, however. As technology advances, perhaps it will be incorporated into handheld VHF sets, and this would be a worthwhile development.

Until recently, it was possible to receive weather forecasts by SMS on a mobile telephone in the UK, but this service is unavailable at the time of writing. An excellent way of obtaining detailed weather information is to carry a smartphone and use it to access meteorological data on the internet. There are a number of specialised maritime weather apps that can be used. Decent mobile reception is necessary, however, which is not always available when you need it most. For the dinghy sailor, there is still no reliable alternative to setting the alarm for the crack of dawn and listening to the marine weather forecast on the radio, so a compact battery radio should always be carried just in case.

Mains electrics

Most maritime electronic devices can be obtained as handheld units, and these are very convenient on a dinghy. An alternative is to fit 'mains power' to your dinghy and use the fixed devices designed for use on larger yachts. This adds much complexity, but has many practical advantages. Fixed equipment tends to be more robust and easier to use in rough conditions. Also, you can use the 'mains power' in your dinghy to recharge the batteries in any handheld units you have aboard. This is invaluable on a long passage.

On my dinghy I have a purpose-made plywood 'battery box' which contains a 12-volt leisure battery. The box runs my chartplotter as well as recharging various handheld devices. It has a tight-fitting lid that clamps down onto a neoprene gasket, so it can withstand a swamping without wiping out the electronics. Inside there is space for the charging cradle of my handheld VHF. I have two batteries for my main VHF. When sailing, the VHF is generally on, monitoring Channel 16, while a spare battery remains in its charging cradle, ready to use if the first runs out of juice. This tends only to happen if I am doing a lot of transmitting.

OTHER ELECTRONIC DEVICES

Mobile telephones

A mobile telephone is an effective means of alerting the rescue services, assuming you are sailing along a coastline with good mobile coverage. Unless it is water-resistant (as they increasingly are) the phone should be kept in a waterproof bag. It is also prudent to pre-program the telephone number of the local coastguard into the phone's memory, so you don't need to look it up while swimming after a capsize. A mobile phone should not be seen as an alternative to a marine VHF set, however, as it does not give you access to general maritime radio traffic and you cannot guarantee you will have a mobile signal when the chips are down.

Smartphones and tablet computers

Many smartphones have compass and GPS capability, and can be programmed with apps that turn them into fully featured chartplotters. I have used a smartphone as an emergency means of navigating on a couple of occasions, and I was surprised how effective it was. The big brothers of smartphones are tablet computers, and these are now used for serious navigation on seagoing yachts. A tablet programmed with navigation software can match anything a dedicated marine chartplotter can do, and is also capable of doing everything you might want to use a computer for, like reading your emails and updating your social media profile while at sea.

In less than a decade, tablets and smartphones (and social media) have taken over our lives. Even a little cruising dinghy is no escape from them – they are too useful. Clearly this is a fast-moving subject. All I can do is report on what I do now, and try to predict what I suspect will happen in the future. At the time of writing, in 2021, I still use my fixed chartplotter. It purports to be waterproof, and so it is in normal conditions, but it is not immune to being slowly destroyed by seawater after a capsize (although it continues to work for a few weeks before finally dying). As a backup I also carry a GPS-enabled tablet in a waterproof pouch. This is a truly amazing object for passage planning ashore or at anchor, but I find that its touchscreen interface is impossible to use while bouncing around at sea. I also have a smartphone loaded with navigation software.

A chartplotter is loaded with chart software via little memory cards, so always retains everything in its memory. A tablet or smartphone, by contrast, downloads

AVEL DRO's battery box is in the bows and has space for a VHF in its charging cradle.

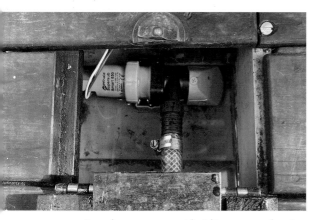

There is an automatic bilge pump in the lowest part of AVEL DRO's bilge.

its charts from the internet, so before you set out on a passage make sure it has downloaded the relevant charts for use offline, or you will suddenly find you have no internet and no electronic charts at all, just at a crucial moment. Now and then these devices have an annoying habit of quietly dropping things from their memory, especially if it is getting full, so keep checking what charts you have in your device's memory.

I imagine the time is coming when cruising dinghy sailors will all just use tablets to navigate on, and the specialised chartplotter will no longer be seen on dinghies. But for me it is not here yet.

Electric bilge pumps

Cruising dinghies with 12-volt power aboard can fit an automatic electric bilge pump, to deal with any spray that comes aboard. This is a very civilised innovation, which I have fitted on my own dinghy. It must be admitted that it runs the battery down rather faster than when it was only used to power a chartplotter and to recharge my VHF sets, however. I have found that the pump must be wired separately, directly to the battery, so it does not affect the operation of the chartplotter, which is very vulnerable to voltage drops in its electrical supply, and used to reboot itself every time the pump turned on.

Echo sounder

If you have gone to all the trouble of fitting a 12-volt power system and a chartplotter to your dinghy, as I have done, fitting an echo sounder is simply a matter of purchasing the transducer from your local chandlery and finding somewhere to mount it. Many chartplotters will also operate as echo sounders if they are connected to a transducer. I have never bothered with an echo sounder on a dinghy, preferring to rely on a simple lead line, but friends who have done so consider it one of the most helpful instruments on board. It comes into its own when tacking up a narrow drying creek, they say.

AIS receivers

The Automatic Identity System (AIS) is an automatic tracking system used on ships and by vessel traffic services (VTS) for identifying and locating vessels. An AIS receiver shows the bearing and distance of nearby vessels on a radar-like display. Other information includes the ship's unique identification number, position, course, and speed. SOLAS requires that AIS is fitted aboard all ships of over 300GT on international voyages, and all passenger ships regardless of size.

AIS technology is also becoming popular on yachts. At present it requires a VHF aerial, 12-volt power and a suitable receiver. An AIS equipped yacht is able to detect other shipping, even over the horizon, giving her the ability to take evasive action well in advance. If the yacht also has an AIS transmitter, its signal will also be received by surrounding ships.

AIS apps can be purchased for smartphones, but they require a decent signal and are unlikely to work in the middle of a shipping lane, so they are still little more than toys. Recently though, AIS receivers have begun to be integrated into fixed VHF sets, and the potential of this technology is very exciting. A dinghy simply needs to fit a VHF transceiver with AIS capability and link it to a chartplotter. The plotter would then display the locations and tracks of the surrounding shipping, almost as if the dinghy were fitted with a radar scanner. This quantity of electronic kit may be regarded as excessive on a small dinghy, but would be comforting when crossing a shipping lane.

AIS provides a solution to the perennial problem of fitting an effective radar reflector to a small dinghy. Instead of passively relying on surrounding ships to notice her reflected echo, a dinghy equipped with AIS would be able to detect approaching ships well in advance and take the necessary evasive action. It would be excellent if this technology could be fitted to a handheld VHF, but seemingly there is not enough demand.

The tides of Porthmadog

We feel our way slowly up the Afon Dwyryd, our dinghy's sails spread wide. The water is murky, the channel steep-sided, and the ochre sands of the Porthmadog Estuary are drying fast on each side of us. Richard prods the water with an oar, trying to find the narrow entrance to the creek.

'It's deeper here!' he calls.

'Gybe-oh!' I cry, and put the helm down.

Soon Baggywrinkle's *bow is pointing towards a wooded headland on the north side of the estuary. The Snowdonian Mountains stand tall against the blue sky. The sunlight washes the crags with highlight and shadow. It is a view of quintessential Welsh coastal beauty, except for an implausibly picturesque accretion of spires, domes and loggias encrusting the hillside opposite. We beach* Baggywrinkle *and walk up the shore towards this exotic vision.*

We have arrived at fabled Portmeirion, the Xanadu of North Wales, and one of the most remarkable coastal sights in Britain. Climbing up into the folly village, we discover an enchanting sequence of architectural spaces, gardens and terraces. At last we emerge onto a high balcony where we can look down on our little dinghy, dried out proudly on the sand far below. The tide is just beginning to creep back up the channel towards her, flooding the sandbanks. It is time to return to our boat.

Richard is excellent company and a good crewmember, but he always mopes if he does not get to a pub each evening. Fortunately, the OS map marks an inn, reachable by a footpath across the saltings from the nearby island of Ynys Gifftan. We moor Baggy beside the island, throw the boat tent over her boom, lay out the sleeping bags, and then pick our way across the salt marsh to the village and its hostelry.

It is a heroically excellent pub, and we stay there until the landlord eventually calls out 'Time, ladies and gentlemen, please.' Then we walk back down the lane and climb the earthen dyke at the edge of the saltings. Reaching the top, we see moonlight shimmering on an unbroken expanse of water, stretching from the foot of the dyke in front of us all the way to the distant island where our boat is moored. Clearly, we have seriously miscalculated the tide!

We look at each other in alarm. It must only just be high water, and we will have to wait for hours in the cold and the dark before the salt marsh is dry enough to walk back to our boat. We hunker down in the shelter of a wooden hut nearby to wait for the tide. The night grows darker and colder with Welsh obdurateness, but at long last the water level falls sufficiently for us to pick out a path back to our little dinghy. We snuggle straight into our sleeping bags and fall fast asleep.

The sunlight shining through the tent door awakens me. I roll over, look at the clock and groan. We have heavily overslept. The ebb is already gurgling past on its way out of the estuary, threatening to leave us high and dry if we don't buck up, and Richard is due to leave the ship this morning. My original plan was to take him back into Porthmadog harbour, but there is no time for that now. Baggywrinkle is bound out to sea on her first true coastal passage, and she must be at the mouth of the estuary before conditions on the bar become untenable. As Richard's boozy nature was clearly the root of the problem, I tell him he will have to do a 'pier head leap' in reverse.

Baggywrinkle sets off towards the bar at the mouth of the estuary, late on her tide. When the river channel swings close to the Porthmadog shore, I haul up the plate and sail straight into the shallows.

'Jump!' I shout.

Richard leaps over the side into thigh-deep water and splashes his way ashore, carrying his dunnage. I spin Baggy round and tack back into the channel.

The ebb tide is very strong now, sweeping my dinghy sideways into the steep standing waves on the river bar. I luff Baggy up into them, smashing through their hissing crests and then bearing off down their backs, trying to keep her moving. One menacing wave catches me unawares and hits her full on the beam, smashing over the gunwale and crashing down heavily into her hull. A few more like that and we will be swamped. But this is the bar's parting shot – a salutary reminder not to underestimate it again. The waves ease and I escape out into the smooth waters of Tremadoc Bay.

I shape a course to the south, towards my destination 12 miles down the coast. I had intended to sail to Barmouth in company with other boats in the Dinghy Cruising Association, but I am now so late that there are no other boats in sight. Where are they all? I feel lonely and exposed, out in the open sea in my dinghy for the first time.

Eventually I espy a small white speck, close inshore under Harlech Castle. A sail! It gets larger very rapidly, so it must be very slow, or it would not be being overhauled by a 12ft dinghy. Soon I can make out a boxy hull, rather like a packing crate. As I get closer it is revealed as a ketch-rigged packing crate, dwarfed by a huge yellow inflatable tender. Eventually I come close enough to see two bearded men perched inside it, surrounded by clouds of pipe smoke. Then I recognise it as a West Wight Potter – a 14ft cabin dinghy of eccentric design and celebrated quirkiness. As I sweep up abeam of her, one of the men takes his pipe out of his mouth and wishes me 'good morning', as insouciantly as Stanley did when he met Livingstone.

I pull in a reef to keep pace with her, and we sail along very amicably, chatting together about boats and voyages, while the Welsh coast slips lazily past a mile off our port beam. It appears that two other boats have attended the rally, but one stayed behind in Porthmadog and the other has gone on a detour into Mochras Lagoon, and will catch us up later on. Indeed, by the time Baggywrinkle and the West Wight Potter arrive at the red and white buoy marking the start of the channel into Barmouth, we can see a blue-hulled Wayfarer coming up fast astern of us.

We raft our three boats to the quay at Barmouth and clamber up the steel ladder. Just across the road is a chip shop.

'We've fallen on our feet here!' we cry, before we all pile in.

We take our food back to our boats, to sit and watch various yachts entering the harbour and manoeuvring to pick up their moorings in the strong tide. The little cabin of the Potter is revealed to contain an extensive drinks locker, so we decide to stay aboard our boats all evening, lounging against our cushions in the open air, talking and drinking as the night falls and the masthead lights of the yachts shine like stars around us.

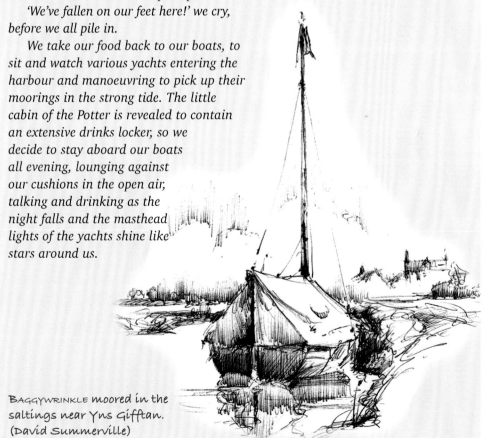

BAGGYWRINKLE moored in the saltings near Yns Gifftan.
(David Summerville)

7 OUT TO SEA

Out on the great ocean, icy spray lashes over her bow. It takes
every ounce of concentration to keep way on her as she plunges
into the steep seas. Better reef her down now, before the sea
state gets any worse. She lies comfortably hove-to while sail
is reduced, the coastline a distant smudge between sea and
the sky. The halyard runs fairly and cleats sweetly with the
familiarity of long use. Soon the reef is tied down and she is
sailing again.

She swoops through the troughs and over the sea ridges more
comfortably now, sailing drier and under better control. At last
there is chance to look about you. The open sea is a wild and
majestic place. An iridescent swell rolls in from the west, flecked
with breaking water. A sudden flash of black and white breaks
the sunlight as a flock of guillemots scud low over the waves on
short stubby wings.

A dinghy at sea must be
completely self-reliant.

Nothing is more exciting than taking your dinghy on a coastal cruise. Long before you get afloat, the anticipation builds as you pore over the charts and work out courses, consult the nautical almanac, mark up the tidal atlas and monitor the weather forecast.

If you have already done a reasonable amount of sailing in sheltered lakes or inlets, you will have gained confidence in your ability to deal with conditions in open water. The basic techniques of sailing do not alter just because the scenery gets bigger. Indeed, navigating on open waters is often less stressful than sailing in more confined places. Out in the open sea the wind is more consistent, the waves are more regular, and you are much less likely to bump into things.

LEAVING HARBOUR

Compared to the wide sea beyond, harbour entrances have many perils. The wind is often deflected by enclosing headlands or breakwaters, and sudden squalls can punch into your sails from unexpected directions. Tides and currents interact in strange and unsettling ways, creating difficult seas and overfalls. In busy harbours there are likely to be large boats manoeuvring, which will exercise a right of way over your little dinghy, whether they actually have a right to or not. When a dinghy clears the congestion of the harbour mouth and sets course along the coast, the crew always feels a sense of relief.

Once you are out at sea, all you have to worry about are the waves and the weather. Compared to the manifold hazards of a crowded harbour, these are comparatively predictable in their behaviour. There really is nothing out there to be afraid of, as long as you know what you are doing.

This Wayfarer is tacking out of a narrow harbour. The crew are expecting rough conditions and already have their waterproofs on. (Mark Broadwith)

ON PASSAGE

Safe coastal passagemaking means planning for every contingency. Most disasters that befall seagoing craft do not appear suddenly out of a clear blue sky, but are the culmination of a chain of escalating events starting with a small problem, which was not properly addressed at the time.

In an emergency, it is important to act swiftly and decisively, but it is also important not to panic. When in doubt, it is usually best to seek sea room and give yourself time to work out the best course of action.

THE HITIA CATAMARAN

The Hitia catamaran was designed by James Wharram, a pioneer of lightweight, low-cost catamaran design. If you like to get places fast, catamarans are an ideal choice. A Hitia can reach a speed of some 12 knots on a reach and will show a clean pair of sterns to most ordinary dinghies even when working to windward. Hitia Cats are stable, seaworthy vessels, but very wet in rough weather. Like most catamarans they do not have anything in the way of a cockpit. You usually sail them by sitting on a trampoline stretched between the hulls. There is plenty of space for four adults to spread themselves out in comfort, though.

Hitias are sloop-rigged with a jib and a typical Wharram 'wingsail', designed to give good drive but with a low centre of effort. This is a tall boomless sail set on either a short gaff or a sprit. Instead of mast slides, the sail luff is a sleeved pocket that encircles the mast.

There is nowhere to put anything out on the exposed flat deck, so any cruising gear needs to be put into waterproof bags and stowed in the hulls, rather like a sea kayak. If you want to sleep aboard, a standard land tent can be erected on the hull, and the trampoline forms a comfortable bed.

Navigating a small boat is mostly just applied common sense. A good skipper will assess each situation as it arises and keep an open mind, rather than blindly follow a standard solution. The ability to keep a cool head is particularly important in an emergency.

Tactics on passage

An effective cruising dinghy will always try to take maximum advantage of the tidal stream. You can never get up too early to catch a fair tide. It is a good idea to be out at sea at least an hour before the tide turns in your favour. Sailing against the last of a foul tide is not usually too difficult, and you are well placed to take maximum advantage of the fair stream when the tide turns.

Keep close inshore when fighting a foul tide. Once the tide has turned in your favour, keep in the fast tide offshore for as long as possible. Remember that the tide turns first close inshore, and that a strong tidal stream often creates back eddies close to the shore. A canny dinghy skipper can make use of these to sail against the prevailing current, hopping from back eddy to back eddy. In the days of working sail, back eddies were marked on the chart to assist the passage of sailing craft, but this level of fine detail is sadly missing from modern charts.

Wind over tide

The direction of the wind relative to the tide has a major effect on the sea state, particularly in areas with a very strong tidal stream, such as my local sailing waters of the Bristol Channel. When the wind blows against the tide the waves become steep

Avel Dro in rough conditions on the Rade de Brest. (Ronan Coquil)

and may even break. After the tide has turned the waves will flatten and lengthen, giving much more pleasant conditions.

Sometimes it is prudent to anchor in a sheltered bay to sit out a foul tide, before continuing on passage. In the Bristol Channel the fastest way to sail against a foul tide is invariably at anchor. A dinghy with facilities for sleeping aboard has an advantage here, as the crew can get some kip while they are waiting for the tide to turn in their favour again.

Tidal races and overfalls

Serious tidal races and overfalls are marked on the chart by the appropriate symbols, but you should expect them anywhere there is a strong tide running against the wind

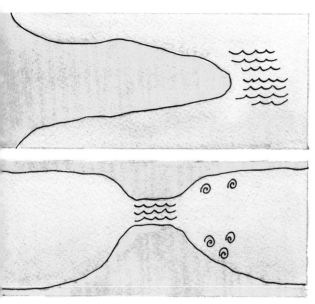

Races are commonly to be found off exposed headlands, while overfalls are created at narrows in tidal inlets.

in shallow water. They will form a belt of rough water across your path, and should never be underestimated. Virtually any headland where the tide runs will have some sort of race off the end of it.

Dangerous races are best passed at slack water or with a good offing, which may mean having to go at least 5 miles offshore. Sometimes there is a narrow belt of flat water very close to the shore, inside the race. Local fishing vessels can often be seen using these inshore passages, using their 'local knowledge' to cut the corner. A sailing dinghy using the same tactic should beware of the sudden gusts that can strike down from high coastal cliffs.

Overfalls occur wherever the tide flows over a shallow area on the seabed, such as a belt of rocks close under the surface. The rough water tends to occur downtide of the obstruction, and changes position when the tide turns. Overfalls are also created where there is a narrowing in the channel. At the

mouths of Scottish sea lochs the tidal stream can run at 10 knots, creating localised rapids. The narrow straits in the Golfe du Morbihan in France are famous for their swift currents and steep waves at full ebb and flow.

Sailing at night

If you make regular coastal passages, you will inevitably end up sailing at night. If there is a bright moon and a clear sky, it can be almost like sailing during the day. On a pitch-dark night, night sailing becomes very disorientating: the boat seems to be sailing much faster than before, rushing forward through the blackness, with the white crests of the waves looming up alarmingly close alongside.

During a sunny summer's day there is usually a sea breeze blowing onto the land, which grows stronger as the day progresses. This is because the land heats up faster than the sea, and sucks in cooler air from over the water. Normally this wind drops during the night, to be followed by a period of calm. As the land continues to cool relative to the sea temperature, a night breeze eventually develops, blowing off the land – although this may not happen until well after midnight. The night breeze is very useful for vessels making night passages. Because of it, the sea is often flatter at night, as the coastline becomes a windward shore.

CLOSING WITH THE LAND

One of the excitements of a coastal passage is arriving somewhere new, but this also means that you will approach an unfamiliar coast late in the day, when you are tired and night may be falling. It is too late to start consulting the pilot book for details of off-lying shoals and harbour buoyage at this stage. A dinghy at sea is

As much chartwork as possible should be done before setting off on passage.

not the ideal environment to read a book. All your preparations should have been completed before setting off from harbour that morning. The salient navigational information should have been noted down concisely in your logbook, and you may even have marked up the chart to indicate the best course into harbour.

River bars

Almost all tidal rivers will form a bar, generally well out to sea, far beyond the mouth of the river. A bar is formed because the water coming down the river is brought to a halt by the greater mass of water in the sea, and the silt that is suspended in it falls to the seabed, forming a shoal. Some river bars are so shallow that they dry completely at low water, with only a stream of fresh water flowing over them, unnavigable even for a dinghy. Other rivers still have a channel deep enough for a small boat to enter even at dead low water, and this can be an ideal time to enter an unknown river, as you are able to see the edges of the channel clearly.

Yachtsman's pilot books are aimed primarily at deep-keel yachts, and they are invariably a hopeless source of information about the depth over a bar at dead low water. The crew of a cruising dinghy just have to investigate for themselves.

When entering a narrow river against the wind, you will find flatter water if you do it against the tide. This is fair enough if you have a powerful outboard, but can be difficult under sail. A boat with no engine can often be towed in against the ebb by wading in the shallow water near the bank of the river, pulling your dinghy behind you. Entering a river against the wind and the last of the ebb is often a better choice than waiting for the flood tide, which may create overfalls as it flows against the wind.

River bars are at their most dangerous when an onshore wind meets an ebb tide, especially if there is a big swell running. You are most likely to encounter these conditions when leaving a river rather than entering from the sea. Suddenly your path is blocked by waves breaking right across the channel. If the ebb is running strongly, it may be difficult to sail back into the river to escape from the surf.

When approaching a river bar on the flood tide from out at sea, any surf on the bar may not be visible until you are practically upon it. All you see are the smooth backs of the waves. As the tide rises, the breakers on the bar usually die down. Most rivers are safe to enter at high-water slack. The trouble is that if you are a little late, the ebb will start to set in, and you will not only be entering against the tide, but if there is an onshore wind overfalls can quickly start to build up on the bar.

A clear patch in the breakers will mark the deepest water. Invariably this is not in the centre of the river, but well over to one side. If at all possible, avoid sailing through breaking water on a bar. If you do, your dinghy will start surfing down the faces of the breakers. This is exciting or alarming, depending on your sensibility. The danger of broaching is ever present, however, so try to keep your dinghy's stern perpendicular to the breaking waves.

HEAVY WEATHER

Everyone worries about being caught out by bad weather at sea. Unlike a well-found yacht, a dinghy cannot remain on the open sea whatever the conditions. If the weather deteriorates, she must eventually seek shelter. In a blow, a prudent yacht skipper will gain sea room, batten down the hatches and await a break in the weather. A dinghy cannot do this. An undecked boat is always vulnerable to swamping or being thrown upside down by the waves.

In a well-crewed yacht in bad conditions, half the crew can be sent down to their bunks to rest, while the rest remain on deck to work the vessel. In a dinghy, everyone is out there in the weather, all of the time. The crew of an open boat have no respite from the elements and soon become tired in a big sea. Weary, wet crews become prone to seasickness and to make mistakes, which could be fatal ones.

The best way to deal with bad conditions in open water is to avoid them. With careful passage planning and judicious attention to the latest weather forecasts, a prudent dinghy sailor can usually avoid too much of a dusting. If conditions begin to worsen while out at sea, begin running for shelter long before things get too bad. Experienced skippers make contingency plans for such an eventuality. If they encounter unexpectedly heavy weather, they alter course for a safe haven already identified in their passage plan.

Getting 'caught out'

Despite every prudent precaution, the day will inevitably come when you are 'caught out' by dirty weather at sea. The most alarming features of a big sea are the noise and the incredible violence of the motion. Everything becomes vicious: a flogging sail will batter you around the head, loose sheets whip with malicious force, and your boat suddenly feels very small and fragile before the awesome might of the great ocean. Incapacitation due to fear and sheer exhaustion are dangers that should not be underestimated.

This anchorage is not sheltered from the wind, but as there is high ground to windward the water is flat enough to anchor and tie down a reef. (Ronan Coquil)

When things cut up rough out there, it is a great comfort to be in a boat you have faith in: well found and shipshape. You need to have confidence in your boat and in your ability to bring her safely into shelter. This comes not only from experience of similar conditions, but also from faith in your passage planning and your navigation. If you are certain of the accuracy of your position fixing and the course you are steering, the situation will feel much less threatening. You must remain in command.

Weathering a rough sea

The undulating surface of a great ocean is a combination of the swell, which heaps up great 'seas' tens of metres apart, and smaller wind-driven waves that run across them. A small boat can deal with a high sea amazingly effectively, swooping down into the troughs and lifting up onto the crests, as long as she can maintain sufficient steerageway when her sails are blanketed in the troughs.

If the wind veers, the waves will begin to run across the direction of the underlying swell. Sudden steep waves begin to break up the even pattern of the swell, leaping up abruptly, smashing into your boat and stopping her dead in the water, or hitting you full in the face. A confused sea is much more difficult for a dinghy than one with regular, even waves.

Steering a course among great seas in heavy weather means concentrating on the heaving water, picking an easy path through the ever-changing waves, concentrating on keeping way on the boat, nursing her along. Even so, you will not be able to avoid every white crest. Inevitably, waves will break aboard.

Luffing up in order to slow down, while I assess the best approach into harbour in rough conditions. (Ronan Coquil)

As the wind rises above a Beaufort Force 6 in open water, you will encounter an increasing number of breaking seas. By the time the wind reaches Beaufort Force 8 (a gale), the crests are numerous and the faces of the seas become streaked by spindrift. White water does not have enough buoyancy to lift a boat. Your dinghy will simply crash straight through the crest, which will smash heavily aboard. The weight and power of white water is awesome. A big breaking sea will nonchalantly punch your dinghy aside or turn her over, crushing her down under tons of water.

It is not the strength of the wind that causes a small open boat to seek a safe sheltered haven, but the deteriorating state of the sea. A dinghy can survive strong winds in sheltered waters, but not out at sea. The seas created by winds of Force 6 and above, blowing across open water, are dangerous for a dinghy. The prudent skipper should avoid being at sea in these conditions.

Running off

A serious sea boat will have an effective method of reducing sail in heavy weather, but as a dinghy's sail area is reduced, so is her power to punch through the waves. Eventually it will become impossible to work to windward. The combination of a loss of drive from a reduced sail area, especially when the sail is blanketed in the troughs, and the slowing effect of waves smashing into the bow, eventually makes upwind progress impossible.

Unlike a yacht, a small dinghy does not have the weight to keep punching through big waves. Eventually she will be unable to make any headway through a heavy sea, and her only choice is to run off the wind under storm canvas, or even under bare poles. If you have made a proper passage plan, you will have identified a sheltered refuge to leeward you can run into.

Running before a big sea is much drier and faster than plugging into it. The motion of the boat is far smoother, and the waves look smoother too. The backs of seas are much less rugged than their faces. It can feel deceptively benign. But running off is perilous. No matter how fast your boat is moving through the water, she will never move faster than the seas. They rise up under her stern, lifting her high, until she swoops exhilaratingly forwards in a churning froth of white water. Then the crest passes under her and she settles down into the next trough. There is a brief moment of comparative peace before the next sea rises up under her and the mad headlong rush begins again. In those swooping surges down the seas, you must be extremely careful not to let her broach.

Running off under jib in a big sea. (David Summerville)

THE NAVIGATOR

John Welsford of New Zealand designs small vessels capable of sailing along the unprotected shorelines of his South Pacific homeland. The Navigator is typical of his shapely and seaworthy craft.

'Performance wise she is a real surprise,' John writes, 'very fast in most conditions, close winded and easily handled. The hull, though light, is seaworthy and stable, powerful enough to drive through a big wave, and she has a surprisingly comfortable motion in the open sea – a real bonus on long coastal passages.

'I began cruising in small boats because that was all I had at the time, but eventually I graduated to a nice ocean cruiser. Trouble was, I spent a lot of time maintaining the boat: antifouling, replacing worn ropework, painting, engine maintenance, sail repair and so on. She was endless work.

'I found myself dreaming of my little boats while working on the bigger one. I would sail past the little creeks and sheltered inlets that I used to frequent, wishing that I could sail into shallow waters forbidden to my deep-keeled boat. Gradually I realised that I'd been much happier in a small open boat.

'Over a period of eight years I designed and built a new cruising dinghy each year. I learned a lot from sailing those boats. Navigator was the last in that series. Years of experience went into her. Speed was not so much a concern as a boat that would reward good sailing and handle very rough conditions. I drew a comfortable cockpit, and a big sloop rig, as well as the alternative yawl rig that has become so popular among dinghy cruisers. She has glued plywood lapstrake sides on a narrow flat bottom, sawn plywood frames with light stringers, built-in buoyancy tanks and wide side decks which make for a relatively quick build: a pretty boat with a traditional air about her.

'Now there are Navigators in more than forty countries, with over 700 sets of plans out there. They are highly thought of by their owners and some have completed astonishing voyages. They have introduced their owners to "real" cruising in small boats – a couple of airbeds, warm dry sleeping bags, space on the bow thwart for the cooker to make the morning mug, and a calm corner in a tiny forest-clad cove. What a view, waking up from a comfortable night camping aboard! That's as close to paradise as you'll get on this Earth.'

Running directly downwind with three reefs in the sail. (Ronan Coquil)

Avoiding a broach

Broaching happens when the boat tries to travel faster than the hull is comfortable with. The first signs of an impending broach are the bow digging in and a strange lightness to the helm as the rudder loses grip. Suddenly she will be flung broadside onto the sea and rolled over onto her beam ends. Many a good windjammer was lost that way in the great seas of the Southern Ocean, running her easting down with a cargo of wool from southern Australia. But you do not need a Southern Ocean greybeard to roll a dinghy.

To avoid a broach, sit as well aft as you can. If your rudder is a lifting one, make sure it is fully down. The centreboard should be fully raised, to stop her tripping over it. If possible, lower the mainsail and run under a headsail only. It is good to have a boom-less storm sail that can be gybed accidentally without endangering the boat. If you judge

that the speed is too high, sheet in to spill wind. When running dead downwind it is the act of sheeting in, rather than letting out the sheet, that spills wind and slows the boat.

As each following sea rises up under your stern, you will reduce the risk of a broach by heading straight down the face of the sea. If your desired course is not completely downwind, and you want to steer a quartering course across the waves, you must alter course back to your desired heading when the crest has passed. The sinusoidal helming often necessary in a big sea makes it hard to maintain a clear sense of your overall course by traditional dead reckoning. Fortunately a modern GPS can take care of that. As conditions worsen, it will become increasingly difficult to maintain this snaking course, and you will have to run dead downwind. Hopefully shelter also lies in that direction.

A dinghy lying to a sea
anchor over the bows.

Running off,
towing a drogue.

Avoiding an accidental gybe

The requirement to run straight before
the seas is often in conflict with the desire
to keep the wind on the quarter in order
to avoid a gybe. This is why running off in
heavy weather is best done under a small jib
or trysail that can gybe accidentally, without
creating any difficulty. If your mainsail is still
set, you will have no choice but to steer a
quartering course – the risk of an accidental
gybe is too great otherwise.

Before conditions get really bad, a
sensible dinghy will have rounded a
headland into sheltered waters, and her
crew will already be considering where
to moor, and how to get back to base.
If conditions become too dangerous to
continue running off under sail, and you
are still out there in open water, you will
have no choice but to lower all sail and
run 'under bare poles', using the windage

of the mast alone. At least you no longer
need to worry about gybing.

Using a sea anchor

My own dinghy has a broad buoyant
transom that slopes aft, and generates a
huge amount of lift in a following sea. If your
dinghy is not endowed with such copious
buttocks, she may be in danger of being
'pooped' by a big sea, and swamped. Should
this be a concern, the only remaining course
of action is to wait for a flat patch between
seas, turn your vessel head to wind and lie
to a sea anchor.

Once the sea anchor is set over the
bows, the boat will make sternway, driven
backwards by the wind and waves. Very few
cruising dinghies ever experience conditions
so severe that they need to set a sea
anchor, but Frank Dye used to do this in his
Wayfarer in very rough seas, with success.

Setting a sea anchor is similar to lowering a conventional anchor, and should be done under control, with the rope carefully flaked out clear of all obstructions and made fast to a secure strong point. Conical drogues suitable for use as sea anchors can be bought from good chandlers, in various sizes.

When lying to a sea anchor, your sails should be lashed down. If you have a boom, take it off the mast and place it on the side benches. Your dinghy will not lie head to wind, but with her bow perhaps some 45 degrees off it. As she is pushed downwind, her hull will leave a slick of flat water upwind of her, which will give her some protection from breaking seas. You should raise the plate and remove the rudder, which would otherwise be damaged, as your boat is moving backwards through the water. If it is possible to do so, you should also lower the mast. In very bad conditions you may need to wrap some cloth around the warp to 'parcel' it against chafe from the fairlead.

It is a feature of very difficult conditions that your options reduce markedly. Deciding to lie to a sea anchor is one of these situations. It is the very last thing you can do to keep your boat safe. Once the sea anchor is deployed and the boat is lying to the warp, there is nothing more to do other than lie on the bottom boards, keep pumping out the spray, and wait for the weather to moderate.

My own feeling, for what it is worth, is that a seaworthy dinghy with buoyant stern-quarters would often be better to continue running off under bare poles, towing a drogue to slow her down and to keep her stern to the seas, rather than risk turning round and setting a sea anchor over the bow.

Should you intend to make a habit of this sort of thing, it would be worth making a flat canvas dodger to put over the boat, with just a small opening to steer from, which would protect her from spray and breaking seas. It would need to have a low ridge amidships to shed the water, perhaps formed by the boom. Ships' lifeboats were sometimes equipped with such a cover.

Frank Dye capsizes when lying to a sea anchor

On his second major sea passage in his Wayfarer dinghy, a crossing from Scotland to Norway, Frank Dye and his crew survived four capsizes and a broken mast during a severe gale (Beaufort Force 9). In *Ocean Crossing Wayfarer*, Dye recalled the scene:

'It was impossible to look into the wind. It was screaming and the tops of the waves were blown completely away, feeling like hail. Within our limited vision the whole sea seemed to be smoking. Just to see such seas break away on the beam was frightening – 25ft of solid water, with another 12ft of overhanging crest above it. It was only a matter of time before we got one aboard … She rose gallantly, but it was an impossible position: she seemed to be rising at 60 degrees and there was still a 15ft crest curling above us. Down it came and we were driven bodily under. With ears roaring under immense pressure, and swallowing water, I fought back to the surface, only to find Wanderer was lying bottom up.'

After three more capsizes, Dye reflected:

'Possibly we were the only people alive to have taken an open dinghy through a Force 9 gale, but we felt no elation, just a reaction of wetness, coldness and extreme tiredness.'

The pair recovered the mast from the sea, made a jury rig and went on to make landfall in Norway without further incident. This experience is exceptional. Few cruising dinghies would want to put themselves in conditions like this, but it is interesting to see how much a dinghy can put up with, and still survive.

ROUND BRITAIN IN A WAYFARER

In 2014, Jeremy Warren and Phillip Kirk sailed a Wayfarer around the island of Great Britain in 32 days. This seemed an amazing achievement, which halved the previous record. Their time seemed impossible to beat, but this new record only lasted 5 years. In 2019 a lovingly refurbished 60 year-old wooden Wayfarer *Nipegegi* did the trip non-stop. Will Hodshon and Rich Mitchell set sail from Salcombe, Devon, on 15 June and completed the 1,390 nautical mile journey on 1 July, in just 18 days. As with Jeremy and Phillip, the off-watch crewmember had to kip down in the open dinghy in a drysuit, a dodger protecting their face from spray.

These were record attempts, and inevitably displayed a more gung-ho attitude than the defensive approach I tend to take to open water sailing. I asked Jeremy Warren to write a few notes about his approach to sailing in the open sea in his Wayfarer:

'The challenge is the waves rather than the wind. On a flat sea, a dinghy reefed down to a sail area, not much larger than the area presented by the side of the hull, can still keep going. A Wayfarer dinghy, with a tiny triangle of reefed mainsail no more than 2m high and a matching scrap of rolled genoa, can still make ground to windward in Force 7 winds, and when so reefed, there is little strain on the rudder and rigging.

Breaking seas are the most hazardous. A 4m sea, but with 60m between the tops, is uncomfortable but manageable; the boat simply bobs over the crests. However, when a wave breaks it unleashes its ability to shove the boat, sometimes violently. If the breaking sea is on the bow, the crew get wet, and progress is slowed. A breaking sea on the beam can roll the sturdiest of hull types, and need not be much higher than the side of the vessel to do this, so the tactic with beam-on waves is avoidance. A following sea provides a surfing sleigh-ride, a steady hand on the helm to steer straight down the waves works, until the boat surfs so fast that it catches up with the back of the next wave, risking nose-diving and broaching. Reducing sail to slow the boat mitigates this scenario as the wind rises.

In the severest conditions, of Force 7 and above, the boat will surf even under bare poles. Tactics for survival include lying bow-on to a sea anchor on a very long stretchy rope, towing a drogue or warps/sheets to slow down the boat, and lying-ahull, even including lowering the mast. These conditions are so rarely experienced in dinghies that no clear winning tactic has yet emerged. If the wind changes, and a new sea builds on an old one, the resultant sea becomes chaotic, making a coherent choice of tactics even more challenging.

Those who have experienced these conditions agree that an analytical approach wins out, based on observation and cool-headed thinking. Practising in big seas is recommended, which builds confidence in your boat and enables you to gain experience should you get caught out at a future date.'

CALLING FOR HELP

Frank Dye always maintained that he would never call for help when out at sea. No matter how bad the conditions, he would solve the problem without outside assistance. I disagree: I believe that it is more seamanlike to ask for assistance before things have got really bad, rather than waiting until a life-threatening situation has developed, and putting your rescuers' lives in danger. There is no dishonour in putting out a PAN PAN call and advising the coastguard of your situation.

TAKING A TOW

Taking a tow in a dinghy is not without its problems. The forces involved can be huge, even in flat water. If the dinghy is towed too fast, it may cause structural damage or even pull her under the water. So do not accept a tow from just anyone, and especially not a high-speed power craft. These vessels are used to belting along on the plane, and are unlikely to travel slowly enough to be a safe towing vessel. Given the choice, I prefer to be towed by a sailing yacht, as her

crew are more likely to have sailed a dinghy themselves, and will be more sensitive to the needs of a small vessel.

When being towed, it is better to use a spare rope, rather than your dinghy's painter. Alternatively, you can accept a rope passed to you by the towing vessel. Take it through a fairlead up forward, then once around a strong point, and either keep hold of the end or cleat it. Do not make it fast with a knot, as you may need to drop the tow in a hurry. It is difficult to untie a knot under load, and cutting a loaded towing rope can be dangerous.

It is good to establish VHF communication with the towing vessel early on. You will be able to hear them when they shout at you, but they may not be able to hear you over the noise of their engine. Agree a working channel, and tell them that you do not want to be towed at more than 5 knots, which is a good maximum speed for a dinghy.

Lower your sails and lash them down, lift the centreplate and then sit at the stern to steer. The crew weight needs to be kept well aft. Aim the bows of your boat directly at the point where the towrope is made

Avel Dro has just picked up a tow off Douarnenez in a flat calm. I am stowing the sail and making all secure. (Solène Canuard)

fast to the towing vessel. Do not allow your boat to take a sheer off to one side, or the towrope may capsize her.

Being towed can be unpleasant in anything of a sea. The towrope will slacken and then snatch sharply, the exhaust gases of the towing vessel will envelop you, and you risk losing control of the situation. Once you have accepted a tow, you become the client vessel. The crew of the towing boat may believe they have 'rescued' you, and make choices on your behalf that are not the ones you would have taken for yourself.

I do not accept tows at sea very often, but every now and then they have got me back to base in a flat calm when otherwise I would have had to stop short of my intended destination. I have also made some good friends that way.

AVOIDING BEING 'RESCUED' WHEN YOU DON'T WANT TO BE

Cruising dinghies are admirable sea boats, and you should have no worries about taking them out on coastal passages. In our dinghies we sail in a way that was perfectly normal in the nineteenth century, when coastal waters were full of open sailing craft. But nowadays people in bigger boats seem to regard our mere presence on open waters as convincing evidence of recklessness. They expect to see dinghies in sheltered waters, not out at sea.

If you take down your sails in a dinghy at sea, even if it is just to put in a reef, you run the risk of being seen as 'in difficulties'. Modern yachts never stop in the open sea with their sails down, and they cannot conceive why any boat should want to do this, so they will approach you offering assistance, perhaps forcibly.

All this is a tiresome distraction from whatever you were doing before the self-styled 'rescue boat' came along (especially if it was sitting on the loo bucket), and it is easy to become annoyed by this unwanted attention. But always remember that the other vessel has the best of motives. They do not know that you are an experienced dinghy cruiser. They probably think you are going to get into trouble, call out the rescue services, and give all small-boat sailors a bad name.

So do not get angry. Refuse their offers politely, with lots of 'thumbs-up' signals and broad grins. They will probably interpret this as meaning that you do indeed want a tow, so you will have to do lots of head shaking too. If you can read the name of their vessel, call them up on the radio and confirm that you are not in any difficulty.

Various friends have been pressurised into accepting unnecessary tows from lifeboat crews, who judged that they were in potential danger. You may encounter similar problems from military or police vessels. I once ended up having to accept a tow from a patrol vessel of Les Affaires Maritimes in France. It meant that I lost virtually all control over the situation and basically had to accept being towed to the place they wanted to take me. But generally things have to be pretty serious for the wishes of a vessel's skipper to be overruled, even by a grey ship bristling with guns. The best policy in these situations is not to be intimidated, to remain devastatingly polite at all times, and to refuse any offers of unnecessary help with effusive thanks.

Politeness is a powerful force, effective even with military officials. But if you are going to refuse proffered advice in this way, you must be absolutely certain that you know what you are doing.

My crazy escapade with Roger Barnes

by Jacques van Geen for Le Chasse-Marée *(translated and abridged by Roger Barnes)*

INTRODUCTION

After the publication of the first edition of this book, I was contacted by the impressive and prestigious French nautical magazine *Le Chasse-Marée*. They wanted to write an article about dinghy cruising and the activities of the Dinghy Cruising Association. A journalist was going to be sent all the way from France to my house, to come out sailing with me! I needed to find another boat to join us and organise a mini rally, somewhere that would be suitably impressive to this experienced gallic sailor.

Where to take him, though? It was late September and the settled summer weather had already broken. Jacques and I sat in my house and discussed the options.

Jacques continues the story:

A good cruise is a well-planned cruise – everyone knows that. Soon charts, almanacs and coastal pilots covered Roger's dining table and, after we have pushed the furniture away, spread across the floor all around us. We note the tide times and tidal flows. This is vital, because the tides that flood into the Bristol Channel are among the largest in the world.

The original plan, for the three days I would be in England, was to sail out of Appledore and across Bideford Bay to the small port of Clovelly, as well as venturing to Lundy Island, which lies out in the Bristol Channel to the west. But the forecast is for strong winds, veering from south to west: 25kn to 30kn, with gusts up to 35kn. This is on the edge of what is sensible for the crossing of Bideford Bar, and once out in the Bristol Channel our options are limited if we need to seek shelter.

We contemplate a more tranquil voyage on a sheltered river or an estuary. But then we receive a vaguely soothing weather report, and our original plan is back on again. 'It will still test the limit of our boat's capabilities,' Roger explains soberly. But I know Roger; his approach to life, to sailing; his long experience of these coasts and of his boat. I know that he is no more interested in testing his prowess to an idiotic level than I am. And we have already thoroughly checked over Avel Dro. So I have confidence in our decision, and if our 'not unreasonable' plan proves to be not so reasonable after all, I will at least have a chance to test the qualities of the man and his boat.

Plans are prepared, and alternative ones explored exhaustively in the light of a pessimistic weather forecast. We weigh up every option, but ignore the one that really makes sense, to snuggle down in a comfortable corner by the wood stove and stay here in the dry for three days, fortified with cups of tea and a stack of sea books.

Arriving at Appledore the next morning, we meet up with Little Jim *and her owner and builder, Alastair Law.* Little Jim *is a Paradox, a small coastal cruising boat with a cabin. She is already afloat at the bottom of the slipway, tethered by her painter. Alastair stands alongside her in bare feet and shorts, laughing at our planned escapade. It is reassuring.*

The wind, channelled between the riverbanks, blows out towards the river mouth. It takes us along with it, our sail well reefed down, the last of the flood tide flowing ever more weakly against us. Soon Bideford Bar comes into view, relatively calm in the main channel, but bordered by impressive breakers on the neighbouring shoals. Roger sheets in our sail to spill wind and take some way off her, in order to prevent the bow from plunging too deeply into the steep waves. Once clear of the Bar, we harden up and set a course towards the southern shore of Bideford Bay. Now were are close-hauled, and it is easier to control the boat's speed as she pitches into the seas.

We had planned to sail to Lundy, but there is no question of pressing on towards the island in these conditions. The wind and the waves would be even greater in the open waters of the Bristol Channel, out beyond the bay. Out there, the southerly swell rolls in unhindered from the other side of the Atlantic, and the fierce currents throw up a steep sea.

(LEFT AND RIGHT ABOVE) Leaving Appledore. We follow LITTLE JIM towards the seas breaking on the bar. (Jacques van Geen)

(RIGHT) Out in Bideford Bay we decide the conditions are not fit to sail out to Lundy, so we sail close on the wind, tacking towards Clovelly. (Jacques van Geen)

It is fast sailing in Avel Dro, and the pumps get a good workout too. Spray crashes in over the bows and the rain batters down on the choppy seas of the bay. We punch bravely onwards towards the indistinct coastline enclosing the bay to the south, vague in the wet murk.

We can see nothing clearly on the smudgy line of black cliffs bordering this almost deserted coast. Then eventually, here and there, we pick out the white glow of waterfalls that cascade from the green fringe separating these dark walls from the sky, pouring over the edge and plunging into the sea. We approach closer, keen to gain the shelter of these fantastic ramparts. Suddenly we enter their wind-shadow, the wind drops and the sea becomes calm. And then, like a strand of lichen rooted in a thin crevice of granite, we see a handful of houses clambering up the cliff face. There is Clovelly!

It is just a curved breakwater, a quay, and a small slipway: barely a port. We cover the last half a mile under oars. We must arrive before the fair current abandons us and before the harbour dries completely at half tide, rendering the port inaccessible.

AT THE SIGN OF THE RED LION

Oh Clovelly! – Your single street paved with black, slippery cobbles, too steep for wheeled vehicles to dare to venture, where your inhabitants must go about their business on foot, dragging sleds made of fish boxes on wooden skids. We climb the sinuous street in continuous heavy rain. There is no one else about. The village is deserted by the tourists, who flock here en masse on sunny days.

Avel Dro just slips into Clovelly before the harbour dries. Little Jim arrives with the flood, after nightfall. (Jacques van Geen)

The next morning the
weather is deceptively
fair under the shelter
of the cliffs, as we
wait for the tide.
(Jacques Van Geen)

We must wait for the flood tide to refill the harbour before we can haul our boat higher up the strand for the night, so we take refuge in the pub – at the sign of the Red Lion. Oh warm and tranquil haven, with its stone-flagged floor on which our boots and oilskins drip abundantly! Here, where a blazing fire warms our bodies and our souls! Soon we're devouring fish and chips, accompanied by local ales to restore our hearts.

The time has come. Now we must haul up our boat high up the pebble strand, and moor her by bow and stern to the huge ground chains that are stretched across the harbour. Then we set up the boat tent for the night.

It rains. It pours continuously. And the cover was already sodden when we unrolled it. Drops of water bead on its underside and then dangle, trembling menacingly. At first hesitant, they swell and sway, and then ultimately lose their grip. But soon we sleep.

I do not notice when Roger delicately moves my feet clear of the stove, so that he can prepare our morning coffee. Nor do I hear the soft gurgles of the Italian moka pot, as it goes about its business brewing our morning coffee. But, waking at last to a radiant dawn, I discover another aspect of life aboard this Ilur: far from the easy comforts of a campervan or their floating plastic equivalents. In that fair morning, with my coffee mug in my hand, the humble Avel Dro feels like a palace.

We review our plans for the day while we wait for the tide to refill the harbour; and discuss them with the harbourmaster as well as the coxs'n of the Clovelly lifeboat, just back from a training trip around the bay. The weather forecast is still unsuitable to continue out to Lundy. Indeed, the wind is forecast to veer and strengthen over the next 24 hours. We would end up trapped on the island, unable to return. Everyone agrees we should have time to return to Appledore before the wind has increased too much and veered into the west, sending deep swells rolling into the bay.

AVEL DRO IN THE BOILING CAULDRON

By 11 o'clock we are in the thick of things. Out of the shelter of the cliffs, the wind is stronger than ever. It pushes us quickly towards the Bideford Bar buoy. The waves seem bigger than yesterday, yet not too threatening. They are high, definitely, but long and only lightly breaking. Arriving off the Bar buoy, we round Avel Dro up into the wind so we can lower the reefed lugsail. We hoist a small storm sail in its place. Then we bear her off again and gybe to come onto the transit over the bar.

There are frequent white crests on the waves now, which grow ever higher and are breaking hard over the shoals to each side of us. Their height is difficult to estimate, as always, but they are much taller than the 5m mast-height of Little Jim. *She is still accompanying us, disappearing completely between the summits of the seas.*

Returning across Bideford Bay, three reefs in the sail. (Jacques Van Geen)

Having changed down to our storm sail, we head into the big waves on the bar. (Jacques Van Geen)

We are just abeam of the second starboard hand buoy in the entrance channel, when a wave, rather higher than the others, suddenly breaks just under the starboard quarter of Avel Dro. It trips her over, throwing us both out into the foaming sea. I land close to the boat, and grab at the gunwale with one hand, reaching out with the other to catch Roger, who is bobbing about entangled in the sheet. Roger is more concerned about stopping the yard and sail from floating away.

We clamber back aboard the Ilur. She has already righted herself, virtually on her own, even with the plate up, (thank you and bravo, Monsieur Vivier!). We put her back on course without delay. I begin to bail again with the bucket, aided by the electric pump, which has diligently started running. Roger guides Avel Dro down the channel once more, and she behaves surprisingly well, even with her hull flooded. Soon the water level inside is dropping visibly. I am just pumping out the last centimetres of water, with my back to the great seas rising up astern of us, when suddenly the boat takes off ...

Avel Dro is rolled over by a breaking crest and we are thrown into the sea.
(Roger Barnes)

ROGER SENDS OUT A MAYDAY

A huge wave has swept us upwards. We are surfing forward at a hallucinatory speed, vibrating, whirring, jets of foam spurting from both sides of our prow. We fly onwards through suspended time. Thirty seconds of eternity perhaps: 15kn, then 16kn and even 17kn, (as attested later by the chartplotter). There was just time to shout, 'grab hold!' and then we're sent on this mad dash – onwards and onwards, in an endless rush. I am grabbing hold so hard, I can feel the nails of my clenched fingers embedding themselves in the thwart beneath me. Then the wave finally breaks around us. We settle down in a foam of bubbles, filling the boat and spreading all around, leaving us sitting dazed and half deafened in a hissing froth. 'Champagne!' the billions of bubbles seem to sing. All is well. We are still here. Drunk with foam, incredulous and stunned, but we are still here!

We look into each other's faces. No doubt Roger can see in my eyes the same stupefaction I see in his. Without losing a second, I grab the bucket with tenfold ardour. Roger, fearing that another wave like that could pitch us inescapably into the breakers on the beach, grabs the VHF and puts out a Mayday call. He continues to steer us into the shelter of the river mouth, while calmly informing Swansea coastguard of our situation. In fact we have already passed the crux of the passage, so by the time the Atlantic class RIB, Glanely, from Appledore lifeboat station appears, things are well under control on board Avel Dro.

The lifeboat arrives only ten minutes after Roger's Mayday. I have long admired the application, vigilance and professionalism of the volunteer crews of the Royal National Lifeboat Institution. But I am blown away by the speed of this response.

Jacques steers Avel Dro into Appledore, accompanied by the inshore lifeboat. (Roger Barnes)

By their civility also, because we had clearly found ourselves at the wrong place and at the wrong time. Yet they refrain from any critical remarks. And I am sure that not one of those impressive rescuers, escorting us into port, blames us for calling them out – not even the crew of the second and larger lifeboat that joins us soon after, the All Weather Lifeboat, Mollie Hunt. *One of the rescuers inquires about our life jackets, as they are out of sight under our oilies, but that is all. The deployment of this maritime rescue force around little* Avel Dro *is rigorously professional, but without exaggerated severity. Beyond them we see* Little Jim *and Alastair's impassive face, as he navigates the chop insouciantly, with his boat's sail rolled down into a deep reef.*

Back in Appledore, it is but a moment's work to get our boats out of the water. We change into dry clothes – then off to the teashop to order a Devon cream tea with half a dozen big warm scones.

And then finally we are back at Roger's house, with the woodstove humming. We drink more good hot tea. Our sleeping bags, clothes, charts and other kit is rinsed out and hung everywhere about the house to dry. The boat is already laid up under her tarpaulin, and we are gently regaining our composure. We begin to relax. Now we can smile about our struggles together. We can take the time to reflect, to draw lessons from our experience. And already I find myself dreaming of future passages, while my socks are not yet dry. Whatever mad folly infects the Dinghy Cruising Association, it is certainly very contagious.

The adventure with Jacques was the second time I capsized *Avel Dro* in the open sea in two years. The first time was off the French coast, and the experience forced me to recognise that I had become too relaxed about the possibility of a capsize.

I had come to rely too much on the innate stability of *Avel Dro*. I suppose I had become complacent. As I righted the dinghy I watched helplessly as things that were not lashed down floated away or dropped over the side and sank. There is nothing like a real capsize to test how well your stowage works aboard your boat. I learnt from that experience and spent some time fitting catches to every locker and lanyards to every loose object aboard. So when we capsized in the huge seas on Bideford Bar, the boat was as well prepared as could be expected. This was fortunate, as it was a far more perilous place to capsize.

The entrance to the estuary at Bideford required us to turn slightly to starboard, relative to the waves on the bar, and this is why we capsized. I was trying to nudge *Avel Dro*'s course slightly to the south, to prevent us running into the beach directly ahead of us, on which the waves were breaking in a vicious surf. So her course was not completely perpendicular to the waves. A breaking crest came up behind us, tripped *Avel Dro* over her forefoot and pitched us both out of the boat into the sea.

The boat righted herself and lay alongside us full of water, the storm sail flogging. We clambered back aboard, I went back to the helm and bore her off the wind again. While Jacques and the electric pump bailed, I kept *Avel Dro* rigorously perpendicular to the seas. This meant we were heading directly for the surf beach however. I was hoping that once we had cleared the bar the waves would lessen sufficiently for us to turn to starboard, before we were piled onto the foaming strand. Then we were suddenly picked up by a huge sea and sent rushing towards the beach at tremendous speed, the whole boat vibrating.

As we settled into the foam behind the wave, the interior of the boat once more completely awash, I rapidly considered our options. Should the boat end up being cast onto the beach by another great sea, she would certainly be smashed up and it was very doubtful that Jacques and I would be

able to scramble ashore through the surf. The undertow would certainly overwhelm us. Our best option would be to jump over the side of the boat into the sea well before the boat hit the surf, allowing the boat to carry on to her doom without us. And if we were going to do that, it would be very handy if there was a big lifeboat right behind us, poised to pluck us out of the waves.

I reached over for the handheld VHF, already monitoring Channel 16, held it close in front of my face and pressed the transmit button:

> 'Mayday, Mayday, Mayday, this is *Avel Dro, Avel Dro, Avel Dro …*'

Swansea Coastguard responded immediately. A calm female voice with a strong Welsh accent asked me various supplementary questions. I was steering with one hand in large seas, trying to keep the boat perpendicular to the breaking crests, and holding the VHF with the other. After summarising the situation, I needed to stop talking and concentrate on my steering.

'Don't worry,' she said: 'I have already called out both Appledore lifeboats. They will be with you shortly.'

The inshore boat reached us first, shortly followed by the all weather craft. But by that stage we had already cleared the breakers, bailed out the boat again and were sailing into the harbour. Two crews of RNLI volunteers had been disturbed from their ordinary lives to come and help us, which was very humbling. So do I regret making the call? Not at all. Jacques has a young family, and I was not going to risk depriving them of a father out of embarrassment in calling for help in a perilous situation that was getting rapidly beyond us.

Out into the West

Every memorable voyage needs an objective: long-desired and perhaps also feared. The remote Île de Sein became mine many years ago. My dinghy lay becalmed in the Raz de Sein, off the western cliffs of Brittany, surrounded by great lighthouses. The island floated seductively on the Atlantic horizon, a thin shimmering line that beckoned me onwards, out into the west. But I was already late on my tide. Soon the waters of Biscay would begin to rush northwards, shouldering their way between the island and the mainland, and the silky sea beneath me would become a torrent.

The Celtic west of Brittany is rich in legends. They tell of Gradilon, King of the ancient realm of Cornouaille, who reigned in the fabulous coastal city of Ys. And also of the stunning beauty of his daughter Dahut, the despair of her aged father. Dahut was dazzlingly fair but also duplicitous. She broke the heart of many a good suitor. But eventually she found a man to her taste and, maddened by desire, she yielded unto him the keys of the sluices that protected the great city from the sea. In that instant, her lover was revealed as Satan himself. And in his malice he opened the gates, and the great waters swept in, drowning the inhabitants and covering Ys forever. The Île de Sein is the last sad remnant of that long lost city, they say.

Like Dahut, the Île de Sein is perilous, but intensely seductive. My Baggywrinkle *was a good boat, well found and weatherly. A traditional clinker 12ft dinghy from one of the last traditional English yards to build such craft, we had shared many adventures. I knew her capabilities, but also her limitations. I knew I could*

not risk a voyage out to sea so late in the day. Instead I rowed her close inshore, seeking somewhere to spend the night. The western buttresses of mainland Europe towered over my little dinghy. The ocean swell sucked at their barnacled feet, and swirled over underwater rocks.

Rounding the Pointe du Van, a broad bay opened out ahead, the Baie des Trépassés – the Bay of the Dead. Local tradition holds that the bodies of druids were taken from here to the sacred island of Sein for burial. But the real reason for the name is clear to any seaman. With its maw gaping wide towards the prevailing wind and teeth-like promontories on each side, the bay is a death trap for sailing vessels.

BAGGYWRINKLE anchored at the
uttermost edge of mainland Europe.

On the northern side of the bay I found a little cove bounded by high crags, where a handful of local fishing boats were lying on mooring buoys. I anchored as close in as I could. Too afraid of the great ocean to the west to erect my boat tent, I slept out in the open, ready to make sail suddenly if the wind shifted. All night long my boat swayed and tugged at her anchor, as the Atlantic swell snored on the cliffs around me.

I awoke early, sodden with dew. It was a bright clear morning. There was a light wind off the land, so I hoisted sail and set a hopeful course towards the distant island. But the wind failed to live up to its early promise, and then the tide turned against me. Eventually I admitted defeat and returned to the cove. I was trapped in the Bay of the Dead – at least until the next slack water.

As I dropped anchor a group of men in yellow fishing trousers hailed me from a boat on one of the moorings.

'Voudriez-vous de la liqueur anglaise?'

I smiled and waved back, wondering what this 'English liquor' might be. They sent a dinghy over to get me. I clambered aboard their workaday vessel and we all shook hands. One of them fished a bottle of 'Paddy' out from under their lobster pots. Glasses were filled with generous measures of the Irish whiskey. I could barely understand a word of their strongly accented Breton French, but we were all buddies well before the second round of drinks. So it was that I never got to the Île de Sein, but I had discovered a great truth: you are never short of a welcome if you sail a small open boat along the coast.

8 COASTAL NAVIGATION

'Qui voit Sein, n'a plus peur du lendemain' (Miossec)

Seven years after I failed to sail to the île de Sein in my old Tideway dinghy, I returned to Brittany with the larger dinghy I still own, confident my new boat would take me safely out to the island. I set out alone from the adorable port town of Douarnenez. All day I sailed slowly westwards, across the deep bay of Douarnenez. Finally I cleared the Cap de la Chèvre and emerged into the open sea. As I did so, three British square-riggers rounded the point under full sail: the PHOENIX, the EARL OF PEMBROKE and the KASKELOT, a poignant vision of the days before great sailing ships were swept from the seas. They braced their yards and bore away northwards towards England, while I continued into the west.

AVEL DRO leaving Douarnenez.

The Île de Sein, in hope and fear

The familiar lighthouses of the Raz de Sein were bathed in sunlight: the tall white tower on Sein itself, grey castellated La Vieille, and cottage-like Tévennec perched on its shoal. Avel Dro lifted to the ocean swell, the bosomy curve of her brown lugsail swaying across the sky. The coastal cliffs stood out crisply in the evening light, and yet it seemed as if the Île de Sein was inexplicably indistinct. Then the island vanished altogether. Suddenly the sea fog rolled over me too. It grew cold and clammy. Avel Dro slid silently onwards, surrounded by a claustrophobic circle of mist, like a bully circling for a fight.

Swirling eddies upwelled from the deeps, sending my vessel shearing off her compass course. I realised that Avel Dro must be entering an area of tidal overfalls, caused by the close proximity of a shoal. I plotted a GPS position. We were close to the Tévennec reef, invisible in the murk.

Tévennec has an evil reputation. Before the lighthouse was automated, the posting drove its lonely keepers to madness or death. They claimed that the unquiet souls of the dead groaned around the shoal in rough seas. I imagined the swell surging over its cruel rocks. What if a back eddy took my boat and sucked her helplessly in among them?

At that moment the mist lifted to unveil Tévennec itself. The reality was far worse than my imagination. Sharp shoals swarmed around the lighthouse rock, seas pouring off them in streams of white foam. Now that I could see them, I was aware of their ominous roar. And behind the noise of the waves, at the uttermost edge of hearing, an intermittent cry hung in the mist. It was a groan of ineffable melancholy. Did the shipwrecked dead really haunt this lonely shoal?

Fog plays tricks on the mind, they say, and perhaps also the ears. But just in case I was not imagining the noise, I scoured the chart for a whistle buoy. Eventually I found one close by, called Cornoc-an-ar-Braden, marking the start of the passage through the shoals into Sein harbour. This old-fashioned piece of navigation raised my damp spirits, and I sailed on with renewed confidence. Soon Tévennec vanished into the mist astern.

The Tévennec shoal in fair weather, seen from AVEL DRO. The distant lighthouse on the far left is La Vieille, which stands in the middle of the Raz de Sein.

Alone again in my ring of fog and water, I continued to make frequent GPS plots. A line of pencil crosses crept across the chart towards an intricate belt of shoals called la Chaussée de Sein, that surrounds the Île de Sein and extends a further 10 miles into the ocean beyond.

After some time a green buoy resolved itself from the miasma ahead. It heaved towards me over the seas, howling like a dog. At that moment, the fog lifted to uncloak the island itself – revealing an indistinct grey line punctuated by lighthouses and radio masts. Scattered rocks poked alarmingly out of the sea in all directions, but it was the ones skulking underwater that I really feared.

The safe passage into Sein harbour is marked by a white beacon on the quayside, which must be aligned with a vertical black line painted on a house beyond. Inevitably, this transit was straight into the eye of the wind, with shoals swirling in the swell on each side. I close-tacked up the transit, judging my turns between the rocks, that heaved beneath the swell like whales.

Snug at last inside the drying harbour and with darkness falling, I laid out a stern anchor and a long painter to the quay. I had just finished putting up the boat tent when a stout bearded figure in a faded yellow smock appeared on the quayside. His name was Abel, he said, and would I like to join him for dinner that evening?

I waded ashore and we shook hands.

'There is no time to lose,' he said, 'if we are to get home before my wife starts cooking.'

My new friend hurried me down a series of narrow passageways, squeezing between the plain rendered houses that enclosed the little harbour. Eventually we came to Abel's house.

Avel Dro moored fore and aft in Sein harbour, with her temporary tarpaulin tent.

Abel in the first Ilur, passing the Men Brial beacon at the mouth of Sein harbour.

Externally as austere as all the others, inside it was a cosy den, comfortably furnished from items of driftwood. Here the three of us ate the fish Abel had caught from the shoals around his island home, earlier that day.

Abel explained that it was his habit to stroll along to the Men Brial beacon at the harbour mouth each evening, and gaze over the sea. From there he had seen my dinghy emerge out of the northern mist. Despite the red ensign flying from the peak of her brown lugsail, he recognised her as a French vessel. Surely she was one of François Vivier's 'Ilur' class? I confirmed that this was the case. He smiled and passed me a photograph album. It was full of images of Abel building the prototype Ilur dinghy for the magazine Le Chasse Marée, many years before. This very boat was lying on a mooring in the harbour, not far from mine.

It was as if we had discovered we both loved the same woman. We yarned late into the night, swapping tales of our adventures. We compared our boats' abilities, shook our heads at their idiosyncrasies, and shared what we adored about them. It was very late before I returned down the sinuous passageways of Sein to my little dinghy, dried out in the harbour. The sky above the shadowy rooftops was a meadow of stars, swept by the powerful beams of the tall lighthouse of Sein.

I would have loved to stay longer on this remarkable island, but I had to rush away to catch the tide early the next afternoon, bound north towards Camaret, eight hours' sail away. Abel accompanied me out of the harbour in his own Ilur. As we sailed companionably past the Men Brial light at the entrance to the harbour, a school of dolphins played in the water around us. Eventually our two luggers parted beside Cornoc-an-ar-Braden, still moaning in the rolling swell. Then the tide swept me away rapidly northwards, and the faded orange sail of Abel's dinghy quickly dwindled to a speck among the rocks.

DINGHY NAVIGATION

A few intrepid voyagers take their little dinghies across the wide seas, but most dinghy cruising takes place in sight of land.

Coastal navigation is often simply a case of checking the scenery to make sure you know where you are, but even a modest coastal passage can become menacing if the weather changes or visibility suddenly reduces due to a rain squall or dense sea fog. You must never become complacent about navigation and always keep track of your position, even in familiar waters.

It is not the purpose of this book to replace a general navigational textbook. Look elsewhere if you need to know the shapes of buoys and the characteristics of navigational lights. I assume that you know all that already, or you will make it your business to find out. In this chapter we will concentrate on the particular techniques required to navigate a dinghy on the wild ocean waste.

Ideally, anyone planning to take a boat out of sheltered waters will take a formal navigation course, such as those offered by the Royal Yacht Association in the UK. A good grounding in general navigational theory is vital for anyone taking a boat to sea. You need to know the textbook technique even though you will hardly ever use much of it in a dinghy. The reality of navigation in a dinghy is a complete contrast to classroom methods. Experienced dinghy navigators reduce chartwork to a bare minimum, not out of laziness, but because it is difficult to navigate accurately in a small boat on open water.

Passage planning

I seem to keep saying this, but on any passage, the most important navigation is always done before you set off. You should always make some sort of passage plan. Study the pilot book, pore over the chart, identify any critical dangers and familiarise yourself with the local tides. Then work out a programme for the passage, with estimated times for departure, arrival, and for all the vital stages in between. Depending on the complexity of the passage, and how familiar you are with the local waters, a plan for a coastal passage may only be a note of the tide times and heights for the day, but usually it will be rather more detailed than this.

On most passage plans, the objective is to identify the 'zone of safety' that you intend to remain in throughout the passage, and the various landmarks, clearing lines or transits that you plan to use to ensure you do not stray outside it. Navigation does not mean knowing exactly where you are at all times, but you must be absolutely certain where you are not.

We have already dealt with tidal planning in Chapter 3, when we looked at sailing in sheltered waters. The tidal plan for an open sea passage is very similar. With good planning, you should be able to ensure that the tides generally work in your favour. I also like to minimise windward sailing, as far as possible. It is also vital to devise at least one escape route to a safe harbour or refuge, preferably on a course that will be both downwind and downtide.

This chapter opened with the description of a passage to the Île de Sein, off the west coast of Brittany. The passage was done with the aid of GPS, but without a chartplotter, so I used a combination of GPS waypoints and bearings to keep track of my position. This is how it was done.

The island is separated from the mainland by a sound called the Raz de Sein (the Race of Sein), and it was absolutely

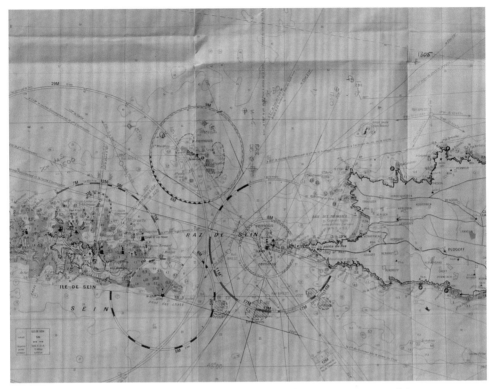

The French chart of the Raz de Sein, marked up with Avel Dro's positions on passage to the Île de Sein. The frequency of the positions increased when she was in the fog. (Éditions Grafocarte)

vital that I crossed this channel at slack water, so my passage plan hinged around the tides in the Raz.

According to my tidal atlas, slack water was at 14h00. I stepped off the distance on the chart from my starting port of Douarnenez with my dividers, opened at a scale distance of 3 nautical miles. The island was six steps of the dividers away, so it would be a passage of six hours at an average speed of 3 knots. This meant leaving Douarnenez at 08h00. Leafing through the tidal atlas, I noted that the pages between 08h00 and 02h00 showed a slight tide in my favour. In the event, I sailed slower than my predicted 3 knots due to the light wind, so I amended my passage plan before I reached the Raz.

GPS waypoints

Not so long ago, all my navigation was by compass, chart and lead line, but now my passage plans generally include the creation of GPS waypoints for critical points of the passage. I always mark my waypoints on the chart as well, so I have a picture in my mind of where they are.

On passage to the Île de Sein, my crucial waypoint was in the middle of the Raz at the point I intended to be at 14h00. Like most of my waypoints, it was placed at a major lat and long intersection, so it would be easy to check that I had inputted it correctly into the GPS. It was also right in the middle of a patch of sea, well away from rocks, buoys or anything else I did not want to bump into.

The first part of the passage was straightforward. I simply sailed along the southern coastline of the Bay of Douarnenez about a mile offshore. I could clearly see the coastline, so I simply marked GPS fixes on the chart every hour or so.

As I approached the Raz de Sein, it became apparent that I was an hour late on the tide, and an hour makes a lot of difference to the tides in the Raz. On the relevant page in the tidal atlas, a huge arrow was visible in the middle of the Raz, showing a strong current setting northwards. The wind was also blowing in the same direction. My emergency escape route involved sailing off to the north-east with the wind and tide, towards a sheltered bay in the lee of the Cap de la Chèvre, so my original intention of passing south of the rocky shoal of Tévennec began to feel misguided. The tide could set me into the shoal, which would also cut me off from my escape route.

Revisiting decisions

Navigation is about making firm decisions, but it is also about changing your mind. If the situation changes, you should not stick rigidly to a passage plan made hours beforehand. I needed a new course to steer, passing to the north of Tévennec. So I laid my Breton plotter on the chart and read off the compass bearing from my present position to a point in the sea close to the Île de Sein, but north of the shoal. Then I adjusted Avel Dro's heading until the GPS 'course over the ground' (COG) readout agreed with that bearing. The correct course to steer, allowing for the cross tide, was the one that had appeared on the steering compass.

This technique for working out a 'course to steer' is crude and simplistic, and you will be warned against using it in any formal navigation class, because it does not allow for future changes in the tidal stream, and simply reflects what the tide is doing at the time. Nonetheless, it can be extremely useful, if you recognise its limitations.

Half an hour later, I was enveloped in thick fog. Fortunately, my change of plan had put me comfortably downtide of any dangers. Just to be sure, I plotted another position at 14h45. Tévennec was a mile to the south-west. I spilled the wind from the sail and lay to. I needed to think things out carefully, while I still had the time and the sea room.

Closing with the land

I had to close with the land somewhere. One option was to continue to the Île de Sein close by, but upwind and surrounded by rocks and fickle tides. The alternative was to run off to my emergency refuge, a small cove in the lee of the Cap de la Chèvre, back in the Bay of Douarnenez. According to the excellent Almanach du Marin Breton, Sein harbour was a safe anchorage, but I knew that there would be a tide setting across the entrance channel, and even the Breton almanac could not tell me precisely how fast that current would run.

I try to avoid plotting GPS positions while I am sailing in confined waters. By the time you have plotted a position, it is already out of date. Instead, I like to navigate using a series of visual transits or compass bearings. But that technique is no use in fog. Nor could I simply sail along a GPS bearing, as I would have to tack all the way down the narrow channel to Sein harbour. I have sometimes been able to sound my way into a safe anchorage by following a depth contour, but the entrance to Sein harbour is half a mile long and less than a cable wide, with rocks rising directly

The transit out of Sein harbour, with Abel's Ilur in the foreground.

from the seabed on each side. Soundings could not get me into there.

Fortunately, the chart marked the white sector of the Men Brial lighthouse at the entrance to Sein harbour, delimiting the clear passage through the rocks. Fortuitously, the French yacht chart I was using also gave the compass bearings of the edges of the white sector. These were ready-made clearing lines. If I inputted the position of the lighthouse as a GPS waypoint, and tacked when the GPS gave the same bearing for the lighthouse as the bearings of the edges of the white sector, I would stay in the channel.

Making contingency plans

It's always good to identify what might go wrong in any passage plan. The main flaw with this one was that it relied totally on my GPS. But the GPS I used at that time was waterproof and could operate on either an internal battery or the 12-volt supply on board. I also had a spare handheld GPS. If the global satellite system were suddenly to go down (something we still worried about in those days), the sea was calm enough for me to anchor and wait until the fog lifted.

Without this convincing plan of action, it would have been foolhardy in the extreme to press on for the island, in zero visibility and in notoriously treacherous waters. But my new passage plan gave me confidence that I could get into a harbour I had never entered before, in a dense fog.

In the event, by the time *Avel Dro* got to the Cornoc-an-ar-Braden whistle buoy the fog had lifted, and I was able to tack down the 'cone' between the clearing lines in full visibility, watching the rocks slip by on each side.

You will notice how much of this account of my navigation is about contingency planning and strategic decision-making, and how little formal chartwork was carried out. This is how it should be. Good navigation should be like a test cricket match – lots of subtle strategy behind the scenes, but not always much drama on the pitch.

Today, using my chartplotter, I could tack into Sein harbour in a dense fog, totally 'blind', simply by watching the screen and tacking when the symbol of my dinghy approached the rocks on each side of the channel. It is almost too simple! In fact this technique would assume a level of precision in the charting of the rocks that cannot be relied on. It is always better to rely on charted clearing lines when sailing in shoal waters, as they will have been checked for accuracy, whereas the charted position of rocks themselves may be less accurate. None the less, the chartplotter allows me to make changes of passage plan on the fly, in a much less laboured way than when I had to manually input the lat and long positions of waypoints into the GPS.

On a chartplotter you can simply scroll the cursor across the screen, place it at the entrance of a haven you have decided to sail to, select 'Go To', and the plotter will give you the course and distance to the new destination. It is tempting to say that you should not do this unless you have gone through a schooling in traditional paper navigation first (as I have done – simply because I am old enough to remember when there was nothing else). That would be ridiculous though. Chartplotters are undoubtedly the key piece of navigation equipment on a modern boat, supplanting even the compass. But they need to be used intelligently, with an understanding of the underlying principles of navigation.

EQUIPMENT FOR SEA NAVIGATION

I have already listed various items of navigational equipment in Chapter 2 that should be carried aboard any cruising dinghy, even in sheltered waters. These need to be augmented for sea navigation.

1. A watch

I have my chartplotter display set to show the current time. But I still carry a watch. In the past an accurate timepiece competed with the compass for the status of the most important instrument on any vessel at sea, and even now I would not be without one. Make sure you have a decent watch that is fully waterproof, with a secure strap so it will not get flicked off your wrist. It is easy to be caught out at sea by nightfall, and most luminous watches only work for about an hour before they need to be refreshed by an external light source, which is hopeless. I have never regretted investing in a watch with tritium markings that glow all the time.

Older GPS sets are sometimes only capable of displaying the time in UTC (effectively the same as GMT or British winter time), and so a watch set to the current local time saves any confusion.

2. Charts

On passage, you may need more than one chart. It is good practice to carry one at a small scale showing the whole passage, supplemented by larger-scale charts of your destination and departure ports. Official charts are excellent, and you cannot really go wrong with them. In UK waters these are Admiralty charts. The corresponding ones available in France are published by SHOM, and other countries have their equivalents. Official charts use the same symbols throughout the world, and most of the abbreviations are in English, whatever the language of the country.

Various independent publishers produce specialist yacht charts, which have a number of advantages over the official ones. Typically, they will include large-scale insets of popular harbours and anchorages, and often incorporate pilotage notes and tidal stream information. They may also be waterproof or water resistant, and overprinted with a grid of squares to make the plotting of GPS positions much simpler.

3. Steering compass

All sea boats should have a proper steering compass, fixed in one position and visible from the helm. The selection and fitting of these was fully covered in Chapter 6.

4. Waterproof chart case

Although some charts are waterproof, it's wise to keep your chart in a waterproof case as well, to protect it from damage and from being blown away. Chart cases are sized to take either a half-folded or quarter-folded Admiralty chart. The smaller size is best in a dinghy. Sadly, I have never been able to find a suitably robust chart case. They are either not completely waterproof, not quite the right size or they inevitably break. I usually have to buy a new chart case every year because the previous one has been damaged and is no longer waterproof.

It is possible to mark positions and bearings on the outside of a chart case with a chinagraph pencil, but the chart tends to move around within the case and makes these inaccurate. For this reason I usually open the case, push my hand inside and mark the positions directly on the chart inside with a normal pencil. This is

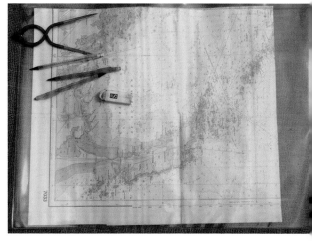

A waterproof chart case, pencils, dividers and rubber.

Positions can be marked on the chart by putting your hand inside the chart case.

rather annoying in heavy rain, but it seems to be unavoidable.

Some people cut up their charts to a handy size and then have them 'heat sealed' in plastic film, so they become completely waterproof. Then they use chinagraph pencils, to write on them. This is an excellent idea, but complicated to arrange if you sail in lots of different places and have a drawer full of charts at home.

5. Pencils and dividers

Even in the age of electronics, making notes and plotting courses is still a vital part of navigation, so you will need pencils. Take a good number of them, as they love exploring the bilges. I tend to use 'non-stop' pencils, which have long, continuous HB leads, never need sharpening, and come with a soft rubber on the other end. A pair of 'one-handed' brass dividers is also useful for measuring off distances. They should be fairly blunt, so they do not puncture the chart case.

6. Transistor radio

The traditional way to receive weather information is by a small transistor radio, tuned into the waveband for the local shipping forecast. In UK waters this means listening to BBC Radio 4 on long wave (LW). The BBC broadcast an inshore forecast outrageously early in the morning, when you are still in bed. In case you oversleep, they transmit another one very late at night, long after you are back in bed again. On passage, you just have to get used to setting an alarm for 05h15, and ensure that you are sitting up awake in time for the 05h20 forecast. I often stay in my sleeping bag, write the forecast in my logbook, then lie down again and go back to sleep again for another hour or so. You will often be able to use an app on your smartphone to obtain a weather forecast, but the radio shipping forecast is still one of the most reliable ways of receiving weather information. For this reason it is vital that your radio set has LW in addition to the more normal FM and MW channels. Many small radios do not do so. If you are sailing alone, a radio is also good company.

7. Logbook

The logbook is a key part of your armoury of navigational tools. You can buy impressive ones from yacht chandlers, with embossed covers and columns to fill in, but these are rather out of place on a workaday cruising dinghy. I use the A6 artist's sketchpads made by Moleskine.

Be firm with yourself and try to make a log entry at least once an hour if in the open sea. Then if fog descends or your GPS goes down, you will be able to work back through the information recorded in your logbook and plot a good estimated position.

A proper log entry should take the following form:

> Time. Course. Wind direction and strength. Event.

The 'event' may be a GPS position (which should be written in the book before it is plotted on the chart), a note to record that you are abeam of a certain buoy or headland, or a course change. I usually put my log entries on the right-hand page of the logbook, and my passage planning notes on the facing page. I also use the left-hand page to note down the latest weather forecast.

Since I fitted my chartplotter, I do not plot GPS positions quite as often as I did, but I still write down the time I have passed various landmarks and seamarks, and note down my lat and long position from time to time in the logbook. Even if this position is not plotted on the chart, it remains available for reference if my electronics were to go down. Should I ever need to revert to traditional navigation, I could work back from my last recorded position.

THE ILUR

François Vivier writes of his Ilur design: 'This dinghy was designed for family daysailing, fishing and even coastal cruising. Two Ilurs have sailed to the Île of Sein, at the extreme west of France, one of the worst places to go, with tremendous tides and bad sea conditions. The Ilur is my best-selling plan, with nearly one thousand copies sold.

'If you are choosing the best boat for your intended use, bear in mind that the Ilur is not as easygoing under oars as my other "sail and oar" designs, like the Aber. The Ilur is wider and higher, with a generous freeboard. This makes her a very different boat, with good sea-keeping ability. She is mainly intended to sail, with the oars being used when wind is falling or to enter a narrow inlet.

'A daggerboard was initially preferred in order to give more room, but it has now been replaced by a pivoting centreboard and a low centreboard case. Many other improvements have been continuously incorporated. As an example, the oars may now be stowed under the bottom boards, leaving a free cockpit when sailing.

'Ilur was designed with the simple lugsail in the Breton style (called the "misainier" rig). But a lug sloop rig is also now available and is a valuable option. A single balance lug is another option, and this is an ideal arrangement for river or singlehanded sailing.

'Construction is either strip planked or plywood clinker. In both cases, laminated or steam bent frames give a very traditional and beautiful looking hull. However, very detailed plans and an instruction booklet allow construction by any home builder. Full size patterns may be purchased in addition to the building plan to make construction easier. A clinker kit is also available on demand.'

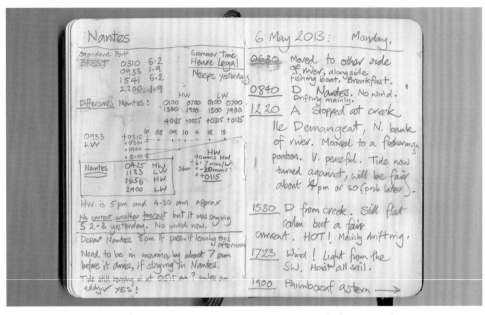

Avel Dro's logbook, with the passage notes on the left. This is for a trip down the Loire River, and an unusually complex tidal calculation was required.

8. Nautical almanac

All seagoing boats should have an up-to-date almanac on board. Tidal information can be obtained from other sources, but the almanac is an encyclopaedic backstop if there is an unexpected gap in any other source of information. Charts have a nasty habit of omitting the sound signals or the light characteristics of minor buoys, but these will be included in the almanac's List of Lights. A good almanac will also have the answer to most unexpected questions that crop up at sea. What is that weird pattern of navigation lights? What is the VHF working channel of the local harbourmaster? Some almanacs also include large scale harbour chartlets. Frustratingly, these are often marked 'not to be used for navigation', but they are still better than nothing if the chips are down.

9. Binoculars

The classic naval binocular is 7 x 50, and this is what you want too. Don't be fobbed off with anything more powerful, or with smaller lenses. Binoculars with more power than x7 cannot be held still enough when

Using 7 x 50 binoculars. These have a compass built in to take bearings.

the dinghy is bouncing around, and 50mm lenses are vital to pick out a distant buoy in poor visibility. Decent binoculars are invaluable for locating transits, identifying landmarks and other vessels, and they can also be used for birdwatching. They must be waterproof, gas filled and rubber armoured. You can spend a fortune on binoculars, and no doubt you get what you pay for. Bearing in mind the rough life they will suffer in a dinghy, and the likelihood of dropping them over the side, I would go for a modestly priced pair.

10. Handbearing compass

Since we all bought GPS sets, we have stopped taking quite so many bearings. But there are still times when a compass bearing is the fastest way to work out

where you are. A succession of identical bearings taken off an approaching ship is unequivocal evidence that you are on a collision course – handy information if you are crossing a shipping lane.

For coastal passagemaking I prefer to use a proper handbearing compass, with illumination for taking bearings in the dark. Some steering compasses are designed so that they can be removed from their mounts and also used for taking bearings.

11. Tidal atlas

Tidal atlases are my preferred source of information about the rate and direction of tidal streams. The information is presented graphically, so it is easy to transfer the tidal vector from the atlas to the chart using a Breton plotter. Charts have tidal

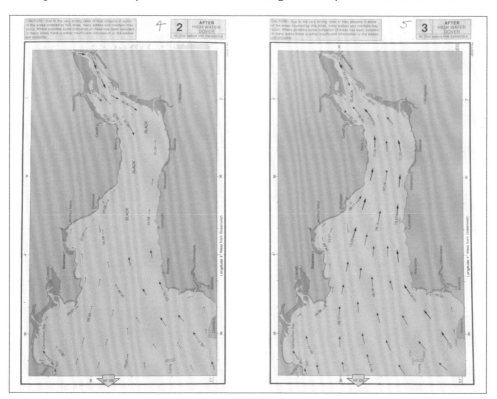

Two pages of the tidal atlas for the Bristol Channel. I have marked the times in pencil for 4 and 5 o'clock. (Admiralty)

diamonds on them, which also give detailed information on tidal flows, but it is difficult to get an overall picture of the currents using this method. When you are in a small boat bouncing about in the waves, it is easy to misread the numbers and get the direction of flow wrong.

Almanacs include tidal atlas pages, but I like to use the British Admiralty booklets. These are A4 size and very easy to read. The Admiralty publish a tidal atlas for each sea area, with a page for each hour of the tide, from six hours before high water to six hours afterwards. Before I set out on an open sea passage, I ritualistically mark each page in pencil with the relevant time for that day, writing the number of the hour on each page. I do not use the 24-hour clock, as the tidal streams during the second twelve hours are nearly the same as the first, so a page marked '9' can be considered to apply to 9am and 9pm.

Chartplotters can be set to show arrows displaying the current tidal streams. These are extremely useful, but in my chartplotter's software the arrows have been pointing in the wrong directions in the waters off La Rochelle for many years, and one wonders where else this is the case.

12. Breton plotter

Complicated chartwork is difficult when out at sea in a dinghy, which is why most chartwork is done before you set off for the day. But when you do need to do it, a Breton plotter is the simplest way of transferring bearings onto the chart and to plot vectors. I am never without mine, and I take it with me even when I am sailing on other people's boats, just in case.

If you have a GPS device, you will rarely need to plot a tidal vector in order to work up an Estimated Position (EP)

in the traditional way. It is still helpful to be able to plot vectors for a 'course to steer', however. I do this by drawing a line showing the course I want to make over a specific number of hours. I then plot the tidal vectors for the whole passage all at once with my Breton plotter, using the information from the tidal atlas.

If you need to do it, a Breton plotter is also the most convenient way to plot a GPS position on the chart. Assuming you have set your GPS to show the bearing and direction of the waypoint you are sailing towards, and the position of the waypoint is marked accurately on the chart, the quickest way to work out your position is to use the GPS range and direction readings, rather than lat and long. Use a pencil against the edge of your Breton plotter to draw a line marking the bearing from the waypoint. Then plot your distance from it by referring to the latitude scale on the side of the chart. This can be measured with your dividers, or even with your thumb against the side of the plotter.

13. Pilot book

A good pilot book is an extremely useful source of navigational information. It will tell you all about the local harbours and anchorages; it will warn of any dangers and give courses to steer; it will even provide photographs of transits and aerial photographs of the entrance channels. Some pilot books even include accurate chartlets.

There are good pilots and bad ones. Bad ones are encumbered with too much froth about local history, the scenery and places to eat. Good ones stick to the necessary navigational information, are curt and to the point. They give you the information you need clearly and succinctly, in the middle of the night, in the rain and a big sea.

A traditional Walker log mounted on Avel Dro. The coil in the foreground is the impeller rope that must be trailed astern.

14. GPS or chartplotter

Handheld GPS sets are so cheap and so fiendishly accurate nowadays that it is crazy not to carry one, and it will inevitably become your main means of navigation. As has already been mentioned, I have now fitted a chartplotter in my dinghy. This amazing device is not only loaded with fully detailed charts of my usual sailing area, but also gives me up to date information about tidal heights, even in a secondary port. It is a wonder and a revelation.

You can generally alter the settings of a GPS or chartplotter to show particular information on the screen. Other than your position in lat and long, the most useful outputs are the bearing and distance of the waypoint you are sailing towards, your COG (Course Over the Ground) and your speed. I also like to know my ETE, (the

Estimated Time that will Elapse before I get to a waypoint or my destination). This is far more useful than an ETA (Estimated Time of Arrival). My chartplotter is also set to display the current local time.

15. Ship's log

Now that even the most traditional sailors have bowed to the inevitable and bought a GPS or a chartplotter, a traditional yacht log may seem unnecessary. But the GPS speed readout only tells you your geographic speed relative to your lat and long position, and not your speed through the water. If you want to maintain an old-fashioned DR plot, as we all did in the tough times before GPS, you will need to know your 'distance run' through the water, and this is provided by a traditional ship's log. They are still made for use on yachts and usually require an impeller to be mounted through a hole in the hull, as well as a source of 12-volt power.

An alternative is to purchase an old-fashioned trailing log, such as the famous 'Knotmaster', built by Walkers in the UK until the 1990s. Thousands of these were made, and they are still widely available second-hand. The most modern type was moulded in Bakelite and is less sought after by collectors than the earlier brass models, so it is rather cheaper. It has a clock face on one end, containing a series of dials clearly visible behind a hinged glass window. It will not give you a speed readout but just counts off the nautical miles.

A Walker log locks into a special bayonet fitting that should be mounted near the stern of the boat. A long line trails astern, on the end of which is a weighted impeller, which rotates the mechanism. Walker logs need no electricity and never go wrong (as long as you remember to oil them occasionally and check that the impeller has not become fouled by weed). They will count the miles with quiet efficiency, just as they did for Robin Knox-Johnston, Bernard Moitessier, and all the great yachtsmen of old.

Streaming the trailing log as you leave port is a hallowed ritual of the sea. It symbolises the moment when you stop grovelling around in the shallows and begin deep-water navigation. But remember to bring in the log line before you enter harbour, or it will undoubtedly foul the bottom and you will lose the impeller.

As I revise this book for the second edition in 2021, the fitting for my Walker log is still in place on my dinghy. But I no longer normally carry the log, its line and its impeller, as the space seems better allocated to other things. I now assume that I will always to be able to use one or another of the many means of electronic navigation I have on board, and it is improbable I will ever have to run a dead reckoning plot using a log, tidal atlas and compass bearings, as we used to have to do when sailing out of familiar waters. So the world has changed, and the old ways begin to be forgotten.

16. Anemometer

It is the convention on big ships to note down the prevailing wind speed in the logbook, and this is generally estimated by looking at the prevailing sea conditions. I often suspect that other sailors are wildly overstating the wind strength when they recount their adventures in the bar afterwards.

If you want to be truly accurate, you will need to take real wind readings with an anemometer. Only then will you know for certain what a Force 6 looks like in the open sea, and the next time you are caught out in one, you will not claim it was a Gale Force 8 in the pub afterwards. The risk is that your tall stories may have to reduce in stature.

SAILING AMONG SHOALS

Pilot books have a tendency to give sailing directions as a series of compass courses. These are only helpful if you always navigate in shoal waters under power, as modern yachts usually do. A dinghy under sail will invariably diverge from a series of compass courses. It is better to keep track of your position with reference to landmarks. Rocks make very good ones. Seeing rocks all around you is scary, but a rock that can be confidently identified on the chart is the best position fix you can get. Navigation buoys can drag their moorings, GPS sets may go on the blink, but rocks are rock-solid.

When you were learning to drive a car, perhaps your instructor advised you to aim at the space between other vehicles, rather than fixate on the vehicles themselves. Navigating between rocks is just like that. You must learn to see the gaps, not the rocks themselves.

It is not necessary to know the exact position of every rock in the water around your boat. That way lies madness. But you must identify the crucial clearing lines or transits that you will use to keep within an area of safe water. Note these down in your logbook or on the chart. Try to picture in advance how you will sail through confined waters, and the landmarks you will use to keep track of your progress, even while tacking. This is not always easy. Places that look straightforward on the chart can be very confusing at sea level. Rocks, islands

and the shore behind merge into a single line of scenery. Navigational text books generally show someone taking a bearing off a 'prominent white house' or a navigation beacon, but often all you see in real life is a confused mass of rocks against a featureless shoreline. Relating the chart to the view can be very difficult.

Using a chartplotter in shoal waters

Chartplotters are a great help in stressful navigational situations. They give an instant picture of your surroundings and a helpful symbol saying 'You Are Here'. But it is perilous to rely on them completely. They will tell you where you are with wondrous accuracy and clarity, but their little screens

I have found two very clear objects to take bearings off to make a three-point fix: a church spire and a white beacon on the shoreline, but my third bearing line is taken off the cliffs at the end of the point, which is much less clearly defined. The tide sets strongly across the entrance of this thorny French anchorage, so I have also prepared a simple tidal vector for a 'course to steer', once I emerge into the full force of the cross tide.

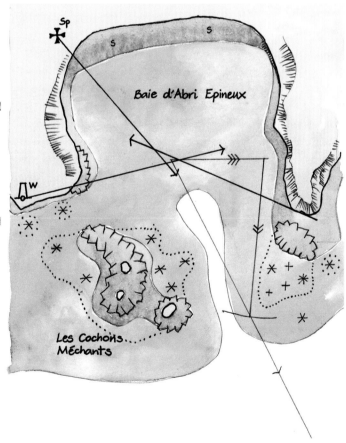

Baie d'Abri Epineux

Les Cochons Méchants

cannot show much of the sea around you. Although you can zoom in and out, this rapidly gets confusing. If you also refer back to a paper chart, you will not lose track of the big picture.

An electronic device will tell you where you are, but it cannot give you counsel. In close-quarters navigation, everything starts happening very quickly, and there is no time to take stock. We all get caught on the hop like this sometimes. The best advice in any stressful navigational situation is to stop where you are. Drop anchor or retrace your steps. Give yourself time to think. A passage plan through an area of shoal water should start with an identifiable safe position. This may be a buoy or a distinctive rock. If you run into difficulties and wonder which way to turn, retrace your steps to the safe position and start again.

FIXES

In traditional navigation, a 'fix' is established by taking a series of bearings off a number of objects that are clearly identified on the chart and also in real life. Three bearings – ideally about 60 degrees apart – are considered the minimum to establish an accurate position.

If you have been accurate in your bearing-taking, the position lines will form a very small triangle or 'cocked hat'. If you are taking bearings from a dinghy at sea, they will usually form a very generous triangle, or 'cock-up hat'. I like to take fixes by using a handbearing compass and then plotting them with my Breton plotter, which can be set to take account of the local compass variation. I also have a compass in my binoculars, which is helpful for picking out distant buoys and then taking an instant bearing off them.

Since the advent of electronic navigation, this traditional method of

taking a fix has become a less vital part of my navigational armoury, but it is good to keep in practice. I still take a three-point fix to locate where I have anchored sometimes, so that a quick bearing will check if my anchor is dragging.

A NAVIGATIONAL CONUNDRUM

This conundrum is not an artificial navigation test. It is a real situation that occurred during a dinghy passage a couple of decades ago, before any of us had electronic navigation. It was not a matter of life and death, and there is no 'right' answer, but it will be interesting to see if you would have made the same choices that I did.

We were on a short trip in my old 12ft Tideway dinghy from Pin Mill to the Walton Backwaters, involving a sea passage between Harwich Harbour and Stone Point, at the entrance to the Backwaters. Although we had a chart and a passage plan, we did not have an accurate method of measuring our speed through the water. We also had no engine on board. What we did have was a good pair of oars, steering and handbearing compasses, a Breton plotter, a lead line, an anchor and the necessary gear to camp aboard.

The relevant chart is still marked with my planned courses, and a section of it is shown here. The courses were marked on the chart before I set off. I had planned two alternative routes from Shelf Buoy to Stone Point, one of 187M to Pye End Buoy, and then turning to 237M for the Backwaters. The other route cut directly across the shallows on 210M. (In both cases the 'M' means 'magnetic'.) Both courses had their reciprocal marked, in case we needed to retrace our route. I also wrote down the

My Stanford's chart of the entrance of Harwich Harbour, marked up with the courses to the Walton Backwaters, as well as the course to Woodbridge we used later in the week.

Pye End Buoy's light characteristics, taken from the almanac, as these were not marked on the chart. (The course of 269/089 going off to the right was for another day's passage to Woodbridge.)

It was a sunny day, with a light NW wind and a calm sea. As we emerged from Harwich Harbour we could see a container ship well out to sea, off our port bow, inbound to Felixstowe. She was nothing to worry about, though. We knew we could keep clear of her. But at that very moment, a sea mist suddenly enveloped us. We were steering 187M and there was no cross tide. Just before the fog blotted out the view, we noted that Landguard Point was directly abeam to port.

If you were in our position, what would you do to sail into safety? The last of the tide was taking us out of Harwich. We could hear a deep fog horn, which was presumably the container ship making her way up the deep-water channel towards us, so we certainly needed to keep well clear of the buoyed navigation channel. Beating back into busy Harwich Harbour did not seem sensible, as it would be too difficult to keep track of our position when tacking upwind. But could we risk carrying on? With no log to measure our speed, how would we know when to change course in order to get into the narrow entrance of the Walton Backwaters?

How we solved the conundrum

The textbook answer to this conundrum is to sail straight into the shallows, then follow a depth contour until we detected the deep water of the entrance to the Backwaters. We could then sail into the entrance. This is a good solution for a vessel fitted with an echo sounder, but more difficult to pull off in a small dinghy with only a lead line. I wanted a much simpler method of finding my way to the Walton Backwaters.

What we actually did was almost ridiculously simple. We altered course to aim straight for the entrance to the Backwaters. We also lowered the steel centreplate, which had been raised as we were sailing off the wind. I had a pretty good idea where we were when the fog came down, so I could work out this course fairly easily using my Breton plotter. I did not make any allowance for the slight cross tide, nor for leeway, so I knew that this 'course to steer' would actually bring us to the coast slightly to the south of the entrance to the Backwaters. This choice also had the benefit of taking us away from the deep-water channel, and into the empty shallows.

After an hour of sailing through the fog, our centreplate started making a clunking noise as it grated on shingle. This signalled that we had reached the shingle bank just south of the entrance to the Backwaters (marked orange on the chart). We immediately turned sharply to starboard and sailed due west until the noise stopped. This indicated that we were in deep water again, just to the north of the shingle bank, so we altered course to 237M, onto the course I had previously worked out, which would take us through the entrance channel into the Backwaters.

Suddenly a red can buoy loomed out of the fog, confirming our position, and we followed the buoys through the narrows into the safety of the Backwaters. It is very satisfying to navigate like this, applying navigational theory in a simple and direct way, to find your way along the coast.

9 DINGHY HOMEMAKING

When I first saw Baggywrinkle, she had the confident air of a real sea boat. She was a traditional clinker dinghy, built of mahogany planks clenched to steam-bent oak timbers with rows of copper nails, faded red sails and an array of wooden blocks. I was seduced and paid the vendor the asking price. As I drove away from his house, with Baggywrinkle following proudly behind me on her trailer, he decided to give me some last-minute advice:

'She may need some time to "take up" after you put her in the water!' he shouted, just before he disappeared from view.

Baggywrinkle lying at anchor with her tent cover erected.

A first night away

My first overnight cruise in Baggywrinkle *was a Solent crossing from Buckler's Hard on the Beaulieu River across to the Isle of Wight. The final reach of the Beaulieu River was a furious beat into a fresh breeze, which threw up steep waves against the ebb. We flew frantically back and forth between the posts marking the navigation channel. Salt spray flashed over the weather bow, stinging our eyes and crashing into* Baggywrinkle's *bottom boards, where it joined the water spurting between her dried-out planks. Distracted by our frantic tacking, we did not notice how high the bilge water was mounting, surging heavily about our feet.*

A big motor cruiser was close astern, a yacht was motoring up against the tide, and various other vessels were entering the channel in the distance. We felt like pedestrians who had strayed into the middle of a motorway. There was no space to stop and bail our flooding dinghy. Out to starboard, seductively close, was the uncrowded expanse of the Solent, separated from us by a narrow belt of breakers where the tide was just covering a shingle spit. Gambling that there was sufficient depth to cut across the shallows, I hauled up the plate and plunged Baggywrinkle *into the breaking water. Weighed down by the mass of liquid swelling around inside her, she wallowed like a tired boxer no longer able to dodge the knockout blow. She barely lifted to the waves. They swept solidly over her varnished foredeck and poured off into her hull like a waterfall. She was settling under us, all fight gone out of her.*

As soon as we were clear of the breakers we bailed like maniacs. Once Baggywrinkle *was more like her old lithe self again, we bore off for the distant island. The wind scattered the clouds and a ray of sunshine bathed my boat in golden light, making her varnish glisten and her sails glow. I looked at her with joy and love. Sure, she needed a bit of bailing from time to time, but that just added to her appeal. She was a proper little ship.*

I had not intended to bring Frances on this experimental cruise. She was lodging in my house at the time, and had never been sailing before. But she looked so plaintive when I was loading up the boat that I had not the heart to leave her. She had no idea what she was letting herself in for.

Hemmed in by hills, the entrance to the River Medina was a confused mass of boats manoeuvring in the narrows. We reached through the melee and sailed on up into the river beyond. It was low tide, and wide mud flats separated the channel from the fields on each side.

We dropped anchor close to the edge of the mud, set up the tent cover and cooked our evening meal. When it was time for bed, we lifted the bottom boards and rested them on the seats to create a sleeping surface, well clear of the bilge water. This was an idea of my own devising, so we could sleep in Baggywrinkle's *leaky hull without drowning in our beds. We rolled out two camping mats and laid our sleeping bags on top. Our beds were a little hard perhaps, but the gentle rocking of the dinghy eventually sent us to sleep.*

A loud roar awakened me. It was pitch dark. I poked my head out of the tent and looked out over the transom. A black shape was throbbing up the river towards us, blotting out the shoreside lights as it passed. It was high tide, and we were no longer comfortably close to the bank. Our unlit dinghy was in the middle of a vast expanse of water. I sprang up, leaning heavily on the springy boards beneath me. There was a splintering noise and the board broke in two, plunging me into the bilge water beneath. I struggled out of my now sodden sleeping bag and flung open the tent doors.

The coaster was coming up fast, her navigation lights clearly visible. She surged past, close by. Baggywrinkle rocked urgently in her wash, setting our hanging lamp crashing from side to side. I jammed the broken boards back in place somehow and settled down to sleep again.

A damp half hour passed. I had just managed to nod off when a metallic crash echoed across the black water close by. A voice was issuing instructions over a tannoy:

'Down at the stern: load more for'ard!' … Crash!

The coaster was being loaded with scrap metal at a nearby wharf. The crashing and the shouting continued for some time, making sleep impossible. Wet and cold, I waited for the dawn.

Imperceptibly, a bleak grey light crept aboard, revealing Frances's haggard face, poking out of her bag. Amazingly, she was sound asleep. I shook her awake.

'Let's drop back to Cowes and get some breakfast,' I said.

It was horribly early in the morning, but by the time we had rowed down the river and moored to the visitor's pontoon, Cowes was beginning to wake up. We found a café and ordered two 'Full English' breakfasts, which we tucked into like trenchermen. Slowly the street came alive. Parties of people in matching yachting kit wandered up and down. One such party took the table next to us. Listening to their conversation, we realised that they were the crew of a racing yacht, and that it must be Cowes week – the social peak of the British yachting calendar.

Grubby, salt-stained and bleary-eyed, we walked back to our little dinghy and slipped away from festive Cowes. A mass of white yachts were dipping to their mooring buoys in the roadstead. Flags flew from the Royal Yacht Squadron clubhouse, glasses clinked and expensively educated voices rang out across the water. Our little varnished dinghy slid through the melee and away into the Solent. Soon all we could hear were the waves swishing past Baggywrinkle's varnished sides.

Back in the Beaulieu River, we hauled out Baggywrinkle at the slipway. A young couple were launching a laden 'Wanderer'. They looked critically at our loaded dinghy.

'We're going dinghy cruising too,' they said, 'but we've never sailed in the Solent before. Do you have any advice?'

'Don't anchor anywhere near the scrap metal wharf on the River Medina,' I said with great authority.

I did not tell them it had been my first overnight cruise.

BEACH CRUISING

There are as many ways to cruise in a dinghy as there are people doing it. Just because Frank Dye sailed an open dinghy from Scotland to Norway, surviving four capsizes and a broken mast, does not mean we all have to make such ambitious passages. Nor does everyone want to camp aboard a small boat. Some people will always prefer to sleep in a comfortable bed ashore.

But there is a glorious freedom in not returning to base each night. A weekend with just a single night away from home transforms two daysails into a real voyage. If you want to test yourself, you can emulate Frank Dye or the other pioneers of extreme dinghy cruising, but more modest passages provide real challenges and are an immensely satisfying way to spend a weekend.

A convenient way to make a first weekend cruise is to pack a small land tent and simply sail off over the horizon to a sheltered beach and pitch camp. The Americans call this 'beach cruising' and it is a magical way to use a small boat. Setting up a tent onshore every night works well on a lake or in a sea area with little tide and plenty of convenient camping places on the foreshore.

In the tideless Baltic Sea there are immense archipelagos of wooded islands through which you can meander in a dinghy, making camp on a different island every night, lighting a fire and cooking your food out in the open. I did this once in a flotilla of little dinghies, and it was a memorable experience. Baltic sailors rarely anchor far away from the shore. Instead they select a sheltered rockface with deep water close inshore, drop an anchor over the stern, bring the bows of the boat close to the rock, then step ashore with the painter and tie it round a convenient tree. The anchor and painter are adjusted to keep the boat afloat just clear of the bank. This is an extraordinarily pleasant way to spend a night, with the boat easily accessible the whole time.

Camping ashore by a lake.

If you are sailing along a crowded coastline, finding a secluded camping ground on the shoreline is rather more difficult than in a Baltic archipelago. A civilised solution is to sail between small harbour towns and check into a local hotel each night. If you plan the trip so that all the harbours have pontoon moorings, it will be easy to get ashore with your dunnage. In peak season it is wise to pre-book your hotel accommodation.

Sleeping aboard

There are many practical advantages to sleeping aboard your dinghy. Landing where there is a biggish tidal range can mean a long trudge across a muddy foreshore carrying all your camping gear. Passage planning is also more relaxed aboard a camping dinghy, as your boat does not need to arrive at any particular place at a particular time. If she is delayed by light winds or foul weather, you can anchor anywhere convenient, erect the boat tent and start cooking your evening meal.

When you first set out on an overnight voyage, you will feel a welling pride in your stout vessel, and a strong sense of self-sufficiency. You will look with pity at the local dinghies. Soon they will have to go slinking back to their slipway, whereas you are free of the land, and bound into the enigmatic waters behind the horizon.

First ventures

Although there are many practical reasons for sleeping aboard a dinghy, the main reason many of us do it is because we really enjoy the experience. Do not be put off if your first attempts are not a complete success, like my night on the River Medina. It takes a while to get into the swing of camping afloat. Ideally your first trip will be in waters you already know well. Plan a passage to a quiet cove that is sheltered in all winds. You will feel rather vulnerable sleeping afloat for the first time, so it is comforting to know that your anchorage is well protected if it blows up during the night.

It can feel strange erecting a tent in the middle of a stretch of water, in full view of everyone sailing past. On land, free camping is of dubious legality in some countries, but afloat in tidal water you can set up your tent anywhere you like, even bang in the middle of a stupendous view.

You will have told sceptical friends that your new boat tent is far more palatial than most backpacking tents, and no doubt this is true, but the first time you try to sleep in it for real, you will discover a vital difference. Unlike camping on land, you cannot just step outside a boat tent to tie down a badly placed lashing. An anchored dinghy is surrounded by a deep moat. All your activities must take place within her gunwales.

After you have snuggled down into your sleeping bag, the unfamiliar gurgles and lurches of a cruising dinghy at anchor may seem rather alarming. Everyone wakes up in the middle of their first night in a sudden panic. Perhaps the wind has changed, and the movement of the boat is very different – more insistent, less reassuring.

Is the anchor dragging? You open the tent flaps and peep out. The shore lights sweep madly across your view as she swings to her anchor. The tide has changed, the boat has shifted, and none of the scenery is in the same place. Do not panic. Locate the transits you noted before going to bed, or check the bearings you took with the handbearing compass. If the transits are still in line and the bearings are the same, you can snuggle back down again, confident that all is secure, marvelling at the contrast between the wildness outside and your homely bedroom, afloat in the black night.

Making a first boat tent in a weekend

If you are going to sleep aboard your boat, you will need some sort of boat tent, but you probably do not want to spend too much time or money on your first one, in case it all goes horribly wrong. A first boat tent should be cheap and quick to construct, so that you can experiment with different designs.

I made my first tent for *Avel Dro* out of cheap plastic tarpaulin sheeting, the sort that is widely available from builders' merchants. It was a simple ridge tent, without any frills, but perfectly adequate for my first nights afloat. Indeed, it was so successful that I continued to use this 'temporary' tent for two years, before I finally commissioned the sewing up of a proper version.

In my dinghy the ridge of the tent is supported by the yard of the lugsail. Dinghies with more conventional rigs normally use the boom, supported by the gooseneck at the mast and wooden crutches at the stern. The height of the ridge is a fine compromise between headroom and windage, but it is worth ensuring that it clears your head when sitting on the rowing thwart, so that the dinghy can be rowed with the tent partially set. My crutches are made from two pieces of planed softwood, 2" x 1" (25 x 50mm) in section, held together by a stainless steel bolt and a locknut. The crutches are set up on the stern deck, and rest inside the gunwales on each side.

To make my first tarpaulin tent, I hoisted up one end of the yard with the halyard and rested the other end on some temporary crutches. Then I threw the sheet of tarpaulin over and tugged at it until it rested flat on both sides of the boat. I cut the

tarpaulin to shape in two stages, the first time rough and oversized, and then again more accurately.

First I cut everything away that was more than 10" (25cm) below the gunwale, sticking down the edge of the cover with gaffer tape as I went along. Then I cut the front and back ends of the tent roughly to shape, so that the ridge of the tent lay flat all along the yard supporting it. The gaffer tape was then adjusted so that the tent was tight against the hull all round, without creases. I took some time over this, making sure everything was just right, before I started on the second cut.

For the second cut, I followed the edge of the top plank land all the way round the boat with my scissors, moving the little pieces of tape up to the cut edge as I went along. If you have a smooth hull, rather than a clinker hull like mine, you will need to go round the boat with a ruler and felt pen, making a series of marks below the rubbing strake and then joining them up to make a guideline for cutting.

Clearly you need a more permanent way of holding down the edges of the boat tent than lots of pieces of gaffer tape. There is much debate about the best way of doing this. The one I used is the most traditional, but often criticised. I fitted a series of short lengths of shock cord at intervals around the edge of the cover, which are hooked down to a line of lacing hooks screwed into the hull and located just under a plank land. Hooks on the topsides of a dinghy are claimed to be vulnerable to damage and prone to get themselves hooked on all sorts of things when you are not looking, but I did not experience any great problems with this method. Indeed, I persist in using it on my permanent tent.

Landing on an
island in the Baltic,
and unloading the
camping gear.

Our campsite on the
same island. Notice that
everything is packed in
waterproof bags.

Making a plastic tent: the tarpaulin is thrown over the yard and lashed down temporarily.

Then it is cut to shape and taped down all round.

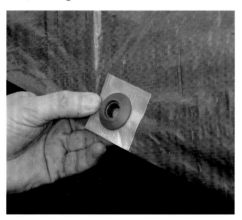

Then eyelets are inserted at intervals, reinforced with gaffer tape.

Finally the tent is ready for use.

The bungees were threaded through eyelets around the perimeter of the tent. The problem with putting eyelets in thin plastic material is that they will tear out in the slightest wind. My solution was to reinforce the tent at each eyelet hole with a small length of gaffer tape, about 4" (10cm) long, folded neatly over the edge of the fabric. Then the eyelets were fixed through these reinforced patches.

Rather than the common soft brass eyelets, I chose plastic ones. These are less attractive but better engineered, as they spread their grip over a wider area, reducing the stress. I pre-cut a hole in each gaffer tape patch and then carefully inserted each eyelet, tapping the two halves tight with a wooden mallet.

Finally I re-cut the flaps where the tent wrapped round the prow and the transom. To do this, I cut each side of the tent so it ended in a triangle and fitted the edge with a line of lacing eyes, to pull the two sides of the tent together.

There it is: a boat tent in a weekend! If you make it with care, you will be surprised how well it will perform.

Professional boat tents

A more permanent boat tent can be commissioned from a sailmaker, or you could purchase the material from a specialist supplier and sew one up yourself. You will have discovered from your plastic tent that internal condensation can be a problem if a tent is made of impervious material. Every time you brush against the inside of the tent, you will get wet. Modern backpacking tents have two skins to combat condensation: a waterproof outer flysheet, and an inner tent that is permeable to water vapour. But a double-skinned tent is extremely difficult to arrange on a dinghy. Boat tents can really only have a single skin, so they are more comfortable if they are made from breathable fabric, which is why traditional materials still have their place.

My old 12-footer *Baggywrinkle* went through a whole series of boat tents, both synthetic and made from natural materials. Her final tent, the 'Mark 4', was made out of traditional 'tent twill' – a fine cotton canvas designed for tent use. Probably the very best bespoke cotton tents are made from 'Ventile', a particularly light and tightly woven fabric. It is wonderful, but very expensive. Only commission a Ventile tent when you are absolutely certain you know exactly what you want.

Avel Dro's present boat tent is based closely on the shape of my tarpaulin prototype. It is not made from Ventile or tent twill, but of traditional cotton duck, to reduce the cost. Cotton duck is heavier and more bulky than more technical tent fabrics, but also more robust. Perhaps I should have been more radical in my choice of material. The technology of man-made fabrics is evolving all the time, and they have many advantages compared to cotton duck. They are lighter, pack smaller, and they do not absorb water when wet. Set against this, they tend to be more vulnerable to abrasion, their fabric will slowly decay from the ultraviolet component of sunlight, and they are still markedly less breathable.

Despite the wonders of synthetic tent fabric, cotton still has its advantages. Apart from its wonderful ability to breathe, it will not flap about noisily in a breeze and keep you awake all night. Be careful about the colour, though. *Baggywrinkle*'s Mark 2 tent was made of thick blue canvas, and my breakfasts were always gloomy. Nowadays I have a tan-coloured tent and my mornings are always blissful. Every day dawns sunny and golden, until I open the tent flaps and discover otherwise.

Avel Dro's tent is set over the yard, rather than slung underneath it, just as *Baggywrinkle*'s was set over her boom. Boat tents designed in this way are much simpler to erect, but they also mean that the sail ends up inside the tent, just above the crew's heads. If the sail was wet when it was furled, it will keep dripping for some time, and this is why some people go to the trouble of suspending their tents below the sail. But I am prepared to put up with a few drips for simplicity and speed of setting. A canvas sail cover would solve this problem for good, and one day I will get round to making one.

Some dinghy tents are much more sophisticated than mine, with hoops or frames to create more internal space. People who have a boat tent with vertical sides, can sit on the side benches when the tent is up, rather than having to keep to the middle of the boat or slouch on the bottom boards like the rest of us. I have even seen boat tents with transparent windows, and presumably some sort of curtaining inside to provide privacy when required.

(ABOVE) Camping dinghies on the Rade de Brest, just begining to dry out. Alongside my boat is Didier Cariou's Druscombe Lugger with his sophisticated tent.

(LEFT) A cheap hooped tent can be purchased from an outdoor shop and adapted to become a dinghy tent.

Perhaps the most clever boat tent is the one on Aidan de la Mare's little yawl, *Jady Lane*. It is essentially two golfing umbrellas, one leaning forward towards the bows and the other towards the stern. He can erect it in less than a minute.

The design of commercial land tents is improving all the time. Modern tents are light, spacious and easy to erect. They can also be purchased at very advantageous prices compared to the cost of commissioning a purpose-made one from a sailmaker. Most modern tents have some sort of hooped configuration, which tensions the fabric and provides substantially more space to move around in than a traditional triangular tent.

A simple way to use such a tent is to carry some pieces of plywood cut to size to deck over the well in your dinghy, between the thwarts. Slide the plywood out to create a flat deck and simply erect a carefully chosen tent on top of it, ensuring that you lash it down to the the gunwales with its guy ropes to prevent it blowing away.

Well worth looking at are the various designs of Pop-up Tent. These tents pack down into a flat circle and can be erected in just a few seconds. They do indeed simply 'pop up'. This ease of erection is a boon on board a boat. Better ones are double skinned and hence avoid problems of condensation. As a quick, simple and inexpensive way into camping aboard they can hardly be bettered, and their pragmatic simplicity should also commend them as a longterm solution.

(LEFT) *Aidan de la Mare's umbrella tent, half erected as a sunshade.*

(BELOW) *Aidan's tent fully deployed. (Aidan de la Mare)*

Bed-making aboard

In bigger dinghies, over some 15ft (4.5m) long, there is usually sufficient space to lay a mattress on the bottom boards either side of the centreboard case. On smaller dinghies, such as my old 12-footer, it is more usual to create a bed platform at thwart level, whether or not you use the level platform so-created to support a land tent. This can be achieved by making dedicated bed boards or by lifting the bottom boards into a raised position each night, to span

between the rowing thwart and the stern seat. After I broke a set of bottom boards during my first night on *Baggywrinkle*, I strengthened her bottom boards by laminating them to a sheet of plywood underneath. This worked a treat.

Numerous types of camping mattress have been developed in recent years, and the choice is now vast. I have used a number of different types and prefer the so-called 'self inflating' mattresses to an air bed, as they provide a more comfortable

(LEFT AND BELOW) Mary Dooley uses a pop-up tent on her Mirror dinghy, laid on plywood boards that she stows on the stern seat when sailing. (DCA)

living surface for other activities like cooking and eating, other than just sleeping on. As the mattress will be laid on hard wooden boards, it is worth getting one with a good degree of cushioning.

Down bags are utterly wonderful things. They seem to have a spooky ability to be cool in hot weather and warm when it is cold. But they rapidly lose their insulating capabilities when wet, which is a disadvantage for use afloat. I used to use synthetic bags, but recently managed to find some down bags with a square foot which are much easier to get in and out of than a mummy bag. The biggest disadvantage is that a down bag cannot be easily cleaned if it gets dirty or impregnated with salt. Synthetic bags, by contrast, can be put in a conventional washing machine, but they are bulkier than a down bag of equivalent insulation.

(RIGHT) Inside a Wayfarer tent. The oars are hung from the shrouds to support the vertical sides of the tent. The yellow objects on the bottom boards are bed boards, which are unfolded and set up between the thwart and the sternlocker when the beds are made. Notice the waterproof hatches to the large storage lockers under the foredeck.

(BELOW RIGHT) Inside Avel Dro's tent, looking forward.

Interior design in a camping dinghy

In my old Tideway, virtually every item of gear had to be moved from its sailing position to another location when in 'camping mode'. This may seem a trivial matter, but the constant packing and repacking rapidly became tedious. I had to allow at least an hour between waking up and starting sailing – or two hours if I also wanted breakfast.

This is why my overriding priority when planning the interior of *Avel Dro* was to make her as simple and streamlined as possible. The interior of the boat is divided into zones for different purposes, based on the traditional hierarchy of a wooden man o' war: from the squalid fo'c'sle in the bows to the plush officers' quarters in the stern. On *Avel Dro* this naval hierarchy had to be compressed into just 15 feet, but it is still discernible.

Muddy and smelly stuff stays in *Avel Dro*'s fo'c'sle, right forward. This is where sea boots, wet waterproofs and the 'stout bucket' live. Amidships there is the galley area, and astern of that you enter the salubrious zone for lounging and sleeping, where no squalor ever penetrates. This at least is the theory.

HOME LIFE ON A DINGHY

As soon as I have got the anchor down at my destination, I erect the tent cover, which provides shade and keeps off the wind. To enjoy the view, I unhook two or three of the bungees on one side of the tent, lift that edge of the cover and tuck it over the ridgepole but under the rest of the cover, so it stays in place.

After that, I lay out the camping mats on the bottom boards and inflate them. This creates a comfy surface to lounge on. I carry two waterproof cushions aboard my dinghy as well as a camping pillow for each crewmember. These are scattered about the saloon, creating a sumptuous boudoir effect.

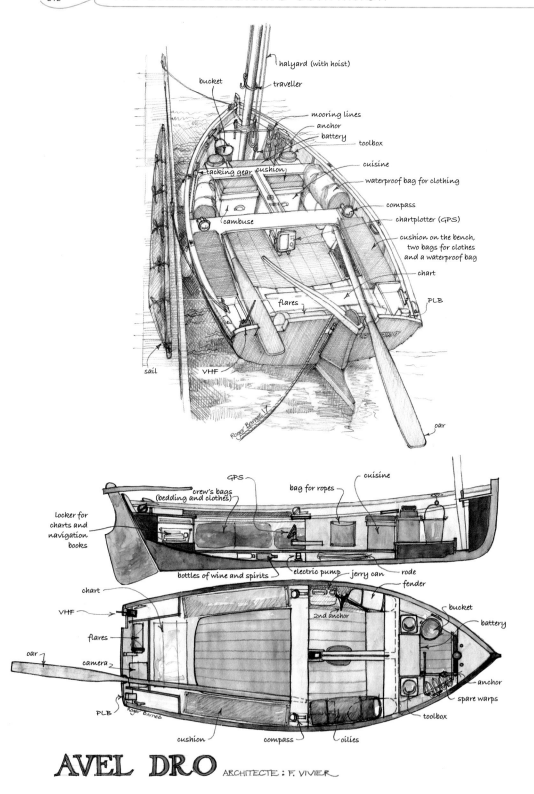

AVEL DRO ARCHITECTE: F. VIVIER

Dinghy internal design, showing the zoning of the interior.

The side benches form useful shelves for any discarded clothing. But small objects that might roll into the bilges are placed in two deeply fiddled trays at each quarter of the dinghy. The torches are always kept here, so they can be located quickly when feeling round in the dark. It is a good idea to develop a routine on a camping dinghy, and always put everything in the same place. For general lighting an LED camping lantern is hung from the ridge of the tent.

In my dinghy we prefer to sleep with our heads at the stern and our legs under the rowing thwart. On a flat beach the dinghy lies slightly bow down, so this orientation is ideal. Sometimes the dinghy dries out at the wrong angle, and we have to sleep the other way round to stop the blood going to our heads. This is much less comfortable.

My dinghy has quite a deep skeg and slightly slack bilges, so unless she dries out into very soft mud, she lies over to one side, at an angle of about 10 degrees. This can be corrected by wedging the big fenders under the bilges on each side, (and tying them on so they don't float away), but I only bother if there is someone else on board. Otherwise I just sleep on the downhill side. One day I will get round to making a pair of 'legs' so that the dinghy always dries out level.

ANCHORING OVERNIGHT

If you want to sleep well aboard a dinghy, you must be confident that nothing nasty can happen to you overnight. Once the tent is set up and the crew are snug in their sleeping bags, it takes a good while to convert the boat back to sailing condition. It is best to anchor the dinghy somewhere that is sheltered in any wind direction, as you don't want to shift anchorage during the night.

When anchored in deep water, there is no chance of getting ashore unless your dinghy has a tender. This is why I prefer to anchor in the shallows, and take the ground during the night. With careful planning of tides, the dinghy will dry out in time for the crew to get ashore to check the quality of the food in the local pub, so that Cook can have a night off. On an ideal tide, the dinghy will stay on the beach all night and then float off again in the morning.

In a narrow creek the sides of the channel can often be very steep, and you must ensure that you either anchor over the middle of it or well over on the mudflats to each side. Otherwise you will wake up in the middle of the night with your dinghy lying at a crazy angle. Just before my dinghy settles onto the bottom, I prod round with an oar to check that the depth is the same on all sides, and we are not anchored over

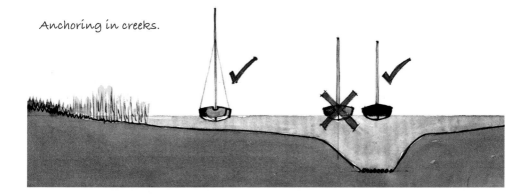

Anchoring in creeks.

a precipice. If we are, we shift anchorage smartly to somewhere more congenial.

On a rocky beach, it is often necessary to anchor in deeper water first, and then pull the boat in towards the shore until she lies directly over the level spot you have selected to dry out on.

COOKING

The cooking arrangement I used on *Baggywrinkle* was transferred almost unchanged to *Avel Dro*. I made two plywood boxes to fit under the forward thwart, either side of the centreboard case, to form a larder and galley. On *Baggywrinkle* the cooking stove had to be moved onto the stern seat each time I wanted to cook, but on *Avel Dro* the galley always stays in the same place and is designed so the stove can be used *in situ*.

Just astern of the galley and larder boxes are the water carriers, one on each side of the boat. These are ordinary 5-litre jerry cans. As they are quite heavy when full, ideally they would be mounted alongside the centreboard case, but that location was already taken by my anchors and their rodes, so the jerry cans are suspended from hooks and hang against the sides of the hull.

STOWAGE IN THE LUXURIOUS 'SALOON'

Aft of the rowing thwart is the 'saloon' area where the officers lounge in luxury. At night, two mattresses are laid out on the bottom boards, extending forward under the main thwart as far as the larder and galley boxes, but during the day, this area is cleared for the business of sailing. Under the side seats, extending along both sides of this area, there is space for four waterproof bags – two for each crewmember. These not only act as stowage but also buoyancy if the boat capsizes, so they are securely lashed in.

I used to use the roll-top waterproof bags that can be purchased from camping shops. But I discovered in recent capsizes that although they may call themselves 'waterproof' they don't really mean that. They are designed to keep rain out, not prevent the contents from getting wet from prolonged immersion. Not only did all my clothing and bedding get damp with seawater, but gradually the buoyancy of the boat became compromised.

This is why I have replaced all my previous bags with a new set that are guaranteed waterproof, even from full immersion. They are made by the American company Watershed, and they differ from ordinary roll top bags by the incorporation of what they call a 'zipdry' closure. They are not cheap, but are astonishingly well made from quality materials and worth it if you want to keep your kit perfectly dry. They open on their long side, so it is easy to locate items inside.

One of my new Watershed bags – completely waterproof even against full immersion. This is the 55-litre Yukon.

THE RS VENTURE

The Venture is a typical modern dinghy design, first launched in 2011. Although RS are best known for their class racing dinghies, the Venture was designed as a training boat, for family sailing and cruising, and is not an extreme racing type. There is ample space on board for a whole family to sail together. Nonetheless it has racing features such as a retractable bowsprit to fly an asymmetric – its hull also has the fine bow and wide stern quarters, which are the modern fashion, designed to plane readily off the wind but maintain excellent windward performance.

Cruising-friendly aspects of the dinghy include a high boom, in no danger of hitting the crews' heads in a sudden gybe, and generous storage in a large stern locker and dry stowage forward. There is a roller reefing jib and a mainsail with single line jiffy reefing: one reef is standard, but a second could easily be added.

The dinghy comes in three versions with different keel configurations. The lightweight GRP centre board on the dinghy I tested can be substituted for a heavier metal one, or even a vertically lifting ballast keel. The hull is in fibreglass, (not rotomolded plastic like many modern dinghies), and is robustly laid up.

Although I do not know of anyone who sleeps aboard the RS Venture at present, at least one person is said to be planning to do so shortly. The interior of the hull is spacious and uncluttered, and there would be ample space for two to sleep on the bottom of the wide, self-draining cockpit.

The dinghy can take an outboard, but at present is manufactured with no provision for being rowed. This would be a relatively simple adaptation however, and there is certainly space to stow full length oars in the cockpit.

The Venture is shiny, sleek, unashamedly modern and fast. It would not suit everyone, but could make a rewarding and responsive fast cruising dinghy.

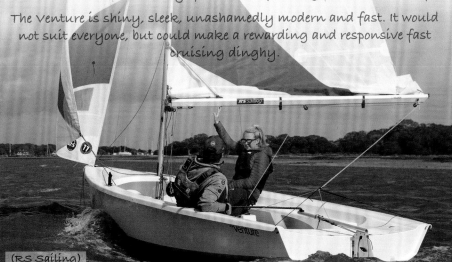

(RS Sailing)

THE COOK, THE SKIPPER, HIS BOAT AND HER CREW

A good skipper makes for a happy ship, they say. But hoary matelots know that the most important person on board ship is always the cook. Hot and nutritious meals at regular intervals are fundamental to crew contentment. This is as true for a windjammer off the Horn as a cruising dinghy in coastal waters.

Equipping a cruising dinghy means reconciling many conflicting demands in a small space. The skipper wants a clear, seamanlike expanse in which to work the ship, and no cook is ever satisfied with the size of the kitchen. In a small boat, the 'skipper' and the 'cook' are often the same person, so this can lead to psychological tension.

In *Baggywrinkle* the skipper persona got things his way. The cooking arrangements were fairly basic, and the cook always complained. Cook is famously profligate with space, and was never happy unless his extensive *batterie de la cuisine* was spread all over the stern of the boat. Pots, plates, cutlery and comestibles would cover virtually every surface. If a sudden nautical crisis

required immediate action, everything got trampled underfoot and Skipper despaired.

When *Avel Dro* was being commissioned, Cook had wistful visions of a state-of-the-art galley area. The crew thought this was a great idea, and looked forward to hot meals prepared on passage, even when green seas were sweeping the decks. The crew is a number of different people at different times, but they all claim to be badly treated by Skipper, who drives ship and crew hard.

'It's wetter than a racing tea clipper, when you ship with Bully Barnes,' they grumble, 'and the food is our only consolation.'

There was loose talk in the fo'c'sle of a properly gimballed yacht stove with twin burners, but Skipper pointed out that dinghies don't sail at great angles of heel, so gimbals were unnecessary, and that two burners would just eat into space that could be used to store more food and drink. So what was finally installed in *Avel Dro*'s spanking new galley was a Swedish single-burner alcohol stove with adjustable fiddles, designed specifically for the nautical environment. These stoves are simple and robust in design, and made entirely out of stainless steel. They are so constructed that they will not flare up or spill fuel, even in extreme circumstances.

Avel Dro's galley was designed so that the stove can be used inside the galley box, which is lined with heat-resistant material. The galley box protects the stove from draughts, and also from being kicked in any desperate nautical crises. In a side compartment there is space for pots, crockery and cutlery. Cook's

Avel Dro's galley in use. These popular marine alcohol stoves, (formerly branded Origo and recently discontinued), are available once again from the German chandlers Compass24.

A Wayfarer on the beach, with the crew cooking supper. (Liz Baker)

precious kitchen tools are stowed here: a good sharp knife, a cafetière, a peppermill filled with real peppercorns, a wooden spatula and a corkscrew.

'There is no dish that isn't improved by a slug of wine,' he says.

Avel Dro's larder is a plywood box, a similar size to her galley. As she was originally a French boat, this is called *la Cambuse* and the galley is called *la Cuisine*, and they carry fine brass plaques to this effect. Both boxes have a removable lid with a deep lip all round, to keep rainwater and spray from spoiling the contents.

While cooking, the lids of the two boxes are inverted and placed on a nearby thwart, to become trays with deep fiddles all round. These contain cooking ingredients and any pots not in use on the stove, and stop Cook spreading stuff around everywhere. Cook sits on the rowing thwart to create

his famous meals, and pumps any water he needs out of the jerry cans using a cheap plastic pump.

Cook has strong opinions about victuals. *La Cambuse* contains a number of standard ingredients that Cook buys before every voyage, to make victualing easier. These include a bottle of olive oil, fresh pasta, rice, bacon, eggs, tinned fish, fresh tomatoes, a loaf of good bread, real ground coffee and some small jars and tins of his special ingredients. There is also usually some good cheese, a selection of fruit to ward off scurvy, muesli bars for the crew to munch when underway and some Tunnock's Caramel Wafers in memory of Skipper's school tuck shop.

Cook is something of a food snob, but even he has to accept that instant meals have their place aboard a seagoing vessel. At the end of a hard day at sea, it is good to

Breakfast on the River Tamar.
(Josephine Street)

There is no point aboard a boat – quite apart from their dull taste and tedious texture, rehydrating them only depletes the boat's supply of precious fresh water.

Despite Bully Barnes's tough reputation, and the privations endured by anyone foolish enough to ship 'before the mast' on *Avel Dro*, his regular crews keep coming back for more. This can only be because of Cook's famous food.

Breakfast afloat

A cooked breakfast at anchor in a dinghy is the supreme gourmet experience available on the planet, or so say the lucky people who have experienced it. You roll back the stern of the tent and look out onto a fresh new world. Soon the smell of cooking and fresh coffee drifts across the anchorage. Then you lounge in the boat savouring your hearty repast, enjoying the view and making plans for the day.

be able to have a nutritious and comforting meal ready in less than five minutes. Tinned food is especially useful, as it can be left in the boat over the season and only used if necessary. Curries are especially popular aboard *Avel Dro*. Unlike our mountain-climbing cousins, we never eat dried foods.

The boat tent on a Hitia Catamaran: there is enough space for the whole family.
(Hughes)

Favourites from the *Avel Dro* cookbook

Cook was producing dishes inspired by provincial Italian cooking long before London's famous River Café, and has contemplated suing them for plagiarism. Italian peasant dishes are swift to make, with everything going into one big pan:

'Now *that's* what I call Fast Food!' he says.

Important note: Skipper will not have a weighing scale on board, so Cook has to measure most of his ingredients in cans, packets or 'slugs'. If you use his recipes and the dishes do not turn out successfully, it is because you have not followed these measurements with sufficient accuracy.

Tortellini e pesto: 'probably the fastest dish in the world'

Boil some water and chuck in a packet of fresh tortellini. Bring back to the boil and cook for one minute. Drain and then stir in a couple of dessertspoons per person of pesto (basil sauce – available in jars). Then grate a generous mound of fresh Parmesan cheese over the dish.

'Not the powdered stuff – tastes like dandruff!'

Add some black pepper. Serve and eat.

Penne alla carbonara

Boil a pan of water and cook the pasta 'al dente'. (Cook uses penne pasta, but any shape can be used except spaghetti, as experiments have proven that it is incompatible with camping dinghies.) Drain and leave to one side in the covered pan. Cut three slices of bacon per person into small pieces, and fry in olive oil. While it is cooking, crush one clove of garlic per person, then chop them and add to the pan. Add a metric slug of red wine per person. Bring to the boil and reduce for a minute or so. Chuck in the pasta. Keep the heat high, and stir. Add ground pepper. Crack an egg per person over the mixture, and stir until the egg cooks. Serve with freshly grated Parmesan cheese, accompanied by the rest of the wine in a large glass.

Penne alla puttanesca

'This dish is prepared by the prostitutes of Naples,' says Cook, who has been there and knows about these things.

Serves two, or one very hungry singlehander. Boil the pasta 'al dente' and drain, then leave it to one side in a covered pan. Open a tin of anchovies in olive oil, and put in a second pan together with their oil. Crush a couple of cloves of fresh garlic, then chop them and begin to fry them gently alongside the anchovies. Now add a dash more oil. When the garlic is golden brown, add a normal-sized tin of tomatoes and half of a half-sized can of olives. Then stir in 4 dessertspoons of capers and a freshly chopped chilli pepper.

'Simmer for the time it takes Skipper to calculate the depth of water in a Secondary Port using the classic Admiralty method, interpolating between Springs and Neaps.'

Then add ground pepper and the pasta to the pan. Continue cooking until the pasta is heated through. Serve with chopped herbs picked on the littoral, and a chunk of bread to mop up the juice.

OTHER CHOICES

In describing the conversion of a dinghy to a camp-cruiser, I have concentrated on describing my own dinghy, but there are lots of other choices. Cruising dinghy sailors tend to be very individualistic people and their dinghies are as individual as they are.

Some people prefer to use a gas stove rather than an alcohol stove. The flat type of gas stove is particularly popular, as they provide a stable base for cooking on. Petrol and paraffin stoves are probably best avoided on a small dinghy, because of the risk of a flare-up, although I used them in my reckless younger days. The fuel of my present alcohol stove can be extinguished just with water, of which there is an inexhaustible supply outside the boat.

Some camping dinghies are very simple and straightforward, while others are full of sybaritic pleasures. Some have a hinged pram hood forward, which can be raised when sailing to keep off the wind and to provide protection for navigating. Others have built-in water tanks and piped water. There are even dinghies that carry a small chemical toilet. People take their pets afloat with them, or use their dinghies to watch wildlife. Artists shelter under their boat tents to make watercolour paintings, photographers take pictures,

Roger Wilkinson takes Lottie out sailing.

and writers make up marvellous stories. Cruising dinghies are a world of their own, with their own society of interesting and unusual people.

MORNING RITUALS

In the morning, after breakfast has been eaten and plans have been made for the day, the washing-up and stowing of gear inevitably takes some time. Clothes, sleeping bags and sleeping mats must be put into their dry bags and lashed down.

If the bottom boards were raised to form the sleeping platform, they must be replaced on the sole. Finally, the tent cover is folded up and stowed away. Everything has its own special position, secure and out of the way when working the boat.

The sails are hoisted and then the anchor is broken out. The dinghy makes sternway for a moment as her bow falls off the wind, then the mainsail fills and her hull heels to the breeze. For a moment the anchorage is disturbed by her wake. Then she slips silently away towards a new horizon.

Breakfast afloat.
(David Summerville)

10 KEEPING COMFORTABLE AND SAFE

Ever since SWALLOWS AND AMAZONS was published in 1930,
Arthur Ransome's books have inspired generations of children
to sail. But young readers are often perplexed that the young
children in the books are allowed to go sailing and camping
on an island on their own, and without lifejackets too. In this
Ransome was reflecting the practices of his time: few people wore
lifejackets in the 1930s, and children were given much more
freedom to roam around the countryside on their own than is
usual nowadays; but they were also well-drilled about personal
responsibility:

'BETTER DROWNED THAN DUFFERS IF NOT DUFFERS WONT DROWN.'

SWALLOW in the English
Lake District, while filming
'Swallows and Amazons'.
(Sophie Neville)

In Ransome's day, keeping safe was believed to be basically a matter of learning the right skills, not purchasing lots of approved safety equipment. Sailing dinghies of the period generally carried ballast and could sink rapidly if capsized or holed, but they were also heavy and stable craft, and much less likely to capsize than a modern dinghy. Although they were effective sea boats, they carried nothing in the way of secondary safety equipment. Instead young dinghy crews were taught that they were ultimately responsible for their own safety. Times have changed, and we are no longer prepared to impose upon children the level of discipline nor accept the level of risk that the pre-War generation considered normal.

KEEPING THE CREW SAFE

Personal buoyancy is totemic of our modern cautious attitude to personal safety. Although statistically the dangers of small boat sailing are very low, it is now considered reckless to go on the water without a lifejacket or buoyancy aid. This is a gloomy subject, but in an age when even lock-keepers are issued with auto-inflating lifejackets, in case they tumble into the canal, we need to address it.

Modern research into the dangers of sudden immersion in cold water has found that drowning is not the greatest initial risk if someone falls into the water. An ability to swim is no protection against the incapacitation caused by 'cold shock', which causes the casualty to hyperventilate when they hit the water, ingesting water into their lungs. The shock of sudden immersion in cold water can also induce a sudden heart attack in the more elderly and less fit. The risk of rapid death is reduced if the water is warm, but at higher latitudes the water in the deep sea remains cold throughout the year, such as off the coast of north-western Europe.

Lifejackets

A lifejacket is designed to turn you on your back and hold your head above water, giving you time to recover from the initial cold shock. On yachts it has now become accepted practice to wear a self-inflating lifejacket combined with a harness, but not necessarily in fair weather. The idea is that if you were to fall over the side, the harness will keep you close to the yacht and the lifejacket will keep you afloat while your fellow crewmembers work out how they are going to get you back on board again. Hopefully they have practised this in advance.

Auto-inflating lifejackets are proven and effective pieces of kit, but they will only save your life if they are the right type. They should have thigh straps to prevent them floating up off your torso and a transparent hood to protect your face from the sea spray. It is also vital that they are regularly inspected and serviced. Many lifejackets do not meet these standards and are probably worse than useless. In random tests, an alarming number failed to inflate, due to elementary faults that could have been corrected by regular servicing.

There are various types of self-inflating lifejacket. Some operate automatically on contact with water; others must be triggered manually by pulling on a cord. Non-automatic types do not address the problem of 'cold shock', as they require you to be fully conscious and capable when you hit the water. By contrast, auto-inflating types do not need any user-intervention.

There are two types of triggering mechanism on auto-inflating lifejackets. The normal type is activated by contact with

Self-inflating lifejackets have their place, but they are more suitable aboard a fully crewed yacht.

A buoyancy aid is more suitable aboard a dinghy. This older model has more buoyancy than is usual nowadays.

water, whereas the better ones for dinghy sailing are triggered by shallow immersion. This older model of lifejacket is activated by contact with water. They are prone to inflate themselves accidentally if they are hit by heavy spray or by a wave breaking aboard the dinghy, so they are not suitable for use on an open boat. The lifejackets triggered by immersion usually use the Swedish 'Hammar' inflator.

All automatic lifejackets can also be inflated manually, should the triggering mechanism fail. They are available in three levels of flotation, 150N, 190N and 275N, depending on the severity of the conditions and the amount of clothing the wearer is likely to have on. A lifejacket should be sized for the worst conditions you are likely to be sailing in.

Buoyancy aids

Most dinghy sailors prefer a close-fitting buoyancy aid to a lifejacket. The floatation incorporated in a modern buoyancy aid is typically only 50N, as compared to 150N for the least buoyant lifejacket. The reason for this difference is that a buoyancy aid is intended to help you to swim, not to keep you afloat when incapacitated. Racing-dinghy sailors always choose buoyancy aids because they need to swim back to their capsized boat, right her, clamber aboard and get her sailing again as fast as possible. It is difficult to swim in a lifejacket, especially the more buoyant versions. Lifejackets are designed to force you onto your back and then keep you afloat while you wait passively for someone else to rescue you.

Larger buoyancy aids are still available with 100N of permanent foam buoyancy, which approaches the smallest size of self-inflating lifejacket. They are worth hunting down, as they are a good compromise between the smaller buoyancy aids and a full lifejacket.

Should you wear a lifejacket or buoyancy aid?

On a well-crewed yacht, a lifejacket is designed to keep you afloat while the rest of the crew bring the yacht back to pick you up. The situation in a dinghy is very different. If you are sailing singlehanded, and you find yourself in the water, there will be no one else available to help you back into the boat, so you must be able to do it unaided. Even if there are other crewmembers aboard your dinghy, it is likely that you will all end up in the sea together.

An auto-inflating lifejacket is not a panacea to the risks of sailing a dinghy. If your dinghy capsizes, it is vital that you stay with her. Should you become separated from your vessel, you must be able to swim back to her. Even if you are unable to right your craft, her buoyancy will keep you afloat indefinitely. A swamped cruising dinghy should be unsinkable. If you have followed the recommendations in this book, she will also contain food and water, a VHF, an EPIRB, flares and spare clothing. She is as close to a liferaft as you can get, without actually being a liferaft. Your chances of survival are improved immeasurably if you can stay with your boat, whereas your prospects when floating free in the sea, even wearing the very best lifejacket, are rather gloomy. Floating in UK coastal waters, the water temperature is so low that most people will expire from hypothermia within an hour, or perhaps two if they are very fit.

Whether you prefer to wear a full lifejacket or a buoyancy aid is a matter of personal choice. It depends on how you assess the comparative risks of each type. But I would think very hard before using an auto-inflating lifejacket in a seagoing dinghy. The idea of floating around helplessly in the open sea, awaiting rescue, does not appeal to me at all. If I fall into the water, I want to be able to get back to my dinghy unaided, and that means being able to swim. Sea kayakers have come to the same judgement. They also prefer buoyancy aids.

I prefer to use a slim-fitting buoyancy aid that is styled as a gilet. (Colin Brady)

Although I usually carry a 100N buoyancy aid aboard, most of the time I wear a 50N version that is styled like a sleeveless waistcoat. It is a proper buoyancy aid, constructed to European CE standards, and even incorporates a thigh strap to prevent it floating up around my head, but it has the appearance of a down-filled gilet. Its great advantage over more conventional types is that it is comfortable to wear, keeps me warm, and has slim pockets for my knife and my logbook.

Some dinghy sailors like to use kayaker's buoyancy aids, as these incorporate large external pockets high on the front in which you can stow a water-resistant smartphone, a handheld VHF and even a PLB. They argue that if they were to end up bobbing about in the sea, they would have innumerable means to call for help conveniently there, already on their person.

I do not like these at all. In my view, if you don't get your boat righted in short order after a capsize and get yourself back on board your longterm outlook is less than rosy. Even if you are wearing a drysuit, you need to get yourself out of the water. It is of vital importance to be able to clamber over the gunwale into your dinghy unencumbered. This is not an issue for kayakers, for whom this particular type of buoyancy jacket is designed, as they can roll a kayak. Dinghy-specific buoyancy aids do not have large chest pockets for a very good reason.

Whenever I need to get back aboard my dinghy after swimming in the water, I inevitably end up with my chest pressed hard against the gunwale, clutching at handholds in the boat to physically drag myself into the dinghy. I am certain that I could not do this while wearing a buoyancy jacket bulging with sundry 'safety' gear all over my chest. It is not just for vanity that I like to wear a buoyancy jacket that enables me to stay looking relatively slim and svelte.

Man overboard

Losing a crewman over the side is much less likely to happen from inside a dinghy than off the deck of a yacht, but the possibility must still be considered. If you sail singlehanded with sheet cleated and the tiller fixed, there is a chance that you could fall over the side and your dinghy will sail on without you, but most dinghies are sufficiently destabilised by the weight of a crewmember that they will luff up into the wind automatically.

If there are two or more crewmembers aboard and only one of them falls over the side, the remaining crew will need to put the 'man overboard drill' into operation. There are various standard techniques, which you can practise by throwing a fender over the side and then trying to recover it. The method I prefer is to go about

immediately into a hove-to position. Unlike the over-complex methods sometimes recommended, this will bring your dinghy to a halt as fast as possible close to the casualty. If you find yourself a little upwind of the person in the water, you can adjust the angle of drift to slide back alongside them. If you find yourself downwind, you can tack slowly back, while keeping the casualty in sight all the time.

To get the casualty back on board, bring them into your lee just forward of amidships, which will put them into the shelter of the boat. Then you should be able to roll them over the gunwale into the boat. In a less stable dinghy, it may be better to bring the casualty in over the stern. Someone wearing a personal buoyancy aid can usually be lifted back on board by pushing them down into the water and then lifting them as they bounce back due to their own buoyancy. Even a light crewmember should be able to bring someone aboard using this method.

Safety harnesses

If you are sailing alone and you are not confident that your dinghy will stop and wait were you to fall over the side, you should wear a harness and clip yourself to the dinghy. You will need a lanyard sufficiently long that you are not impeded while working the dinghy, and this means it will certainly not prevent you from falling overboard. It will, however, keep you from getting totally separated from your boat, which is vital for survival.

Auto-inflating lifejackets can be purchased in 'harness' and 'non-harness' versions. The harness type have an attachment loop for a safety line. One end of your safety line should be snapped onto the harness and the other to a strongpoint on the boat.

Buoyancy aids, by contrast, do not usually incorporate harness attachment points, and a separate harness must be worn on top of them. This is possible with the new gilet-styled models, but not always practicable with other types.

I have tried using a safety harness in my dinghy, but I found that it was always in the way when sailing. Eventually I decided that it was creating more potential danger than it solved. The risk of becoming entangled in the safety line was too high for me. But my dinghy is deep in the hull and hard to fall out of, and I never sit her out when sailing alone. I am also confident that she would not keep on sailing if I fell over the side, even with helm fixed and sheet cleated. Other skippers should assess the balance of risk in their own dinghies.

Capsize recovery

A heavy dinghy carrying a sensible amount of sail is extremely resistant to capsizing, but the crew should still have a strategy for that eventuality. If you sail a Drascombe Lugger, you may decide that the conditions that would capsize your boat would be so extreme that she would be impossible to right and bale out again, so the best strategy is to treat the swamped dinghy as a liferaft. The crews of more sporty dinghies should certainly practise capsize recovery, however. The standard method of righting a capsized dinghy will need to be adapted to each particular boat. In the narrative that follows, there are two crewmembers sailing a normal sloop-rigged dinghy, and their dinghy has just capsized. I have called them 'Helm' and 'Crew' for convenience.

If the dinghy has completely turned turtle, Helm clambers up onto the windward gunwale and grabs the centreboard, if

this is still sticking up out of the hull. Then Helm stands up on the upturned hull and leans back, pulling on the board, using body weight to bring the boat over onto her side. If the centreboard is not projecting from the hull, Crew throws a jib sheet over the upturned hull for Helm to catch. Helm then stands on the upturned hull holding onto the rope, and uses it to bring the dinghy onto her side.

Once the dinghy is on her side, Crew swims into the hull and lowers the centreboard, if necessary. Crew should stay there, floating in the hull. The centreboard will now be parallel with the water's surface and a little above it. Helm now climbs onto the centreboard, stands on it and leans right back, holding on to the jib sheet. This should lever the boat upright. As the boat rights, Crew will be scooped up inside the hull, while Helm clambers in over the side.

The centreboard should now be raised, so the hull does not trip over it and threaten to roll over again, and the sails should be lowered to prevent any further capsizes. Then Helm and Crew can work together to bail and pump the dinghy dry.

The biggest danger is the risk of a further capsize immediately following the first one – the dinghy is righted but proves so unstable that she immediately capsizes again, the crew rapidly tire and eventually cannot right the dinghy at all. After prolonged immersion it can become difficult even to cling on to the boat, and a simple capsize is well on the way to becoming a tragedy.

This method of righting a capsized dinghy is not appropriate for every boat or every cruising sailor. Wet clothing can weigh so much that it prevents you climbing onto the centreboard. The Dinghy Cruising Association's Keith Muscott believes that righting lines are a good solution:

THE PARADOX

Unlike all the other boats featured in this book, the Paradox has an overall cabin. But she is completely different in concept to the usual pocket cruiser, where the designer attempts to shrink a standard yacht design down to a dinghy scale: with cabin up forward and cockpit at the stern. This is never successful. Inevitably, the boat squats on her stern with the crew weight when under sail, and the minute cabin becomes damp with condensation in cooler weather. It is better to cruise in an open boat and rig a camping tent for overnighting, so that the whole hull is available for the crew to use both when under sail and at night.

Matt Layden's Paradox ingeniously avoids the 'pocket cruiser' dilemma by being all cabin. When under sail, the sole occupant slides back the roof and steers from within the boat. All the control lines lead into the cabin. Built in 1993, the first Paradox was designed to be used in the open ocean off the East Coast of America. After cruising down the Florida coast and out to the Bahamas for ten years, she was then entered in the gruelling 300-mile Everglades Challenge. She was not only placed first in her class, but also garnered overall honours.

The Paradox is purpose-designed for one person to live aboard for long periods. At only 13'10" long and a mere 48" wide, she looks bizarrely unstable. In fact, the design is immensely seaworthy and the boat is designed to right herself even if she is rolled right over by a large wave. This is a unique boat with many interesting and innovative features. She has no centreboard to prevent leeway, but instead she relies on the resistance of her rudder and the shape of her hull to go to windward. The sail can be hoisted and reefed without leaving the cabin and without stopping sailing. When the wind fails, she is propelled by a single sculling oar or 'yuloh'. This is not a flexible design: you cannot take your friends out sailing in her, as there is no space for anyone else, but as a purpose-designed cruising boat for one person the Paradox is hard to beat.

Keith Muscott's Topper Cruz moored in Scapa Flow, Orkney. This successful design of dinghy is no longer in production. (Keith Muscott)

'I found it well-nigh impossible to get up to the board on my capsized Topper Cruz (6ft/1.8m beam) with wet clothes. So I have now fitted 'righting lines'. These are ropes coiled and held by Velcro loops, out of the way under the port and starboard ends of the main thwart, to which they are secured. They are 12ft (3.6m) in length and the last 6ft (1.8m) of them has bulky knots at 1ft (30cm) intervals.

'If I end up in the water after a knock down, I swim round and rip the righting line that is attached to the submerged gunwale out of its Velcro and then sling the coil over the boat. I then swim round to the other side of the boat, get under the centreboard, grip the knotted end of the righting line, pull my knees up under my chin, and creep up the bottom of the boat until I can reach the board. The leg muscles take most of my weight, sparing my arms. After that it is simply a question of leaning back on the rope to pull the dinghy upright

and then falling in over the gunwale as she rises.

'Having a dedicated righting line means that you don't need to use a sheet, which you may get cleated off unintentionally when you pull yourself up on it, causing the waterlogged boat to capsize again when the sail fills and draws.'

THE FLOATING SOFA

Comfort when sailing is of vital importance. If the crew are uncomfortable, they will not concentrate properly on navigation and other important matters. This is one reason why I have both fixed and movable upholstery in my boat. The fixed cushions are fastened to the side seats, and the crew sit on them when sailing the boat. In light winds the boat is often steered from the bottom boards, while sitting on various scatter cushions, which enables the helmsman to have a clear view under the unreefed sail.

(ABOVE) *A dinghy designed as a floating bed: Keith Holdsworth's* THE FLYING PIG. (DCA)

(RIGHT) *Cooking arrangements on* THE FLYING PIG. (DCA)

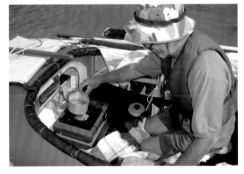

Some experienced dinghy cruisers have built vessels that are even more padded than mine is. Keith Holdsworth sails the sheltered waters of the south coast of England in a boat that is basically a floating double bed. The whole inside of *The Flying Pig* is a mattress, with a padded backrest all round the edge of the well. Keith sails the boat while lying on the bed, lounging against the backrest. *The Flying Pig* is not a boat for crossing oceans in, nor does she have any great turn of speed. She is simply designed for comfortable cruising in the creeks of his local coastline. Keith is a wise and extremely comfy man.

SEASICKNESS

Most people are much less prone to being seasick in a dinghy than when crewing a yacht. Sailors also vary in their vulnerability to seasickness. Some lucky individuals are totally immune, but for the rest of us seasickness is largely a matter of psychology. If you feel warm and secure, you are less likely to feel sick, whereas a cold and frightened crewmember will turn green faster than traffic lights. A classic cure for the early onset of *mal de mer* is to put the afflicted crewmember in the helm, as it is difficult to concentrate on steering a boat and to think about getting seasick all at the same time.

Most people will become sick if they have to grovel on the bottom boards in heavy weather, recovering something that has slid into the bilge water. Inputting waypoints into the chartplotter is a good way of setting me off, which is why I always try to do this before I leave port.

If you are prone to seasickness, you need to find a way to deal with it. I have been sick on many different seas, and have found that I am not incapacitated by it. For this reason I prefer to risk the chance of being seasick rather than take medication every time I take a dinghy to sea. Other sailors may prefer to take preventative medication.

There are many effective pills to treat seasickness, but they must be taken in advance each time you go to sea. There are also various popular remedies based on myth and mumbo-jumbo, which probably have something of a placebo effect if you believe in them.

KEEPING WARM AND DRY

Of all the garments worn by a dinghy crew, lifejackets contribute the least to safety. Personal buoyancy only comes into action if you fall in the water. The rest of the time it just gets in the way. Although a gilet buoyancy aid like mine may be less effective in certain conditions than a self-inflating jacket, it keeps me warm and snug every time I go afloat, and contributes to my comfort and alertness each time I go sailing. I think of it as another layer of clothing rather than a piece of safety gear, and usually wear it under my smock or my oilies.

Exposure is a greater risk to the crew of an open boat than drowning. The undergarments that keep you warm, the waterproofs that keep you dry, the footwear that stops you slipping and protects your feet from cuts and bruises: these make the greatest contribution to your safety at sea.

Unless you do all of your sailing in balmy southern seas, a wet crew will become a cold crew in short order, and rapidly lose capability and motivation. Protection against exposure means having adequate clothing for all conditions and ensuring that you always put on your oilies before a wet passage to windward, and before it starts raining hard. Even the best oilies cannot keep you dry if you only put them on after you are already wet. Warm and comfortable clothes are not only more pleasurable to wear, they can also become a matter of survival.

Finding clothes for dinghy cruising

At one time, yacht chandleries were a cornucopia of cordage, blocks and deck fittings, with cleats, rigging screws and galvanised shackles strewn all over the floor. Nowadays they are more like walking into a fashion boutique, and you rarely find galvanised shackles in them. It is also extraordinarily difficult to buy clothes suitable for dinghy cruising.

The clothes in yacht chandleries fall into three categories: items of yacht-styled leisurewear, basically designed for use ashore, and more technical gear either designed for dinghy racing or offshore yachting. The leisurewear is too insubstantial for active use, and neither type of technical gear is really suitable for our type of sailing.

Racing-dinghy gear is designed to be used for short periods of intense exercise,

John Hughes and his crew shelter from the rain while waiting for the tide.

zooming round the course. It revolves around the wet suit and various forms of dry suit. Both garments are uncomfortable if they are worn all day. In a cruising dinghy, we need clothing that is comfortable to wear continuously for long periods. Most specialist dinghy gear does not fill this role.

A set of modern yachting oilies is a magnificent thing. The jacket is lined with a multiplicity of clever technical membranes, there are numerous pockets, various reinforcement patches in contrasting colours, and a built-in harness attachment. The trousers are equally impressive and laden with clever features. But these are chunky garments, reminiscent of the spacesuits worn by Apollo astronauts, and terribly bulky to stow when you take them off. Yachts have capacious hanging lockers, but even these can have trouble swallowing a number of these multi-layer waterproofs. On a cruising dinghy, we

need to be able to shove everything into a handful waterproof bags. I dread it when friends come aboard my dinghy who have invested in 'a good set of yachting oilies', as I know that their waterproofs will take up more space than the rest of their dunnage put together.

The cruising dinghy sailor has to be a choosy customer. Very few garments that claim to be designed for sailing are actually suitable for our activity. With sufficient diligence you can find lighter oilies than the 'spaceman suits' I have criticised, and other sensible garments may be uncovered in the less-frequented corners of a good yacht chandlery, but there is a more promising source of gear. The best place to find clothing suitable for dinghy cruising is a good outdoor shop that caters for hillwalkers and climbers, as this gear is designed for an activity much closer to what we do in a cruising dinghy.

The layering system

The layering principle has become the accepted norm for outdoor clothing. The concept is to start by putting on a thin base layer next to your skin, which is designed to wick moisture away from your body. On top of that you should don a midlayer, which provides the insulation. In cold weather this may be a number of layers of clothing, to achieve a sufficient thickness for the prevailing conditions. Finally, you cover everything with a 'hard shell' garment, that is designed to protect the system from the wind and rain.

Most yachting clothing still follows this layering system. You are expected to wear oilies virtually all the time, and to adjust the number of layers you wear beneath, depending on the temperature. This may be fine on a yacht, where people mostly sit around all day and occasionally wind on a sheet winch, but in a sailing dinghy periods of frenetic activity alternate with periods of sitting quite still. If you have to remove your oilies each time you need to adjust your insulation layers, you will inevitably spend most of the time either too hot or too cold, because it is such an effort adjusting your midlayer garments, especially if it is raining.

Learning from George Mallory

During the 1924 British Everest Expedition, Mallory and his climbing partner 'Sandy' Irvine disappeared high on the north-east ridge of the mountain during their attempt to make the first ascent of the world's highest peak. The pair's last known sighting was about 800ft below the summit. Whether or not they reached the top before they died remains a subject of continuing speculation, and Mallory's ultimate fate was unknown for 75 years, until his body was discovered in 1999, high up on the mountain.

Mallory's body still rests there, but samples of his clothing were brought back for research. A team from four UK universities collaborated in a two-year project to create replicas of his climbing gear for testing. Until then, it had been complacently assumed that modern outdoor garments were vastly superior to those available seventy years earlier, before modern synthetic fabrics had been developed. The team was surprised to find that the opposite was the case. Mallory's clothes were windproof, waterproof and warm. His garments of silk and wool mix were intelligently knitted and effective. This was probably the lightest kit ever used on Everest, 20 per cent lighter than the equivalent modern high-altitude mountaineering clothes, and the tailoring of his jacket made it more manoeuvrable than those available to climbers of the twenty-first century.

This research was part of an ongoing reassessment of the capabilities of natural fabrics in technical outdoor clothing, and has contributed to a revolution in gear designed for hillwalking, climbing and bushcraft.

From 'hard shell' to 'soft shell'

In recent years the 'soft shell' principle has begun to supplant the old layering theory, pioneered by innovative companies like Páramo. Soft-shell garments are based on the realisation that the body experiences periods of high exertion during which it produces a lot of heat, followed by periods of virtual inactivity, when the body cools down rapidly. The soft shell approach focuses on creating a basic 'action suit' that will keep you sufficiently warm during periods of high activity. When inactive, an additional garment is pulled on top. Typically you wear a base layer and an insulating layer on top, but the traditional all-encasing hard shell is omitted.

Advanced hard shell garments rely on Gore-Tex or a similar membrane. Gore-Tex is an emulsion polymerised PTFE semi-permeable membrane, with pores big enough to let water vapour molecules out, but prevent liquid from entering. The idea is that any sweat will evaporate outwards, but rain won't come in. Unfortunately this process does not work effectively in a cold, damp atmosphere, when sweat tends to condense on the inside of the membrane. This is disguised by giving the garment an internal lining, which contains the dampness within the garment. It must then re-evaporate to escape through the Gore-Tex membrane. This makes the wearer feel cold and clammy, even though the garment is completely waterproof.

The design of a 'soft shell' garment is based on the premise that breathability is much more important than ultimate waterproofness. These garments are windproof but not fully waterproof. Instead of a membrane, they rely on the warmth of the body to keep out moisture, mimicking the way a hairy animal keeps dry. In very heavy rain, a certain amount of rainwater may seep through the outer garment, but the heat of the body soon drives it out again. Technical soft shell garments, such as those designed for mountain walkers, can also be worn in a boat, and they perform well in most conditions. They do, however, rely on the wearer keeping active, and are not ideal for long periods sitting still in the rain. This means that they need to be supplemented by proper oilies in really bad weather, but the principle is still a good one, even if it needs some adaptation for nautical conditions.

As I am sceptical about the inflated claims made for synthetic garments, my own clothing uses a mixture of new and old technology and is mostly made from natural materials. I replicate the 'soft shell' principle using more traditional fabrics, wearing clothes much closer to the ones that George Mallory would have known than the garb of the typical modern yachtsman.

Base-layer garments

Choice of clothing is inevitably a very personal one. Over time, you will find which clothes work for you and which don't. It all depends on your style of dinghy cruising and on your personal taste. I have tried out all sorts of garments over the years, and found what works for me, but I have no intention of forcing my preferences upon the reader. Nonetheless, you may be interested in what I wear.

In cooler weather I put on a base layer of 100g fleece, consisting of long johns and a long-sleeved top. Whatever the claims made for synthetic undergarments, I believe that the best base layers are made of merino wool. This material is very breathable, does not retain smells if worn for long periods, and has the miraculous ability to be cool in hot weather and yet warming when it's cold.

The reason for this is that wool is able to transport moisture in the form of vapour as well as liquid, whereas synthetic baselayers transport moisture primarily as liquid, by a process of 'wicking'. Sweat moves through a wool garment as water vapour and does not need to condense, wick, and then re-evaporate, as it must do if you wear a synthetic base layer. Remarkably, wool also produces warmth when the garment gets damp. This may seem wildly improbable, but it is true. The cause is rather technical, and is called 'heat of sorption'. The overall effect is that you will feel dry and warm when wearing

Merino wool baselayer garments. These are by Icebreaker of New Zealand.

woollens, even in damp conditions. This is why sheep are covered in wool and not a synthetic fleece.

Midlayer garments

Midlayers are mostly worn on the top half of the body. Only in very cold conditions do you need to put an additional insulation layer on your legs. Most people wear synthetic fleece as a midlayer, but my midlayers are various weights of wool fleece. I am a great fan of the garments made by Woolpower of Sweden, designed to combat the long winters in high latitudes. I find these clothes very comfortable in a range of conditions. No matter how long or short the trip, I pack a selection of different Woolpower tops in various weights as well as a pair of Ullfrotté leggings. This provides me with different combinations of clothing that can be layered for different conditions. I can wear every garment all at once in really cold weather, but usually I just put on a single layer.

The wonders of cotton

Modern sailors tend to wear their oilies virtually all the time, even when it is not raining, as this is vital to protect their vulnerable midlayers from the spray. In contrast, I only wear my oilies in very wet weather or a very rough sea. Most of the time I rely on my 'soft shell' system to protect me from the wind and spray, and to keep me comfortable.

I tend to wear the same outer garments the whole time on the boat, even on a cruise of a number of days' duration, rinsing them out occasionally when they become too stiff with salt or clagged with mud. These are not modern technical garments, however. Instead they are made of cotton.

There is much propaganda to the effect that cotton has no place in serious outdoor attire. Nonetheless, my usual sailing top is a canvas fisherman's smock, typical of those once used for fishing under sail. These wonderfully flexible garments can be worn as a shirt in hot weather, or as a windproof top over other garments. If treated with wash-in waterproofing, such as that made by Nikwax, they will shrug off spray and drizzle. They cannot be made totally waterproof, however, so I substitute an oily jacket if it really begins to pour down, but it is surprising how rarely this is necessary.

For many years my standard sailing trousers were of 'Ventile'. I have mentioned this material before in connection with boat tents. Ventile is a tightly woven cotton that manages to be extremely breathable, windproof and virtually completely waterproof, without relying on membranes or applied waterproofing. Developed during the Second World War to keep British antisubmarine aircrew (who had to ditch in the North Atlantic) alive for long enough to be picked up out of the sea, garments made from this remarkable product are still available from specialist suppliers of expedition gear.

Ventile garments are lovely things in all sorts of ways, and I still feel nostalgic for all the years I used to wear them. But they are only made by a few specialist manufacturers and so they are breathtakingly expensive to buy. That would not be a problem if they lasted a long time, and so they do if used on land. But if they are washed frequently to remove caked on salt, which is inevitable for sailing clothes, their life is markedly shortened. Repeated washing weakens the weave and they become prone to damage. Hence, the standard wear on my legs is now a pair of polycotton walking trousers. These are not waterproof, but if they get wet from rain or spray, they soon dry.

I like trousers without cargo pockets, which encumber your legs and tend to get caught on things on board a boat, but with a good number of zips on their other pockets so I do not lose my loose change or my wallet, in case I have forgotten to take them out of the trousers and stow somewhere safer. I wear these trousers on their own, or over merino wool leggings in cool weather.

Oilies

If it starts to bucket down, or when a lot of spray is coming on board, even the best 'soft shell' will fail to cut the mustard. In bad conditions there is no substitute for a full set of marine waterproofs, which we sailors still call 'oilies'. These must be sufficiently robust to cope with rough treatment in an open boat, as you will inevitably damage them when scrambling over barnacle-encrusted rocks or climbing a rough sea wall.

I do not normally wear my oilies over my smock or my trousers, but strip them off and put them on directly over my woollen baselayer or midlayer garments. These

AVEL DRO on a river, drifting with the wind. The mast is down as I have been passing under low bridges. I am wearing my usual get-up of an oiled cotton hat, canvas smock and outdoor trousers. (Ronan Coquil)

Guy Cotten's simple oilies are the standard issue on most commercial fishing boats, as well as many cruising dinghies.

The round-Britain dinghy sailor Jeremy Warren models the Musto HPX Ocean Gore-Tex drysuit. This sort of high-end gear is essential for ambitious offshore dinghy cruising. (Jeremy Warren)

garments remain very comfortable when worn under impervious oilies, whereas cotton clothes would soon feel clammy. Many cruising dinghy sailors use standard yachtsmen's oilies, and there is no harm in that, if you believe their claims for breathability, find them comfortable and you have somewhere to stow them. Personally I prefer the sturdy yellow PVC oilies universally used by professional fishermen, and obtainable in commercial chandleries serving the few remaining British fishing ports. They are invariably manufactured by Guy Cotten, and are more widely available in France, where they are made.

Guy Cotten's range is offered in various grades – the more expensive ones are more robust but also softer and more comfortable. None of their garments pretend to be breathable, but neither is a Gore-Tex jacket in very heavy rain. Guy Cotten's commercial range is made of a robust cloth with a thick covering of PVC. They are best used over wool layers, rather than synthetics, as natural woollen fabric will absorb the moisture created by your perspiration.

Drysuits

If you want to keep perfectly dry even in heavy rain, dashing spray, and to laugh in the face of capsizes, you need a drysuit. These are like a set of oilies, but made in one piece with neoprene seats around neck and wrist holes, and bonded on socks encasing your feet. For dinghy use you need one of breathable material like Gore-Tex. People like Will Hodshon and Rich Mitchell, who do crazy things like sail a Wayfarer dinghy round Britain non-stop, basically wear these all the time, even when sleeping aboard their dinghy.

The great advantage of a drysuit is that you will remain dry even if you end up in

(ABOVE) Wonderful SealSkinz waterproof socks have made wet feet a thing of the past.

(RIGHT) Chris Waite cooks his breakfast wearing his summer dinghy gear: a fleece top over a light cotton shirt, and cotton trousers.

the sea in a capsize. They are effectively a survival suit. If you intend to do extensive, long distance open water passages they are probably essential. Personally I find even waterproofs too sweaty for the sort of sailing I do, which often involves prolonged periods rowing, and I prefer to wear clothes with no outer waterproof membrane. But my clothes would not keep me alive for very long during a prolonged immersion, and a drysuit would.

Clothes for hot weather

In very hot weather my normal woollen garments become too warm, and I wear lighter gear. The role of clothing in hot weather is not to keep heat in, but largely for protection from the sun. This is important. The dangers of skin cancer should not be underestimated. Cotton really comes into its own in these conditions. My standard lightweight garb is a pair of polycotton walking trousers and a long sleeved shirt. The traditional cloth for warm weather is linen, and this has started to

become more widely available. If you are sailing somewhere hot, a long-sleeved linen shirt and some linen trousers are well worth carrying aboard.

Footwear

In hot weather I wear sandals. I find that plastic beach sandals abrade my feet, so I use a cheap pair of ordinary with Velcro straps and accept that they will eventually fall apart from wading in the sea. The rest of the time I wear sea boots. These inevitably get water in them, so I wear a pair of 'SealSkinz' socks inside my boots. SealSkinz are made of merino wool, but contain a Gore-Tex layer, which makes them waterproof and fairly breathable.

Night attire

If you are embarked on an extended cruise of a few days' duration, sleeping aboard your dinghy, it is easy to get into slovenly habits. It is tempting to keep on wearing the same clothes all the time, even in bed. You must make an effort to remain more

soiled work gear, but they prided themselves on looking presentable for special events. Dinghy cruising sailors should have the same proud attitude. We have our reputations to defend. My own shore gear, kept ready for all those swanky invitations, consists of a spare pair of chino trousers, a cotton shirt, clean socks and a change of underwear.

When all your sailing gear is hopelessly dirty, your shore gear comes in handy to wear in the launderette, rather than sitting there naked while your clothes are washing.

civilised, however. Think of the great explorers of the past and how they would change for dinner even in the wilderness! Salt-caked and sweaty clothing irritates the skin if worn continuously, and once your skin has become inflamed, it is difficult to remedy the situation.

I always pack a separate set of base-layer garments to change into every evening. These are kept with my sleeping bag and used as pyjamas, but they look sufficiently 'proper' that I can wear them during a midnight emergency without shocking my neighbours. After breakfast, I change back into my normal sailing gear, often putting on exactly the same clothes that I was wearing the day before, with only a change of my most intimate underwear.

Shore gear

Dinghy cruising sailors are popular, and we are often invited to dinner by people we have just met. Whether this is out of affection, or sympathy for the perceived hardship of our sailing lifestyle, it is difficult to say. In any case, it is worthwhile packing a set of presentable 'shore gear' for the inevitable invitation to dine ashore.

In the days of working sail, open boatmen had no choice but to go ashore in their

PERSONAL HYGIENE ON PASSAGE

It is easy for dinghy sailors to neglect washing on a long passage at sea (yes, even the female ones). Stripping off to wash yourself feels such a pain, especially on a cold day. If the seawater is reasonably warm, you can jump in and swim round the boat, clamber back aboard to lather yourself all over, then jump back in again to rinse off. I did this every day on a cruise in the Baltic once. You will need a soap that works in salt water though. I carry a bottle of special outdoor soap, which works both for washing the body and also as shampoo. It can also be used for washing clothes by hand, and is biodegradable.

In cold weather, it is tempting to stop washing altogether until you get to a sailing club with hot showers. This is normal sailing behaviour, even on yachts. But we should learn from the Marines, who once came to my aid in Poole Harbour. They find washing just as much of a pain as you do. When on extended patrol, these tough troops are trained to wash themselves with a few baby wipes, and I suggest that you do too. If you do not have time or the facilities for a proper wash, you should wipe yourself down with a couple of these amazing products, which are completely wasted on unappreciative babies.

Two or three baby wipes will ensure that you emerge from your boat tent acceptably clean and sweet-smelling each morning. A standard pack of baby wipes lasts for many weeks. Unlike toilet paper, baby wipes do not break down in the sea and so they should not be thrown overboard. Instead they should be placed in the gash bucket and disposed of properly ashore.

If you do feel motivated to have a proper wash, you need a washing bowl. Either carry a folding washing bowl or use one of the other receptacles on board.

For drying yourself, a backpacking towel performs far better than a normal towel, which takes up lots of space and is usually impossible to dry. 'Pack towels' dry you just as effectively, then air-dry themselves in a trice, ready to be packed into a miraculously small space.

Shaving

I gave up shaving during the Great Storm of 1987, as it was incompatible with life onboard the boat I was sailing at the time. The rest of you would be less likely to cut yourselves if you used a battery shaver. Either that, or you should leave off shaving your face or legs until you get to a friendly yacht club.

Public toilets

Sometimes, cruising dinghy sailors need to wash themselves in public toilets. In the UK these vary in their facilities and their charm, and often the plugs have mysteriously disappeared from the hand basins. Wise sailors always carry a spare stopper in their washbag. It is also a good idea to take some toilet paper with you, as this is not always

Bedtime in a Tideway on the Norfolk Broads. (Nick Vowles)

provided either. I always keep a small pack of paper hankies in my pocket for this purpose.

Other items
Sunglasses

If you are a sensible soul and wear a hat with a broad brim, sunglasses are less important than they are for ordinary mortals, as your eyes will be well shaded. Sun glasses are, however, very useful for cutting down the glare off the sea. The ones that curve and clip to your head above your ears are less likely to come adrift.

Spectacle wearers

Spectacles are a problem at sea, as the salt inevitably builds up on the lenses, requiring frequent cleaning. Wearing glasses did not really cramp the style of Sir Francis Chichester, however. Even so, it is best to wear contact lenses if possible. But you will never manage to keep sand out of your lenses if you wear the type of contacts that are reused over several days. The best ones to use on a cruising dinghy are the 'daily replaceable' type, in which you unwrap a fresh hygienic lens every day.

Safely home

The forecast is Force 7 from the south, and gusting more. Avel Dro *strains against her mooring lines, pitching and surging against the concrete jetty, while the fair tide runs to waste beneath its barnacled piles. She cannot stay moored here any longer. I cast off without reefing, and set off down the estuary.*

It is not blowing too hard yet, but the wind is rolling down in gusts from the low wooded hills on my port beam. Out to starboard there is a rocky point, and beyond it the northern shore opens out into a deep bay. On the far side of the bay is my destination, the old fishing port of Tinduff. I should really stop and tie down that reef now, while I have the whole width of the estuary to do it in, but I am eager to get into port before the storm hits. Avel Dro *is making a good speed, slapping purposefully into the waves.*

The first gust hits very suddenly, sweeping darkly across the water and smashing into the sail. Avel Dro *lurches violently. I let the mainsheet out on the run, the rope burning through my fingers. The sail flogs mercilessly, shaking the mast viciously. I yank the plate up to stop her tripping over it, and she starts making tremendous leeway. The waves are breaking on her beam. A larger wave comes smashing over the bow and runs down over the thwarts.*

I nurse her along, pulling in the sheet so only the rear corner of the sail is brought up to the wind. The rocky northern shore is close abeam of me now, and I am fast running out of sea room. I must get her around the point at all costs. In desperation I drop the plate to reduce the leeway. This makes Avel Dro *rather tippier, but she stands up to it.*

Finally we clear the point. At last I have sufficient sea room to risk stopping to reef the sail. Plate up again so she will slide sideways when the waves smash into her. Tiller loose so she lies with the quarter to the seas, lifting lightly to the breaking waves. I drop the sail on the run, without sheeting it in first. Most of it ends up in the sea, so I haul it aboard laden with seawater. It is like handling a net full of cod. Then I reef her right down. Three reefs in the sail. No mucking about now.

The worse the conditions, the more important it is to do things properly. I concentrate on rolling the great wodge of wet terylene, while keeping the foot of the sail tight. It is raining heavily now, pouring off the cuffs of my oilskins onto my hands. At last the sail is rolled to my satisfaction and the long line of reef points are tied around it.

It will be easier to hoist the sail on the starboard tack, so that the lugsail blows away from the mast. I gybe the boat round, steering under the windage of the rig alone. Then I go forward to the foot of the mast. I hoist the sail, swig the halyard tight and cleat the wet rope round the belaying pin, then harden in the tack downhaul. I am fast running out of sea room again. Got to get her sailing now: plate down again.

We are approaching the shore rapidly. She must be put back onto the other tack before I put her on the rocks. I look for a flat patch behind a wave. There: that one.

Tiller down: round she comes, up into the wind. I transfer the sheet to the other quarter, and she pays off the wind. Plate up again and I steer the best course for Tinduff, without gybing.

Some of the waves are large enough to set her surfing. Weight right back to save a broach. Got to keep the rudder well down into the water. I must counteract the lightness of helm that tells me the rig is forcing the hull through the water faster than it can stand, otherwise she'll slew uncontrollably into a capsize.

We cannot make Tinduff without gybing. Unhappy to risk even a controlled gybe, I stay her round twice in the steep waves. Even so I end up rushing in towards the harbour uncomfortably close to the concrete mole.

The waves are steeper now as the water shallows. We are surfing most of the time, the boat swooping down the faces of the waves in a rush of spray. My mouth is dry. But boats like Avel Dro fished these waters for generations. I am not the first little sailing boat to have come thundering in towards this big concrete breakwater, eager for the shelter and the safety in its lee, and this thought comforts me.

Avel Dro running into Tinduff.
(David Summerville)

11 TRAILABLE BOATS AND BACKYARD BOATYARDS

It is deep midwinter. The BBC shipping forecast is for storms and high seas. Outside in the dark the wind howls and the rain lashes furiously. This is when a cruising dinghy needs to be tucked up in a snug berth. Fortunately AVEL DRO's winter quarters are secure and deep inland, so I do not need to worry about her. I can stay at home beside the fire, listening to the wind shaking at the windowpanes and dreaming of the new sailing season ahead.

The dinghy ashore on her trailer. It is best if the cover allows her to breathe.

WINTER PLANS

Unlike those poor yacht owners, doomed to sail in the same waters forever, we lucky dinghy sailors are spoilt for choice. Whenever we feel like a change, we can hitch the boat trailer to our car and drive off to waters new. After a comfortable overnight trip on a cross-Channel ferry and a few hours' drive on the other side, *Avel Dro* can be afloat in places that a cruising yacht would take a couple of weeks to reach.

The fire is dying down. I add another log and it crackles back into flame, reminding me of the sun glistening on the water as my dinghy lay at anchor last summer. Where will we go this year, my boat and I? There is so much choice …

But winter is not only a time to plan for the future. It is also when we can reflect on the year past. In these dark, short days I enjoy rereading the logbooks of last year's passages. Interspersed with the dry record of courses steered and seamarks passed, I find notes to myself: 'Stop the food locker handle from fouling the oars', 'Make cool store for milk and eggs', 'Need dedicated stowage for binoculars and Breton plotter'. So I can't lounge here by the fire all winter. I should be doing some work on *Avel Dro*, putting right all the defects I found last year, so she will operate at the peak of efficiency next season.

Although she is kept ashore, *Avel Dro* generally remains 'in commission' most of the winter. On a bright winter's day I sometimes take her down to the coast for a day out. In the old days there was a distinct 'sailing season'. Dinghies were taken home in the autumn and stripped down. The following spring there was a corresponding 'fitting out' period, when the vessel was re-rigged for the new sailing season ahead.

These Thames skiffs are real works of art, but seagoing dinghies usually choose more robust finishes.

Nowadays fibreglass dinghies remain in the sailing club dinghy park all the year round, ready for the winter racing programme, and epoxy-plywood dinghies like *Avel Dro* do not need the same care and attention as their traditionally built forebears.

Even a modern dinghy needs some routine maintenance, however, or she will let you down when you are most relying on her. At best this will be embarrassing – at worst it could be lethal. If our boats are to remain in commission all year round, we must find a way to fit in some maintenance sometime. Dinghy sailors can learn a thing or two from the way that a seagoing ship is kept running. Every few years she has a

THE TIDEWAY

The Tideway is typical of the older design of sailing dinghy, traditionally built of mahogany planking on steamed oak frames, and fastened with rows of copper rivets. At the time of writing, traditional wooden Tideways are still built in the time-honoured way, for those who appreciate traditional craftsmanship. The design is also available with a fibreglass hull, but even these versions are fitted out with a great deal of wood.

The boat carries a gunter rig of modest area. Although not the fastest of dinghies, Tideways are extraordinarily seaworthy for their size. With their helm lashed, they will steer themselves on most points of sailing, they are very resistant to capsize and they row well. Tideways can be propelled by a small outboard clamped onto the transom, but they row so well that an outboard is not really necessary.

I owned a traditional wooden Tideway for many years, and used her for coastal cruising with two people on board. There was not a lot of space to stow all the camping gear for two people, and packing the boat was inevitably an exercise in minimalism. The dinghy is adequately spacious with only one person aboard. In both cases a bed platform must be set up at thwart level, by lifting the bottom boards or by carrying bed boards.

The Tideway is a pleasing and practical dinghy, easy to launch and recover, and can be stowed in the average garage. They are good-looking boats, with an honest and straightforward character. You grow to love them.

(David Schwartz)

major shipyard refit, when she is taken into dry dock and thoroughly overhauled. The rest of the time any necessary maintenance work is carried out while the ship continues to earn her keep on the oceans of the world. The programme of work is fitted around her maritime duties.

BOSUN'S WORK

On a seagoing vessel, it is the Bosun's job to ensure that the fabric of the vessel and her systems are kept on the top line. The Bosun's store holds sufficient stock of materials and tools to undertake routine work on the fabric of the ship, and the Bosun is skilled in all aspects of ship repair and maintenance, which takes place continually as the ship sails along.

If you have time for a proper winter refit, it is a good opportunity to strip the boat right down, clean her out and overhaul everything systematically. But if you cannot fit a full refit into your packed programme, you should treat your boat maintenance as Bosun's Work, rather than Shipyard Work. Instead of saving up your boat maintenance to be done sometime in the future, it is best to break it down into a series of small items that can be fitted in between your sailing trips. Produce a clear set of priorities and then plan a systematic schedule of work.

When he walks around boat shows inspecting the other craft, the Bosun whistles with admiration as he strokes the decks of a lovingly varnished vessel, glossy as a grand piano. In comparison, *Avel Dro* is as dowdy as a country cousin at a metropolitan ball. But the Bosun does not go for dolled-up city girls. He knows that a cruising dinghy will never win a concours d'élégance. Cruising dinghies are working

boats. A 'yacht finish' is as out of place on them as it would be on a trawler.

When the weather cuts up rough off the coast, and you're trying to keep your feet in a bucking dinghy, fine finishes count for nothing. The Stockholm tar on *Avel Dro*'s bottom boards may smell and look grubby, but it is non-slip, it preserves the timber and it's easy to touch up when it gets scuffed. The Bosun is as likely to replace it with slippy varnish as he would forgo the comforts of a longshore bar at the end of a hard sea passage.

Marlinespike seamanship

Skills in knots, lashings, splices and whippings were once central to the seafarer's craft, but many yachtsmen consider them arcane. What is the point of going to all the trouble to learn how to to splice an eye, when you can buy warps from the chandlery with the loops already turned in the end?

Modern yachtsmen and women can get away with rudimentary rope craft, as yacht sailing often means just hopping from one fully equipped marina to another. In the half-tide creeks and remote backwaters that dinghy cruisers love to frequent, there may be no assistance for many lonely miles. This is why a dinghy cruising sailor needs all the traditional skills of a seaman.

When Captain Cook ran *Endeavour* on to Australia's Great Barrier Reef in 1770, seriously damaging her hull, he jettisoned her guns, ballast and other stores to lighten the ship enough float her off and then put her ashore in the Endeavour River in modern New South Wales for repairs. Cook beached the ship, careened her for underwater repairs and spent six weeks in Australia making her seaworthy again. *Endeavour* was thoroughly self-sufficient, half a world away from the nearest shipyard. Every component could be rebuilt using the skills available on board, materials readily to hand or in the ship's stores. Cruising sailors should model themselves on Cook.

Look at a serious cruising dinghy and you will see few mass-produced fittings. Gear has a hard life on any sea boat, and cruising dinghies take more of a battering than similar sized racing boats. It is generally best to keep the gear simple. If a special fitting is required which is not repairable with the skills and the tools on board, you should always carry a spare.

Ropework

Virtually all the ropes on my *Avel Dro* are conventional three-strand ropes, rather than braided. This is because I like to make all my own splices, and the splicing of braided rope is far too complicated for me. The only braided ropes on board are the main sheet and the fall of the main halyard, as this type of rope is more comfortable to hold for long periods.

All seamen should be able to splice an eye, put a whipping in the end of a rope and know the most common knots: the clove hitch, bowline, fisherman's bend, rolling hitch, reef knot, figure-of-eight knot, sheet bend and lighterman's hitch (or tugboat bend). These will see you through every eventuality at sea.

For tying up a sail, lashing down gear and innumerable other uses on a boat, the humble gasket is invaluable. This is simply a short length of 6mm rope with an eye spliced in the end. When used as a gasket, it is passed round the sail and then secured with a simple slipped half hitch. You should make up your own and have a good supply on board. I have a special canvas bag fixed to the side of the centreboard case to put them in. It is a wonder how many uses there are for these humble objects.

Painting and varnishing

Wooden boats inevitably need more maintenance than fibreglass ones, but even plastic dinghies often have something that needs rubbing down and re-varnishing. Only rotomoulded polyethylene boats seem to have no natural materials at all.

Some people really enjoy varnishing. They delight in building up coat after coat, rubbing down between each one, vacuuming and then wiping down with a tack rag to pick up the last of the dust, before lovingly brushing on the next layer of varnish. I owned a varnished clinker dinghy for many years, so I did a lot of this.

Nowadays, I try to do more sailing and less varnishing, so my present dinghy has finishes that are as low maintenance as possible. The clinker plywood hull is painted inside and out. Her gunwales, thwarts and spars are clear finished, but not varnished. Instead I use a medium-build wood stain (International Woodskin). This is nowhere near as pretty as varnish, but infinitely less work. Its great advantage over varnish is that only two or three coats are required, not ten or twelve. When the coating gets scuffed it can simply be touched up, or lightly rubbed down and an additional coat put on top.

I treat *Avel Dro* as a workboat, with workboat finishes. It is wonderful to be released from the tyranny of varnish. Traditional workboats were never finished with varnish. Their crew would just wipe their spars down with linseed oil. I have friends with traditional boats who still do this, and it is very effective, if rather sticky. On a modern dinghy, modern stains are a better choice.

If you use wood stains on clear-finished timber, choose one with a very light hue, like International Woodskin, otherwise

Making running repairs to Avel Dro's hull, dried out against a quayside.

everything turns a sludgy brown. Just because your gunwales are built of teak or mahogany does not mean you have to use a teak or mahogany stain. A naturally coloured one is perfectly suitable.

My dinghy has a waterline marked on her hull, with a different coloured finish above and below. This means that I do not need to repaint the whole of the hull every time, but can attend either to the topsides or the under-waterline coating separately. The best way to mark a waterline is to obtain a revolving builders' laser level. This will draw a red line with light across your hull. Ensure that the boat is chocked level on her trailer, and then go over the line with a felt-tipped pen. Then you can either 'cut in' the waterline with a paintbrush, or use masking tape.

I have always used proper marine paints on my boats, but some people prefer household paints, which they claim are just as effective and substantially cheaper. I am not sure that this is the case. You get what you pay for with paint, and one of the things you are paying for is the pigment. Better paints tend to have nicer colours.

Paints are designed to work as a system, with their own primers and undercoats. In any paint system, it is the primer that really does the job of protecting the timber. Good primers incorporate lots of metal and form a very effective barrier against moisture. It is worth taking the time to put a decent number of coats of primer on the hull before putting on the topcoat, thinning the first coat of primer so it soaks in. I tend to finish the priming layers with a coat of primer mixed 50-50 with topcoat, which makes the colour change to the topcoat less pronounced.

It is worth laying the sails out once a year, checking them over and carrying out any necessary small repairs.

Maintaining a GRP hull

GRP may not need painting, but it appreciates being washed down with fresh water and detergent a few times a season, and that includes inside any buoyancy tanks with access hatches. While washing down, check for any stress cracks where fittings may be overloading the hull. GRP dinghies that are kept on a mooring may also need antifouling. This should be scrubbed down and recoated every year or two.

Maintaining sails

Cruising sails tend to be left bent on their spars all year. But once a year they should be taken off and scrubbed gently with soap to get rid of the salt. At the same time, it is worth looking them over to see if any seams are becoming unstitched. A little bit of work with a sailmaker's palm and needle can prevent a more serious failure later on. Good sailmakers provide a checking and cleaning service, but if you want your sails dealt with quickly, choose a time when they are quiet, and not just before the start of the sailing season in the spring.

If you need major repairs or a new sail made, remember that many sailmakers only know about racing dinghy sails or yacht sails, not sails for cruising dinghies. Find a sailmaker who is experienced in making sails for cruising boats, and understands arcane matters like reef points.

As with paints, you very much get what you pay for with sails. There is a good reason why cheap sails are cheap. Better sailcloth is more expensive, and better-finished sails often incorporate 'hand work', which is much more time-consuming. Like a well-cut business suit, it is worth investing in a quality suit of sails. Good cruising sails will last you perhaps twenty years, and there is nothing more beautiful than a set of well-cut sails.

Buying boat gear

A dinghy owner has less reason to spend lots of money in the yacht chandlery than a yacht sailor. But even dinghies need chandlery occasionally, and it is tempting to buy gear on the internet, which seems cheaper (at least until you pay the postage). But I like to be able to handle the product before buying it. A good yacht chandlery is also a great source of information and good advice. They know which products are popular with their customers and which have a reputation for failing early.

Boat jumbles are not as common as they once were, but they are a great place to stock up with chandlery. Equipment has a hard life in a cruising boat, so cruising sailors incline towards the old-fashioned and robust rather than the flash and modern. This makes the boat jumble our natural habitat. Jumbles are the places to buy chunky Seagull outboards, which will start on the second pull even after you have dropped them overboard, or a Walker trailing log. Experienced jumblers always take a rucksack or a wheelbarrow with them to carry their bargain purchases back to the car.

The road trailer

The reason a cruising dinghy can be kept snug at home in her 'backyard boatyard' is because she can be transported on a road trailer. Many cruising dinghies live on their trailers all year round. A boat trailer is not just a way to move your boat around; it cradles her boat hull when not in use. Despite this, many trailers often lead a Cinderella existence. Money is lavished on the boat, but begrudged on the trailer. Lovely boats are put on the cheapest trailers.

This is misguided. The boat and trailer should be seen as a combination. Cruising dinghies do most of their passage-making by road, leapfrogging dangerous and tedious bits of sea to arrive directly at the interesting bits of water. If you were intending to make such a long passage by sea, surely you would not begrudge spending money fitting out your boat for the purpose? That's why you should not be stingy about spending money on the boat trailer, when it achieves the same objective. Money spent on a trailer is money well spent.

If your dinghy is traditionally constructed, ensure that the trailer supports her properly, or the hull will distort. Old clinker dinghies often become hogged and leaky after for many years sitting on a poorly designed trailer. A line of close-set rollers should continuously support the keel of a traditional boat, and the bilge supports must not be set too high or they will slowly distort the shape of the hull.

Avel Dro on her trailer, being prepared for the road.

Dinghies using more modern forms of construction are much more stable than traditional wooden boats, and their hulls are often stronger than the trailer itself. A lightly built trailer relies on the strength of the boat to stop it flexing when on the road, whereas a traditionally constructed wooden dinghy needs to sit on a heavy and stout trailer.

A light trailer may weigh as little as a quarter of the all-up weight of the boat, whereas a heavy trailer could be half the weight of its load. To ensure that you are towing in accordance with the law, you will need to know the gross vehicle weight (GVW) of the trailer, which is the weight of the boat and trailer combined. Remember that a dinghy loaded with cruising gear will be substantially heavier than a stripped-down racing craft. If you take your dinghy straight to a public weighbridge on the way back from a cruise, you can check her weight with all the gear aboard. You may be surprised how heavy it is.

Reversing a boat trailer

Boat trailers often need to be reversed down slipways and other places, and you should become skilled in this. Learning how to handle your boat on land is as important as handling her afloat. Practise until you can reverse your trailer confidently, loaded or light. Take the car and trailer to an area of hard standing and keep trying until you have mastered it.

Reversing a trailer is a bit like learning to scull over the stern – difficult to explain and best learnt by trial and error. The following explanation may help, or perhaps confuse. Reversing in a straight line means making very rapid and subtle adjustments to the steering wheel, and is best attempted after you have mastered the trick of reversing around a corner.

To turn a corner when reversing, the steering wheel of the car must be turned the opposite way than normal. This is to give the back of the trailer a 'kick' in the right direction. Once the trailer has started to turn, you can begin to turn the car steering wheel the other way, so that the car follows the trailer around the bend. If you get into difficulties, just drive forward until the whole 'rig' has straightened out, and then try again.

Once you have mastered steering the trailer around a bend, you can try reversing it in a straight line. This also means turning the car wheel the opposite way than with a car on its own, but very subtly. You should never turn the wheel more than about a quarter turn. The trick is to detect the slightest movement of the trailer, and to correct it before it gets too far out of line with the car.

It is much more difficult to reverse a trailer using the wing mirrors than by looking over your shoulder. Reversing using wing mirrors is only for advanced students, or for people who drive vans. Turn half round in the driver's seat so you can look fully over your shoulder. One hand should be on the back of the passenger seat, and your other hand should be grasping the top of the steering wheel. You should now be able to see the boat and trailer clearly through the rear window of the car. If your car is a hatchback or an estate, opening the rear hatch will allow you to see the trailer more clearly, especially if there is no boat on it. It may help if you also fold down the back seats.

Reversing with the back hatch open is particularly useful when bringing the car up to a detached trailer. It is difficult to know how close you are to the trailer's drawbar if you cannot see it below the rear windowsill of your car. After raising the rear hatch, you should be able to see both the car's tow hitch and the trailer's drawbar through the back of your car. This makes it much easier to bring the two together.

TRAILER TYPES

All boat trailers should be hot-dip galvanised, so they can cope with the marine environment. They should also be designed so that launching and recovery is as easy and stress-free as possible. A boat trailer should have a winch, jockey wheel and lots of rollers to support the boat evenly. The trailer should be adjusted so that it is lightly balanced, with only a moderate nose weight. You can adjust the balance of the trailer by moving the wheel axle forward and backwards.

An ordinary trailer may be adequate for a light dinghy, but there are also more sophisticated ones: combi-trailers, break-back trailers and swing-beam trailers. But we will deal with the ordinary ones first.

Ordinary road trailers

An ordinary trailer is simply an axle connected to a drawbar, with some sort of triangulation to stop the whole thing racking. Light trailers have no form of braking and are usually detached from the car for launching and recovery. To launch the dinghy, the trailer is pushed into the water by hand until the boat floats off. At the end of a day's sailing, the trailer is wheeled back into the water, the boat is floated on to it, and then the trailer and boat are hauled back up the slipway by the crew.

There is nothing wrong with this sort of trailer, but it should be fitted with rollers, a winch and jockey wheel, as I have recommended. These features can usually be retrofitted quite easily.

An ordinary road trailer being reversed down the slipway. This trailer is very simple. It has a winch, but no brakes or other refinements.

Braked and unbraked trailers

Below a certain weight, a trailer can be unbraked. Such trailers are cheaper and less complicated than the braked ones, but the trailer wheels should always be chocked if you leave the trailer on a slope when it is not hitched to the car, because there is no handbrake on the trailer.

As a braked trailer does not rely totally on the brakes of the towing vehicle, such trailers can carry much heavier loads. Their brakes are very vulnerable to corrosion, however, and you should take extra care to keep the wheels from being immersed. On the better examples, the brake drums are fitted with a freshwater flushing system. This allows a water hose to be attached to the trailer, to flush any salt out of the brake drums before the trailer is driven off onto the road.

The total weight of trailer that your car can tow, braked and unbraked, will be recorded in the manfacturer's information, and should not be exceeded or you will invalidate your insurance.

Trailer lights

Trailer lights were generally mounted on a detachable lighting board mounted on to the transom of the boat. A wire was taken from the lighting board along the trailer then draped along the drawbar and plugged into the electrical socket on the back of the car. This is still relatively common, but in Europe the newer EC-marked trailers always have the lighting board mounted on the rear of the trailer, as well as small forward-pointing white lights defining the width of the loaded trailer. All the wiring is run inside the trailer. Trailer lights used to be prone to failure, but recent advances in LED technology have made them much more reliable.

LAUNCHING AND RECOVERING A DINGHY

Many dinghy owners simply float their dinghy onto the road trailer. They immerse the trailer in the water until the dinghy can be floated over the chocks. The trailer and dinghy are then pulled out of the water together, by hand. This straightforward method inevitably means wading into the water deeper than your sea boots can cope with, so they get full of water and the bottoms of your trousers get soaked. In hot countries, people wear shorts and sandals to recover their boats. In cold countries, some boat owners change into thigh waders, while others take their shoes and socks off, roll up their trouser legs and put up with the cold.

Spouses who are less keen on sailing often say that recovering the boat is 'the worst bit of sailing'. I do not have the statistics to hand just now, but I am sure that it has led to divorces. The tragedy is that this is completely unnecessary. Immersing your trailer in the water is bad for the trailer, bad for your back and bad for your relationships. Do not do it.

The Lifeboat Method

There is no reason to immerse even an ordinary trailer in the water, and there is no reason to get your feet wet. All you need to do is to equip yourself with a stout rope some 20ft (7m) long, and a pair of wooden chocks for the trailer wheels.

The Lifeboat Method only works on steep slipways where you can take a car virtually right down to the water. Reverse your car and trailer down the slipway until the wheels of the trailer are just touching the

The Lifeboat Method.

The Rope Trick.

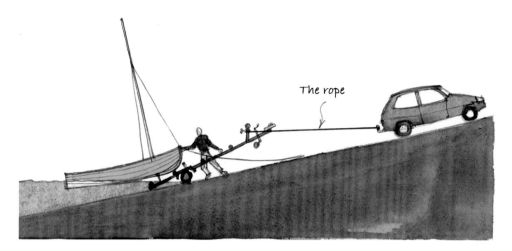

The rope

water, and then engage the handbrake. If the slipway is particularly steep, you should leave the car in gear with the ignition off.

Unfasten the dinghy from the winch rope and then simply push her straight off the trailer, stern-first into the water, rather like launching a lifeboat. There might need to be a little bit of jiggling to get her moving, and then off she will go. But always make sure you have attached the painter to the trailer with plenty of slack before you do this, otherwise the boat may escape your clutches and go off on her own.

If the slipway is less steep and the Lifeboat Method does not work, and you will have to deploy the Rope Trick. This is why you brought the rope and the wooden chocks with you.

Launching using the Rope Trick

Start the same way as The Lifeboat Method. Reverse the car and trailer down the slipway and stop the car some 15ft (4.5m) short of the water. Now chock the trailer wheels and unhitch the trailer from the car. Wind the drawbar of the trailer up

with the jockey wheel until it is well above the tow hitch.

Take a length of stout rope and tie it to the front of the trailer. Round the base of the winch post is a good place. Now also tie it to the car's tow hitch with a round turn and two half hitches knot, so that the trailer is held close to the car by the rope. You can now remove the wheel chocks from the trailer.

Take the half hitches off the rope, so the trailer is only held just by the round turn. Then take off a half a turn from the hitch and gently lower the trailer down the slipway towards the water by letting out the rope, keeping the remaining half turn around the ball hitch. When the trailer wheels are just short of the water, tie off the rope with a couple of half hitches again.

Detach the boat from the trailer winch rope and then give the boat a good push backwards. This will move it beyond the trailer balance point, so that the whole trailer tips up backwards, held in place by the rope connecting it to the car's ball hitch. The boat should now slide off the trailer under the force of gravity. If the water is deep enough, she will float away, so the dinghy painter needs to have been attached somewhere to stop this happening.

Sometimes the dinghy's stern grounds in shallow water. If this happens, you will need to pull the trailer out from under her. Make sure someone is holding your boat's painter or it is made fast to a mooring ring on the slipway (if there is one). Go back to the car, take off the handbrake and gently drive it forward, so it pulls the trailer by the rope. Once the trailer has been dragged clear of the dinghy's bows, it will drop back down level, its drawbar resting on the jockey wheel. The trailer can then be towed back up the slipway, still attached to its rope, until you have reached the flat ground at the top. The rope can then be untied and the trailer hitched directly to the car.

Dinghy recovery using the Rope Trick

The Rope Trick is also a way of recovering a dinghy with an ordinary trailer. Begin by floating the dinghy up to the bottom of the slipway and make her fast if you can. You may have to use the anchor. Reverse the car and trailer down the slipway, bringing the trailer to a stop 10ft (3m) short of the water. Fasten a rope between the trailer and the car ball hitch, as described above. Then push the trailer down to the water's edge. It may be necessary to dip the rim of the wheels in the water, but try to keep the wheel bearings clear if you can. Tie off the rope on the car tow hitch with a round turn and two half hitches, so that the trailer cannot move from this position.

Haul sufficient rope off the winch, so that the winch rope can reach the dinghy when it is at the end of the trailer. Now float your dinghy around until her bows are just touching the last roller on the trailer.

Clip the winch rope to the prow of the dinghy, straighten her up and then start winching. As the rope is tensioned, lift the front of the trailer so that it tips up, pivoting on its wheels, and the back of the trailer dips down towards the water, until the boat begins to ride up onto the rollers. Then she will begin to work her way up the trailer, pulled by the winch rope.

As the boat comes onto the trailer, she will eventually reach the balance point. The front of the trailer will now drop down again. When the boat is fully onto the trailer, return to the wheel of the car and pull the trailer up the slipway, towing it behind the car on the end of the rope. When you are far enough up the slipway to be clear of any mud and slime, chock the trailer wheels, remove the rope, reverse the car back and hitch the trailer directly to the car.

On more muddy and slimy slipways you may need a longer rope, perhaps 100ft (30m) long, which you can use to lower your trailer right down the slipway, leaving your car on the flat ground at the top. The Rope Trick works with any length of rope.

MORE ADVANCED TRAILERS

Combi-trailers

Many dinghy owners prefer 'combi-trailers'. These are a combination of launching trolley and road trailer. They are a bit like the Apollo 11 spacecraft – they divide into a launching module and a road module. Only the launching module descends to the water, while the road module remains far away from anything wet or salty.

The idea is that you park the boat and trailer on the shore near to the slipway, detach the launching trolley from the road trailer and use it to wheel the boat into

(RIGHT) This combi trailer
has been adapted to support
the stern of this traditional
dinghy (a Tideway).

(BELOW LEFT) A Wayfarer being
recovered on a combi-trailer.
Here the boat is being floated
onto the trolley section ...

... and here (BELOW RIGHT) the
Wayfarer is being hauled
up the slipway on her trolley
behind the car.

the water. Recovering the dinghy is done by floating it onto the launching trolley, wheeling it back up the slipway and pulling it onto the road module.

This all works very effectively, but the problem for the cruising sailor is that you have to pull the launching trolley up the slipway by hand, and this can be hard work with a heavily loaded cruising dinghy. Variations of the Rope Trick are sometimes deployed on combi-trailers: a jockey wheel is mounted on the launching trolley and the car is used to pull it up the slipway on a long rope. But combi-trailers are really only advantageous if you often launch your dinghy in a sailing club where road trailers are banned from the slipway, and all dinghies have to be launched by hand.

Break-back trailers

Break-back trailers are slightly more sophisticated than an ordinary road trailer, commensurately more expensive and also heavier. Their advantage is that they can usually be left-hitched to the towing vehicle at all stages of launching and recovery, so you rarely need to lug the boat about by hand or indulge in rope tricks.

Avel Dro being recovered on her break-back trailer. Notice how the trailer remains attached to the car. In seawater I would have tried to keep the wheel bearings clear of the water, but this is a freshwater lake. (Amy Edelman)

To launch a dinghy from a break-back trailer, reverse the whole rig down the slipway until the trailer wheels are just at the water's edge. Then engage the car's handbrake, get out of the car and walk round to the trailer. At this stage the boat should be held on the trailer simply by the winch rope. The mechanism that 'breaks' the trailer is now operated. This is designed to allow the back of the trailer to pivot downwards about the axis of the wheel axle. But nothing will happen until you also release the boat from the winch rope. Once you have done this, the front of the boat can be pushed upwards until the back of the trailer dips down towards the water. If the rollers are well greased and the boat is well balanced, the boat may simply roll backwards off the trailer under her own weight, and into the water. Other dinghies sometimes need more encouragement.

Recovering the dinghy is a similar process. The empty trailer is reversed to the water's edge, the breaking mechanism is operated and the back of the trailer is pushed downwards. Sufficient winch rope is pulled off the winch to attach it to the front of the boat, which is then winched onto the trailer. As the boat reaches the trailer's balance point the mechanism will straighten up. Once the boat is fully onto the trailer, the breaking mechanism is fixed and the whole rig is towed back up the slipway.

Break-back trailers tend to be used for heavier boats. They can also be used with the Rope Trick if a slipway is particularly slimy and treacherous, so that the car is kept well away from the slippy part of the slipway. If you have a heavy dinghy, you tend to be more choosy about which slipways you use, however.

Swing-beam trailers

Break-back trailers are rather crude pieces of technology. If you have a heavy boat and you want to launch and recover her with ultimate ease, swing-beam technology is the way to go. Swing-beam trailers are shaped like a tuning fork, enclosing the boat, with pivoted rollers slung between the arms of the fork. The trailer acts rather like a break-back trailer, but works automatically, due to its clever geometry. This type of trailer is standard for heavy speedboats. They are also popular among the owners of really heavy cruising dinghies, such as the Drascombe Lugger. The only problem with swing-beam trailers is that they do not generally support a dinghy's keel along its full length, so they are not normally suitable for traditional wooden dinghies without adaptation.

Using a swing-beam trailer is simply a matter of reversing the trailer to the water's edge and then pushing the boat off the trailer into the water. To recover the boat, she is simply winched back onto the trailer. Big powerboats often drive themselves straight onto their trailers using the thrust of their outboard motors, and then the crew step out dry-shod. After watching the simplicity of that process, you wonder why so many dinghy owners still struggle with the primitive method of floating their boat onto the trailer.

TOWING AND TRAILER REFINEMENTS

Front tow hitches

If you fit a front tow hitch to the towing vehicle, you do not need to reverse the car and trailer down the slipway. Instead, you can drive the trailer down the slipway with the vehicle facing forwards, and the dinghy in full view. This works very well. But you

A BayRaider 20 being recovered on a swing-beam trailer. This sophisticated type of trailer can be used to launch into very shallow water.

must ensure that the tow hitch is removable and is never left in place when the towing vehicle is used on the road, in order to comply with road traffic regulations.

Electric winches

The owners of particularly heavy dinghies might consider fitting an electric winch onto the trailer. These are plugged into the car's electrics and produce a good deal of torque. They are available with remote controls so you can walk all round your boat checking she is coming onto the trailer in a straight line. This is wonderfully civilised, but on lighter boats a geared winch works well enough.

Wheel bearings

Trailer wheel bearings are vulnerable to corrosion, but if you have a break-back or a swing-cradle trailer, it should not usually

be necessary for the wheel bearings to be submerged. Even so, there will come a day when a wave breaks over your trailer. This is not too much of a problem if you keep the bearings well greased. Some bearings are factory sealed, and impossible to top up with grease, but an engineering works will be able to add grease nipples for you. Never mix different types of grease. I use lithium grease.

I have recently replaced my old trailer with a newer EC-marked model, and I am impressed at the advances in trailer technology over the period, not just its integrated LED lighting, but more sophisticated winches and rollers. The trailer wheels also incorporate oil baths with transparent end caps so you can monitor the oil level within.

For trailers with greased wheel bearings there are special products available called 'bearing protectors', which can be

My brand new EC-marked road trailer, delivered 2021, and built to the latest standards. I have adapted it to have low-level rollers at the rear so it can recover my boat when dried out, like my last trailer. It still needs a little more tailoring to my boat however.

Hauling the boat onto the trailer 'dry'.

substituted for standard wheel-bearing caps. These are short cylinders with a grease nipple in the end. They keep the grease under pressure so water cannot get into the bearing, and are extra protection for your wheel bearings if they have to be immersed.

Dry launching and recovery

It is a great advantage if your trailer is set up so you can launch and recover a dinghy 'dry', so you have the ability to get the dinghy off and onto the trailer when she is nowhere near the water. This is invaluable in your 'backyard boatyard' at home, and also comes in handy if you ever need to recover a dinghy that has dried out.

A winched trailer will have the power to pick a boat up off the beach, but the trailer needs to be able to pull itself under the boat, rather than trying to drag the boat onto the trailer. Some swing-beam trailers will do this; it all depends on their geometry, but other trailers are not usually able to work in this way: the back of the trailer just tips downwards and digs into the ground, rather than moving backwards under the boat. I have solved this problem by adding a light pair of trolley wheels to the back of all my boat trailers. These little wheels only come into contact with the ground when the trailer is tipped up, and allow the trailer to winch itself smoothly under the boat.

Back to Sein

The easterly wind that blew me all the way along the granite coast of Northern Brittany is dying now. Its final breaths took me through the intricate inshore passages that lace the rock-strewn shallows west of l'Aber-Wrac'h. Once I emerged into the open ocean, it failed me. I am somewhere in the heaving gap between the Île d'Ouessant and les Roches d'Argenton, out beyond Finistère, beyond the 'end of the Earth', where the Atlantic swells prowl. They rise under my boat, long and smooth as a caress, but they do not comfort me. I fear this ocean. I should be working south into the Chenal du Four, but for most of the day Le Four lighthouse has squatted stubbornly immobile on the southern horizon, emblematic of Avel Dro's slow progress against this pitiful sou'westerly. And now the lighthouse has vanished too. As so often in these waters, a sea fog has cloaked the view and blotted out the sun. My world is reduced to a cold circle of grey sea, stockaded by mist.

It is already 5pm, and it is getting late to seek a haven for the night. A prudent yacht skipper would probably turn on the engine and seek the safety of the open ocean, out west beyond Ouessant, but I am not aboard a yacht and I have no engine. A night adrift in the North Atlantic in a 15ft dinghy is not an appealing prospect. I must re-enter the shoals and seek a protected anchorage where I can set up the dinghy tent in shelter.

I release the main sheet so Avel Dro lies quietly, spilling the wind, her hull rising and falling on the belly of the deep, while I study the chart. Seven miles due south is l'Île Molène, but that is right into the eye of the wind. The Île d'Ouessant is slightly nearer, but the locals have warned me of the dangerous tide rips around that storm-wracked island. A third option is to head back to the mainland. I punch a waypoint into the GPS off the mouth of Aber-Ildut, a charted inlet a little way down the coast, and then bring Avel Dro round until her heading matches the GPS bearing. It is a broad reach, Avel Dro's happiest point of sailing. The big lugsail embraces the wind, and her hull gurgles like a cuddled child as she picks up speed.

Passage planning in a small open boat is inevitably imprecise, especially if you rely on the good wind and just the strength in your arms to get you about. A new crewmember is meant to be joining me in the port of Brest. Instead I arrange for a taxi to collect her from the railway station, so she can join the ship at Aber-Ildut instead. She has never been on a sea passage before, and I'd planned that her first taste of salt-water sailing would be in sheltered waters. Out beyond the entrance of Aber-Ildut we won't find much shelter this side of New York.

The next day I treat my new crewmember to a good lunch in Aber-Ildut, thinking that if she's going to be seasick, at least she'll be sick on something. I unfold the chart on the restaurant table and explain the afternoon's passage. Our goal is the small island of Molène, some 10 miles away, amidst a mass of shoals.

My plan is to approach the island from the north, tacking between two clearing lines. By the time Avel Dro reaches the first clearing line, the mainland coast is a distant smudge astern. The wind is strengthening and rain begins to pock the sea around us. We lower the sail and tie in a second reef. L'Île Molène is hunched on the horizon like a great beast among a herd of rocks. But every new island is an undiscovered country to explore, and our spirits rise as we get closer and begin to discern a huddle of grey houses clustered below an old semaphore tower.

Avel Dro's keel grounds gently on the shingle of the island, and my crew splashes ashore to lay out the anchor. Then we walk up the beach into the narrow pedestrian lanes between the tight-packed houses, looking for a bar to shelter in. A steamy hostelry, full of bric-a-brac and photographs of wrecks, serves us two hot chocolates and we sit by the windows, looking out over the rain-drenched anchorage.

L'Île Molène is an adorable little island, but after spending two nights slobbing on its beach, Avel Dro's crew are keen to move on. Over the next couple of days we dribble slowly down the coast, against a feeble southerly wind. The hot sun beats down on a flat sea, rippled by our oar strokes. Passing the dramatic rock arch by the Pointe de Toulinguet, we approach the imposing sea stacks of Les Tas de Pois. They rise sheer and rocky from the sea before us, like the gateposts of the gods. Steering between the two highest of them, their tall cliffs frame only empty ocean, but we know that somewhere, way over the horizon, is our destination: the remote, romantic Île de Sein.

AVEL DRO dried out on the beach at Île Molene. Her hull is wedged upright with fenders and the crew is airing the bedding.

The Île de Sein viewed from the lighthouse.

We have run out of tide, so we anchor to wait for the stream to turn fair again. As so often, the turn of the tide brings a change of wind. At last a decent northerly fills our sail. Clearing our anchorage and re-entering the full strength of the tide, Avel Dro picks up her skirts and simply snores along. The Île de Sein is still a good 17 miles away, but we'll just reach it before nightfall if we crack on. The sun has gone. The once-blue sea is a sombre grey, flecked with white. The waves pile behind us like slate mountains, lifting our stern high and thrusting us forward. We surge madly down their faces, our bow wave hissing and the helm humming. This is sailing!

The Île de Sein is part of a long shoal extending out into the Atlantic, forcing the tide to pour through the narrow gap between the island and the mainland, where it breaks into spectacular standing waves. This is the notorious Raz de Sein, and even though I have been there twice before in a dinghy, no one approaches it with complacency.

Soon the lighthouses that mark the Raz rise over the horizon to greet me once again, and the water becomes agitated as we pass close to Tévennec. Wheeling currents grasp our hull and thrust Avel Dro bodily sideways, and she needs a firm hand to hold her on her course.

The familiar whistle buoy marking the passage through the shoals into Sein harbour moans past over the heaving swells. Dusk is falling, and the high light on Sein sweeps the sky with its beams. As we close with the island, the southern horizon is a mass of rocks, but the sectored light of the Men Brial lighthouse guides us safely down the narrow entrance channel. It is fully dark as we glide slowly round the mole into the inner harbour and lower the sail.

We climb the weathered granite steps onto the quay. The bars on the quayside are still open. Light pours out of them, silhouetting the people clustered in front, having a last drink in the warm dusk. A figure detaches itself from the crowd and walks forward with an outstretched hand. Only when it grasps mine do I recognise it as belonging to Abel Touzet, whom I met on my previous visit to Sein, two years before. He tells me that he and his wife walked out to the harbour lighthouse as usual that evening, and looked out over the rocks that surround their island home. They saw a brown sail away in the distance, entering the channel in the last of the light. Guessing that it was us, he had come to welcome us ashore.

Of all the places in all the world you can sail to in a cruising dinghy, the Île de Sein is surely one of the strangest and most poignant. The plain rendered houses of this salty community cluster closely together for protection against the Atlantic gales, on a bleak and rocky island that hardly rises above sea level. There are no cars, no fields and no trees. For centuries this little community has clung tenaciously to this scrap of earth, through storms and calms, peace and war – living off the sea and staunchly independent of the rest of France. It is good to find that Avel Dro still has friends here.

APPENDIX 1:
BOAT DATA

BUYING A DINGHY

It feels unfair to pick out just a handful of dinghies from the wide variety of boats available to the cruising dinghy sailor, but I have chosen a representative sample of available dinghies for the box features throughout the book, which illustrate the choices available to anyone looking for a small boat. In the table below these boats are listed in order of hull length, and I have kept to metric measurements to keep the table simple. The length of a boat is a rather deceptive measurement, however; a better indication of the size of a boat is the weight – a Drascombe Lugger feels like a larger boat than a Ness Yawl. Some of the boats vary in weight depending on how they are fitted out, and two of them carry water ballast.

Boat	Designer	LOA	Beam	Unladen weight	Working sail	Construction
Ness Yawl	Oughtred	5.84m	1.60m	130kg	12.35sq m	Plywood
Drascombe Lugger	Watkinson	5.72m	1.90m	340kg	12.26sq m	GRP
Seil	Vivier	5.40m	1.62m	250kg	11.00sq m	GRP/plywood
Norseboat 17.5	Paine	5.33m	1.57m	240kg	13.00sq m	GRP
BayRaider 20	Newland	6.01m	2.06m	460kg 760kg*	17.6sq m	GRP/plywood
Hitia 17 catamaran	Wharram	5.18m	3.07m	134kg	14.90sq m	Plywood
Wayfarer	Proctor	4.80m	1.85m	170kg	11.50sq m	GRP
Navigator	Welsford	4.50m	1.80m	140kg	12.60sq m	Plywood
Ilur	Vivier	4.46m	1.68m	180–210kg	12.00sq m	Plywood/strip plank
RS Venture	Morrison	4.9m	2m	200kg 325kg***	13.8sq m	GRP/plywood
Paradox	Layden	4.20m	1.23m	640kg**	9.30sq m	Plywood
Tideway	Walker	3.66m	1.52m	125kg	7.50sq m	GRP/trad clinker
Mirror	Holt	3.30m	1.39m	61kg	6.50sq m	GRP/plywood
SCAMP	Welsford	3.63m	1.63m	190kg	9.30sq m	GRP/plywood
Deben Lugger	Watkinson/Haig	5.49m	1.90m	360kg	13.57sq m	GRP

LOA = Overall length of hull, excluding rudder and projecting spars.
Working sail area excludes genoas and spinnakers, if carried.
Unladen weights can vary in some designs.

* The heavier figure is with the water ballast tanks filled.
** With full ballast tanks.
*** With optional ballast keel. A slightly lighter steel centreplate can also be fitted.

A GRP version of the SCAMP sails across a lake in North America. (Debra Colvin)

APPENDIX 2: RECOMMENDED EQUIPMENT

EQUIPMENT FOR SHELTERED WATERS

Compass (an orienteering compass is satisfactory)
Local chart (or perhaps a detailed map)
Lead line
Logbook
First aid kit
Efficient torch
Waterproof handheld VHF
Ship's papers: proof of insurance and other documentation
Bottle of sun cream
Food and drink
Sharp knife
Anchor and rode
Spare clothes

EQUIPMENT FOR COASTAL PASSAGES

Wrist watch
Steering compass
Handbearing compass
GPS device
Local and passage charts
Waterproof chart case
Pencils and dividers
Transistor radio
Almanac
Pilot book
Breton plotter
Tidal atlas
Binoculars
Radar reflector
Table of life-saving signals
Pack of distress flares in a waterproof box
Waterproof handheld VHF
Lead line
Logbook
First aid kit
Efficient torch
Ship's papers: proof of insurance and other documentation
Bottle of sun cream
Food and drink
Sharp knife
Anchor and rode
Spare clothes
Warps for mooring and other purposes
EPIRB
Fog horn
Masthead light
Drogue
Efficient pumps
Stout bucket
Mobile phone

Equipment for sleeping aboard

This is *Avel Dro*'s current inventory for a weekend or a longer cruise, sleeping afloat, which may be of interest to fellow mariners. I have now updated it to reflect changes over the years.

General gear

Fenders small x 2
Fenders large x 2
Stout bucket
Bailer
Drogue
Spare warps
Crutches
Battery box, containing charging leads for portable electronic equipment
Handheld VHF x 2
Tent cover
Burgee
Lead line
Masthead light
Oars x 2
5-litre fresh water carriers x 2
Sail and yard
Sail ties (gaskets)
Chartplotter
Steering compasses x 2
Handbearing compass
Distress flares
EPIRB
Folded radar reflector (kept in the bows)
Waterproof torch (LED)
Anchors x 2
Spare fuel for stove
Rudder
Tiller
Mainsheet
Sponge (for removing water from the bilges)
Comfy cushions x 2
GPS chartplotter
Fog horn
Binoculars

Tool box

Small can of lubricating oil
WD40 (spray oil)
Cloths
Thin line
Wood file
Mole wrench
Saw
Adjustable spanner
Flathead screwdriver (large)
Flathead screwdriver (small)
Electrical screwdriver
Crosshead screwdriver (large)
Crosshead screwdriver (small)
Pliers
Bradawl
Hand drill + bits
Hammer
Cold chisel
Various screws and bolts
Small tin of waterproof stopping
Roll of gaffer tape
Scissors
Tarred twine
Spare blocks (for rigging outhauls or hauling the boat up a beach)

Other box

Sewing kit
Baby wipes
Spare batteries
Antiseptic hand wash
Battery lantern
Bosun's bag containing sail needles, whipping twine, etc.
Battery charger in waterproof box
Adapter for marina power outlet
240V extension lead

Cuisine

Cooker
Pans and kettle
Bowls x 2
Plates x 2
Mugs x 2
Various glasses
Gas lighter
Sponge
Washing liquid
Cutlery
Corkscrew
Tin opener
Sharp knife

Sharpener for knife
Tea towel

Cambuse

Coffee
Tea
Plastic bottle for milk
Salt
Pepper
Olive oil
Oatcakes
Tinned food for at least 2 days
Rice
Pasta
Cereal for breakfast

Stern locker

First aid kit in plastic box
Pencils
Dividers

Chart shelf

Charts
Chart case

Navigation box

Card with distress signals
Spare mobile phone for emergencies (in
    waterproof pouch)
Logbook
Spare handheld GPS device
Certificate of registry
Radio licence
Radio operator's licence
Instruction books
Transistor radio
Pencil sharpener
Rubber (eraser)
Breton plotter
Nautical almanac
Boat insurance information
Navigation books
Pilot book
Tidal stream atlas
Countryside map

Personal box

Head torch
Smartphone

Sunglasses
Drawing equipment and watercolours
Filming equipment
iPad in waterproof pouch – GPS enabled and
    loaded with navigation software
Reading book (in case I am stormbound)
Guidebook
Waterproof box containing car keys and wallet
Passport (when abroad)

Waterproof camera box

Cameras, lenses, spare batteries, microphone

Clothes bag (x 2 if two crewmembers aboard)

Spare underwear
Woollen midlayers in various thicknesses
Woolly hat for cold weather
Waterproof gloves
Polycotten walking trousers x 2
2 pairs waterproof socks
Thin socks (1 pair)

Night bag (x 2 if two crewmembers aboard)

Sleeping bag
Backpacking pillow
Self-inflating mattress
Pyjamas (thin merino wool long johns
    and top)
Pack towel
Washbag

'Oilies' bag

Guy Cotten tops and trousers for each
    person aboard
Sea boots
Sou'wester

Minimum normally worn

Pocket knife
Cotton smock
Walking trousers
Merino wool underwear
Buoyancy gilet
Hat
Long-sleeved cotton or linen shirt
Plastic sandals
Wide-brim oiled cotton hat

INDEX